Roads *in the* Wilderness

ROADS IN THE WILDERNESS

Conflict in Canyon Country

Jedediah S. Rogers

THE UNIVERSITY OF UTAH PRESS
Salt Lake City

The Defiance House Man colophon is a registered trademark of the University of Utah Press. It is based on a four-foot-tall Ancient Puebloan pictograph (late PIII) near Glen Canyon, Utah.

17 16 15 14 13   1 2 3 4 5

Library of Congress Control Number: 2013951256
CIP data on file with the Library of Congress

ISBN 978-1-60781-311-8 (cloth)
ISBN 978-1-60781-313-2 (paper)
ISBN 978-1-60781-312-5 (ebook)

Cover photo: Thompson Pass looking toward Moab.
© 2012 Andrew McAllister / www.lookingatthewest.com.

Printed and bound by Sheridan Books, Inc., Ann Arbor, Michigan.

For Holly

AND

for William and Donna Smart

—in gratitude for sharing your love of canyon country—

Prologue

In the heart of canyon country—the region cut by a stretch of the Colorado River and its tributaries in what is now southeastern Utah—the one-armed former Civil War general John Wesley Powell camped for several days near the junction of the Green and Grand (Colorado) Rivers during his famed 1869 expedition.[1] Powell wasted no time scaling the adjacent canyon walls for a good look of the landscape. It took a few false starts before he located a passage to the top via "a long, narrow rock" that stretched above him. Powell found a crevice wide enough to climb out by pressing his hand and feet against the sheer rock walls. The view exposed the Green and Grand Rivers slicing through their deep gorges, the forested La Sal range hovering in the east, a jagged sea of broken cliffs and ledges to the west, and across the river "rock forms that we do not understand.... Wherever we look there is but a wilderness of rocks; deep gorges, where the rivers are lost below cliffs and towers and pinnacles; and ten thousand strangely carved forms in every direction; and beyond them, mountains blending with the clouds." The second day was spent ascending the opposite canyon wall, and the day following he and his party continued their journey down the Colorado.[2]

Since European and later American explorers first discovered the canyon country centuries earlier, the dominant reaction was fear and even repulsion. This was a place that demanded distance, and for hundreds of years that was precisely how travelers approached it. They peered in and then cleared out. The canyons and deserts were places to shun, obstacles to maneuver around. While Powell found the land lacking from failure to conform to expectations of what good land was supposed to be, with that apprehension mingled awe. For the first time, visitors to this pocket of the Southwest began to view it through a new lens: they saw in the awesome power of nature a hint of the sublime.

Powell's explorations would open the canyon country of southern Utah and northern Arizona for closer inspection. He shone a light on the region's promise and limitations for human consumption. No longer perceiving the area as an immeasurably valueless wasteland, Powell's generation and generations following would discover here great promise in a nation beset with dwindling open spaces and wildlands. But it was still a landscape that defied convention. "Beware, traveler. You are approaching the land of the horned gods," penned Edward Abbey in his classic text *Desert Solitaire*, referring to the images painted on stone by Native people centuries ago. But the warning could also apply to the land itself: this was what Powell called "strange country," a desert sea of rock and sand, tortuously warped into a thousand shapes.[3]

This redrock landscape has been variously imagined and firsthand experienced in the ensuing 150 years. The first permanent Anglo-American settlers were pioneer Mormons on a pilgrimage to "make the crooked places straight." Their quest was to tame the land and make it habitable for human use. In their eyes, the untouched wilderness was foreboding and terrible; transforming it into an earthly paradise would require ingenuity and hard labor. This or a variation on that theme has been put to work here. In San Juan County, ranchers built a large livestock empire in the early twentieth century. Prospectors scoured the desert for gold, silver, and other precious minerals. Settlers laid out towns, planted fields, and constructed roads. Energy companies eyed the region's oil, gas, and coal, and the Bureau of Reclamation its water, with uncommon vigor. By the mid-twentieth century, development interests increasingly viewed the plateau country as a blank slate where they could realize their visions.[4]

Whereas Mormons and other groups looked upon the canyon country as one might a garden plot, to make the land blossom as the rose, others approached it with a very different lens. By the early twentieth century, tourists set out either on horseback or by automobile over primitive dirt roads into the redrock desert for a wilderness experience. They experienced the land contradistinct from Mormon settlers. Theirs was a brief wilderness excursion; the deep canyon gorges were not obstacles but nooks to explore. Native American peoples who had earlier resided there were no longer feared but became objects of study and fascination. The rough contours of the rock and sea of sand produced an intimate traveling experience for those willing to strike out on an adventure. As the twentieth century marched onward, a small but growing cadre of writers, river runners, nature enthusiasts, and tourists looked to the canyon country as a place set apart from the shadow of the industrial machine. In fact, despite grand schemes, industry has yet to touch vast stretches of the region, and even today populations remain scant.

In broad strokes, these are two dominant ways of approaching this country. It is a landscape of dueling perceptions, viewed variously as vulnerable and compromised versus resilient and full of untapped potential, as a scenic wonderland versus a hostile desert, as wild and pristine versus inhabited and productive, as a land ordained by Providence for human labor versus a land ordained by Providence as a refuge for nature. Likewise, some see the remoteness of the region as a liability, while others see it as its greatest asset. These polar approaches to the canyon country endure. Many southern Utah residents are ideological if not blood descendants of the original pioneers who settled here. They cling firmly to a conquest narrative that the land is theirs by birthright and divine decree; theirs is a quest to domesticate the wilderness. Others, both locals and "outsiders," hold a diametric view: that the land demands distance from the human touch and ought to be protected. These dueling visions are consequential; it matters how one thinks about and perceives the land, and the dialectic has contributed to persistent tensions here. Both have been at loggerheads for more than fifty years. And the roots of these conflicts reach back even further.

Writers have filled many pages about modern environmental conflicts in the canyon country. The works of those sympathetic to wilderness—some nationally recognized—are well represented.[5] Historians, to a lesser degree, have addressed environmental battles, notably over water development in Echo

Park, Glen Canyon, and the Grand Canyon.[6] *Roads in the Wilderness* adds to the literature by exploring a topic that has been little studied from a historian's perspective but is central to the conflicts still raging in a subregion of the American West.

Although perceived as one of the last large roadless places in the continental United States, the canyon country actually contains an extensive network of dirt trails and roads. They imprint the land as veins mark a leaf—roads crisscross desert expanses, persist up rocky mesas, and creep along the bottoms of river gorges. Actual paved roads that would appear on a highway map may be relatively few—invoking the perception of roadlessness—but in fact the human presence and impacts are unmistakable. Any county map would show dirt routes running in all directions, weblike, sometimes connecting points, other times dead-ending.

These roads are at the center of a controversy stemming from a one-sentence statute in the 1866 mining laws—three years before Powell's famous descent down the Colorado—granting "the right-of-way for the construction of highways across public lands not otherwise reserved for public purposes."[7] The word highway here may sound out of place to modern ears, but its meaning then was clear enough: "A public road; a way open to all passengers," according to the 1828 Webster's Dictionary. Congress ostensibly had in mind a law that would promote the development and settlement of western lands. Apparently, no one contested the statute at the time; Revised Statute (R.S.) 2477, as it is now known, was adopted as a matter of course.

But by 1976, when Congress repealed R.S. 2477, roads had taken a rather controversial presence on the landscape. In the American imagination, roads—particularly those well groomed and paved—came to signify industrialization of the modern age. Early twentieth-century conservationists regarded roads as intrusive human imprints in the nation's wildlands. Roads had their own impacts on the land's ecological health, but they also invited despoliation. When Congress passed the Wilderness Act, specifically prohibiting permanent roads within wilderness areas, no quality came to define wilderness more precisely than roadlessness. Primitive dirt roads threatened the wilderness experience and potentially the wilderness designation of the redrock backcountry.

The rub was that while Congress repealed the statute, it "grandfathered" roads existing prior to 1976. If local counties could show that a road or trail had been constructed by some means beyond the mere passage of vehicles and had been in continuous use (meaning, according to Utah law, for ten years) prior to 1976, then it would assume ownership and control of the road. Southern Utah county officials have since identified and claimed R.S. 2477 rights to anything from faint pioneer-era trails to oft-traveled thoroughfares across the public lands. As many as twenty thousand "roads" (the majority in San Juan, Garfield, and Kane Counties) are claimed by local governments, though few of these have been officially recognized as R.S. 2477 roads. Meanwhile, the environmental community, led by the Southern Utah Wilderness Alliance (SUWA) and the Sierra Club, has waged a tireless campaign to thwart counties from claiming every two-track route traversing the public lands.

Most of the roads now in contention are backcountry trails, suitable only for backcountry vehicles. In a 1931 report, geologists Herbert E. Gregory and Raymond C. Moore referred to all but the main roads connecting the tiny towns in southern Utah as "roads only for the want of a better name."[8] Many remain in primitive condition, and some claimed roads are nothing more than two (if that) faint tracks. Local communities assert control over them anyway, insisting they continue to serve an important function and represent a vital aspect of history and culture. "Some claim that R.S. 2477 rights-of-ways are nothing more than dirt tracks in the wilderness with no meaningful history, whose only value to rural counties arises from the hope of stopping the creation of wilderness areas," explained Utah senator Orrin Hatch in 1996 during hearings for a bill that would have given states authority to recognize and control R.S. 2477 claims. "Nothing could be further from the truth."[9]

What, then, do these roads mean? Why do southern Utah counties lay claim to them with such energy? Roads facilitate; they are first cause, sine qua non. Wilderness advocates have long recognized this, consciously equating wilderness with roadlessness. Many of the now-claimed roads had an economic purpose at least at one time. Some were paths used by ranchers, others prospecting roads to access claims. Wagon trails provided movement for people and goods. Some roads still serve their original economic purpose, many do not. From a purely economical perspective, roads have a function, but it is debatable whether having more roads or even maintaining existing tracks is economically advantageous. Indeed, it seems that many of the roads claimed by Utah counties no longer serve an economic benefit at all.

In fact, roads are larger expressions of ideology rooted in history and culture. Views of land and resource use in southern Utah are inherited and derive from stories passed down of pioneer settlers braving wilderness and founding communities in the desert. They tap into a conservative tradition that has as its touchstone notions of liberty, sovereignty, and private property. The mix of local culture and heritage with conservative ideology has produced a unique climate where environmental conflicts take on an intense grit.

The dirt roads that owe their existence to this statute remain indelibly imprinted on the landscape in more ways than just physically. The markings tell stories that are more important remembered than lived. These artifacts, steeped in cultural and historical meaning, linger—and nowhere more so than on the windswept redrock deserts of southern Utah.

I would now like to travel a certain stretch of road—one that leads through an iconic American desert. The story is not just of the road; it merely leads the eye to the history, culture, and environment of a place mired in conflict. It is both material artifact and narrative device—both physical object and metaphor for the arc of conflict in the celebrated high desert of the American West.

Taking us along this road allows me to explore a somewhat neglected aspect of canyon-country history and literature. I linger not on some of the more known landmarks but on those less immediately celebrated but no less remarkable. Echo Park, the arches of Moab, Lake Powell, and the Grand Canyon are significant, but the in-between places undergird their stories. Roads connect the landmarks; they are first cause, and in the end are at the heart of modern debates over wilderness and land use.

Chapter 1 recounts two stories—one of the Mormon pioneer Hole-in-the-Rock expedition and the other of the young adventurer Clyde Kluckhohn—that suggest how worldviews and material visions in the late nineteenth and early twentieth centuries are linked to modern environmental conflicts. Those stories betoken a journey on a winding, uncertain path into the heart of American culture's relationship to land and nature. Thus, the road extends backward and forward. A great distance has already been traveled.

By the 1960s, though, the road's contours and direction were by no means certain, and over the subsequent half century the landscape underwent numberless transformations. At times it would be altered unrecognizably; other times it remained virtually untouched—"as it was," as Edward Abbey liked to say. Chapter 2 continues with the story of San Juan County, Utah, and depicts the struggle between development and preservation through the life stories of Abbey and Calvin Black. Using two real-life mortal foes who nevertheless respected one another does more than frame the debate; it humanizes a conflict often characterized as a contest between nebulous abstract ideologies. Subsequent chapters present road controversies in various locales, from the infamous Burr Trail battle to contentions over the web of roads in Utah's newest national monument to off-roading in Arch Canyon. Black and Abbey continue to surface throughout these stories, but new characters emerge who both embrace and depart from those ideological positions.

The final chapter reflects on the meaning of roads generally and of the unique geographic and cultural circumstances that have helped to create and prolong conflict. Most towns bordering the canyon-country edges are predominantly Mormon, and the pioneers who settled here as well as the folks who still call it home hold distinct religious notions of land and nature. The canyon-country geography is unlike any other in the American imagination, sparking diverse notions of its best use or its best defense against the human touch. At the same time, the contending categories of development and preservation have historical and contemporary resonance in American culture. Both are subsumed in the larger American narrative of progress. We value economic growth and technological innovation, but we also appreciate clean water and wide-open spaces. We value the built environment just as we cherish the natural world. These are not necessarily incompatible values, but we often assume they are. *Roads in the Wilderness* explores the manifestation of these two polar approaches to reading the land in an arid corner of the American West.

Each of the stories related here is intergenerational; orientation requires dipping into points along the proverbial stream of history. Part of this is because each road essentially follows existing trails or routes, many dating back to pioneer times. (Brand-new roads are sometimes built, but they are rare—and highly controversial. The proposed Trans-Escalante Highway that would have run north from Glen Canyon City along the west side of Lake Powell received such a stink that it was soundly defeated by the early 1970s.)

Beyond the physical, roads are cultural sponges—artifacts, timepieces of earlier times. If not in physical form, in cultural memory they reveal much about how generations, then and now, thought about the land and acted on it. The routes may have been created randomly, designless and haphazard, but each was premeditated. Before becoming a physical presence on the land, roads existed in imagination, and only later evolved as the products of long-fermented but contentious dreams. They began not merely as trails or wagon ruts but as ideas that stamped a particular worldview on the land. History—how one recounts and understands the past—is as much about remembering as it is about fact. We all tell stories about our past, and the stories—many handed down by oral tradition, others absorbed into culture and tradition—become a major way we identify ourselves and perceive the world. These roads, these material artifacts, have stories to tell about society and culture in an American desert. And the conflicts are just as much about the stories we tell and how we tell them.

The intent is not to be polemic. I see a story that is neither as straightforward nor as black-and-white as we might hope. We see in each road our own bias, a reflection of what we value and how we live. We would do well to exhibit more charity on either side, for roads and the people who created (and still wrestle over) them are not monolithic. The sides are not clearly or morally drawn. We ought to understand the deep undercurrents that induced the conflicts in the first place.

one

Stories of Origin

Just outside the tiny hamlet of Escalante, Utah, off Highway 12, a dirt road veers to the southeast. The Mormons first forged this road in 1879; whether the existing grade follows precisely the original route is unclear. Veering in and out of washes over a relatively flat plain, the road parallels two geologic landforms. The Kaiparowits' rock walls cast a shadow to the west, and the Escalante River, a Colorado River tributary, meanders through a twisted canyon directly east of the road. Any enthusiast determined enough to reach the road's end (which begins as well maintained on the Garfield County side but deteriorates to a rough pass where it reaches the famous Hole-in-the-Rock notch at Glen Canyon in Kane County) will become bewitched by the wildness and remoteness of this place.

This road ostensibly leads to the end of the world, but there are human stories embedded that are not immediately apparent. The road itself is an artifact, the physical remains of a most remarkable nineteen-century migration story, but the nonhuman landforms—the plateau, canyon, and vast stretch of desert in view from the road—also tell stories. Two of these stories are told here. One follows the original route beyond the road's end at Glen Canyon's rim. Eastward, Mormon pioneers set out across a broken landscape in 1879 to make a home "on the San Juan river, at wherever point may be deemed advisable."[1] The second is a countertale of young Clyde Kluckhohn, who in the 1920s sought adventure, wonder, and sublimity in the same desert country traversed by the Mormons a generation before, and whose story (literally and figuratively) intersected with that of the Hole-in-the-Rock expedition. The region, marked by high plateaus and twisted canyon gorges, both defied yet invited travel. Those who variously encountered it feared and celebrated its remote, broken, otherworldly features. Modern travel along the dirt road to Hole-in-the-Rock is sufficient to evoke both emotions.

These two stories are in fact beginning points of a broader modern-day story of land and culture in a distinct American desert. They are foundational stories that I use to explain origins and roots of contemporary environmental conflicts. The Mormon Hole-in-the-Rock tale powerfully connects biological and cultural descendants of the nineteenth-century settlers of southeastern Utah to a homeland. The story is deeply symbolic because it suggests a people's association to a place. Kluckhohn's story is less known, and thus less culturally powerful, but it too explains the abiding attachment to the same landscape. Although distant in time to modern disputes over public land use and access, the symbolic and cultural power of these two opposing stories helps frame the debate about humans' place on the land and responsibility to it and also helps inform the land ethic and perspective that directly developed in their wake.

Although García López de Cárdenas became the first European to see the Rio Colorado (the red or colored river) near the Grand Canyon some four hundred years earlier, the plateau region of southern Utah and northern Arizona did not really become, in the words of historian Donald Worster, "a part of the European and American imagination" until well into the nineteenth century.[2] It was mostly a region of the mind, since few Europeans prior to the nineteenth century did more than peer in from the peripheries. Native Americans, of course, had made their home there, but before the Mormon party in 1879, relatively few explorers, missionaries, and traders had penetrated deeply into the region that is now southeastern Utah. Indeed, the Mormons, intent on establishing settlements along the San Juan River and in the greater Four Corners region, knew nearly as little about the place as had the visitors who had preceded them.[3]

The first task of the newly "called" Mormons was to settle on the precise route to the San Juan country. The party had considered taking a southern route, and an advance party had been organized to travel from the jumping-off point at Paragonah, not far north of Cedar City in southwestern Utah, through northern Arizona and Navajo Country and into the San Juan River region from the south. But that party determined that the route was too dry and the distances between water too great to be feasible for a party of several hundred men, women, and children traveling in covered wagons. Moreover, the threat of Indian attack prompted them to find another route—the advance party's northern return route along the well-worn Old Spanish Trail through central Utah. This route avoided the broken canyons of southern Utah and land thought to be hostile through northern Arizona, but the Old Spanish Trail (famously dubbed "the longest, crookedest, toughest pack trail" in North America) was still dangerous and arduous for Mexican traders carrying goods and slaves to California.[4] The advance party considered this route to be too long to take before the onset of winter.[5]

So instead of taking either the southern or the northern routes, Silas S. Smith, leader designate of the Hole-in-the-Rock expedition, selected a more direct route along the thirty-seventh parallel through Glen Canyon and the region bounded by the Colorado and San Juan Rivers. The settlers, he announced, would travel southeast from Escalante, through the desert, to the rim of the Colorado River's canyon where locals Andrew P. Schow and Reuben Collett had located a two-foot-wide notch—a natural break in the canyon wall that allowed a descent to the river, giving the expedition the name Hole-in-the-Rock—at the western rim of the Colorado canyon that would later be named Glen Canyon. Based on Schow and Collett's recommendation, Smith figured the notch could be widened to allow passage of wagons and horses. The plan was to descend to the river, cross it, and forge a trail eastward. What was beyond the other side of the Colorado, no one knew for certain; Schow and Collett had explored only "a short distance," probably up Cottonwood Canyon. They had not reached the end of the canyon to catch a glimpse of the rough and broken country beyond Grey Mesa and the Red House Cliffs. Instead, they returned and reported favorably on the route they had located.[6]

On the strength of that report, and possibly that of Charles Hall, another explorer credited with locating a route to the river and beyond, settlers rendezvoused at Escalante in the fall of 1879. It had taken some settlers four weeks to reach the town of Escalante from their homes in southern and central Utah, but thus far the trek had passed through a familiar landscape that had recently been settled.[7] With their provisions already dwindling, the settlers bought what they could in Escalante and continued forty miles southeast to Forty-Mile Spring, where the grasslands could accommodate their large number of cattle. Almost immediately, they found that their chosen route would take much longer than originally expected. The road's condition became the perennial concern. Not far from Escalante, the party reached a point on the rim overlooking the country that lay ahead, "and as far as we can see east and south the country looks very rough and broken." Platte D. Lyman, a leader of the company and diarist, noted the condition of the "road." On November 21, it was "a soft sandy road," and three days later a "very heavy road," probably meaning the route was rough and difficult to traverse.[8] As they wove in and out of sand-and-rock washes, the party of men, women, and children encountered a landscape not entirely similar to the desert homes they had left behind. More bare rock and less vegetation blanketed the land.

As the main company traveled in a southeasterly direction along the base of Fifty-Mile Mountain, a small exploring party moved ahead to locate the precise route into the San Juan region. From Forty-Mile Spring, four men reached the notch at the rim and, with no rope in tow, lowered each other over the ledge using blankets. Building on the path forged by Schow and Collett, the party penetrated deeper into the canyon maze—traveling ten miles in six days—but located no obvious route to build a road. Meanwhile, a second exploring party hoped to find an alternative route via the Colorado and San Juan Rivers. Seven of the thirteen men in the party started down the Colorado in a boat that they had lowered down to the river but shortly returned to camp, having encountered "rapids" in Glen Canyon. The men traveled southeast across box canyons, draws, and gulches to the San Juan region.[9] "The country here is almost entirely solid sand rock, high hills and mountains cut all to pieces by deep gulches which are in many places altogether impassable," Lyman recorded in his journal. "It is certainly the worst country I ever saw."[10]

The attempts to locate a feasible wagon route to the San Juan country had failed. The dire prospects now facing the company were not lost on the men who had not only experienced what it would take to descend to the Colorado River but also glanced out to the vast and daunting region beyond the river to the east. Even before seeing that country up close, Lyman felt that "the prospect is rather discouraging"; afterward, he almost certainly expected to abandon the mission.[11]

When the party returned to the main camp, they called back the men working on the road from Forty-Mile to Fifty-Mile Spring and, at a conference, gave the dire report. The consensus, minus one—the ardent George B. Hobbs—was that a road could not be built. Nevertheless, the decision of whether to abort the mission rested with Silas S. Smith, who in a restless night weighed the options and the following day reported, in an improbable verdict, that they would continue moving forward. The country was broken but not impassable. The party had invested too much and traveled too far over too many difficult rocks, and the cattle had eaten too much of the grass along the route to turn back now. Besides, even if they did return, the members of the party had sold their homes and farms. Moreover, the town of Escalante was ill-equipped to support the whole company and livestock through the winter. Unanimously, the company sustained Smith's decision.[12]

The company's task would be to build a road so that others would follow. In other words, they set out not merely to traverse the terrain but to establish a permanent route into southeastern Utah. It is curious to consider why they felt it necessary to build it on this trip—why not send men back to do it after having a better idea of the route? Perhaps the main reason was that sections of the route like the notch at the rim of Glen Canyon could not be used without some roadwork. The other answer is that they believed they had the requisite manpower to do it now. In any case, the task of building the road was all consuming, requiring large amounts of labor and supplies. In fact, in mid-December Silas Smith left his company for what he hoped would be no more than three weeks to get additional gunpowder and supplies, and to convince the territorial legislature to appropriate money for the road construction. (His absence, in fact, lasted nearly five months, and news of the appropriation of five thousand dollars did not reach the settlers until after they had reached their destination.) Lyman, acting company leader, put men to work on the road and sent out yet another advance party "to the

San Juan if it is possible to get through."[13] This time the advance party did press through, northeasterly forty miles to Clay Hill Pass, another forty miles to Grand Gulch, then to Comb Wash, following a Navajo trail over Comb Ridge. The party reached Montezuma Creek after traveling twelve days with eight days' worth of provisions.[14]

Meanwhile, the main party reached the canyon rim of the Colorado River, and men began work to widen the two-foot notch through which 250 people with eighty-two wagons and their livestock would eventually begin a two-thousand-foot vertical descent to the river. The men used what little powder they had to widen the slit and smooth the forty-five-degree grade. A second crew labored to carve a road through loose boulders and steep grades the remaining way to the river, totaling nearly a mile. A formidable obstacle in their descent was a solid wall of sandstone on the left. Using powder and chisels, the men blasted out a shelf for the left-side wheels and, a few feet below, holes for oak stakes to be covered by rocks and tree poles harvested from the top of the Kaiparowits Plateau. They called this section of the road "Uncle Ben's Dugway" after the man who designed it. It was a marvel if not extremely perilous—a road literally suspended on a near-vertical cliff wall.[15]

The treacherous descent from the canyon's rim to the river, for which the expedition is best known, took place over two harrowing days in January 1880. The first day, forty wagons made the descent, and forty-two the next day, with no loss of life or serious injury. At the Colorado, the wagons forded the river in a ferry built by Charles Hall and continued up the opposite cliffs over a road built by a third crew.[16] Elizabeth (Lizzie) Decker's description of the ordeal is worth quoting in full:

> We crossed the [Colorado] river on the 1st of Feb. all safe; was not half as scared as we thought we'd be, it was the easiest part of our journey. Coming down the hole in the rock to get to the river was ten times as bad. If you ever come this way it will scare you to death to look down it. It is about a mile from the top down to the river and it is almost strait down, the cliffs on each side are five hundred ft. high and there is just room enough for a wagon to go down. It nearly scared me to death. The first wagon I saw go down they put the brake on and rough locked the hind wheels and had a big rope fastened to the wagon and about

> ten men holding back on it and then they went down like they would smash everything. I'll never forget that day. When we was walking down [to the river] Willie looked back and cried and asked me how we would get back home.[17]

What remained of the journey was more than 100 miles and more than three months of labor to traverse what Lyman considered "impassable" country. The company regrouped and repaired damaged wagons in Cottonwood Wash while men resumed work on the road up the cliffs out of the wash—in many ways repeating the Hole-in-the-Rock episode. Lyman wrote rather tersely that for several days, they had been "building [the] road over and through solid rock." Beyond Cottonwood Wash, the land became "smoother and more open and looks much better," although Lyman's diary continues to be sprinkled with references to "rough," "rocky," and "sandy" conditions.[18] Writing home to her parents from Grey Mesa, Elizabeth Decker had difficulty describing the land: "It's the roughest country you or anybody else ever seen; it's nothing in the world but rocks and holes, hills and hollows." For weeks the company inched forward, in wintry conditions, over rock and sand encrusted with mud and snow. They traveled in a northeasterly direction from Grey Mesa over Slick Rocks ("the mountains are just one solid rock as smooth as an apple"), to Lake Pagahrit (a natural lake and dam formed in Lake Canyon), and down Clay Hill (the only passage through the Red House Cliffs).[19] From Clay Hill, the company caught a good view of the country, but the route could not be direct: the road would arc northeast around Grand Gulch before turning southeast to Comb Wash. The company would then have to follow the wash south to the San Juan River owing to the north-south Comb Ridge, a sandstone escarpment rising 1,000 feet above the wash that afforded no possible passage for teams and wagons. They would then follow the course of the river around Comb Ridge to their destination.

But there was an unforeseen hitch to this plan, for Comb Ridge ended abruptly at the water's edge. Where they hoped to skirt the ridge along the river, that route proved impassable owing to the sheer cliffs that hung its banks. The only conceivable route was a scramble straight up the rocky face of the nose of Comb Ridge—what the settlers called San Juan Hill. Their earlier passage through Hole-in-the-Rock had certainly been treacherous, but after 170 miles building a road over rock, in canyon gorges, and through thick stands of piñon-juniper, the imminent pull up San Juan Hill to Comb Ridge must have seemed absurdly insurmountable.

As they had at Hole-in-the-Rock, Cottonwood Canyon, and Clay Hill, the company built a dugway, this time a full mile up the slope, with what little powder and willpower remained. That took an arduous ten days. Then came the grueling ordeal of slowly shuttling teams and wagons up the slope. On April 3, they advanced three miles, the next day four along the ridge's precipice. At last, the following day they arrived, ragged and depleted, at the site of Bluff. An unknown member of the party inscribed the words "We Thank Thee Oh God" on San Juan Hill. Beyond that, no one else wrote much of what transpired at Comb Ridge's summit, where—met with a breathtaking view of miles upon miles—the beleaguered pioneers caught a first glimpse of their new home.[20]

What can we glean from the Hole-in-the-Rock story? In southeastern Utah, the chronicle is etched in the Mormon consciousness as deeply as the Mormon Trail, creating what historian Charles Peterson calls the "Hole-in-the-Rock mystique."[21] The overland trek lasted six grueling months through utterly remote and wild country, and for what purpose? It was seemingly to buffer the outer edges of their territory by establishing a Mormon base in the Four Corners region and to extend a religious reach by establishing friendly relations with American Indians who sparsely populated the region. Mormons memorialize the trek as a story of physical and spiritual redemption, of forebears dutifully responding to their prophet's call to bring light, order, community, and God to the wilderness.[22] Historian Samuel Schmieding sets the story of the Hole-in-the-Rock expedition in the context of the Mormon quest to establish a physical representation on earth of the Kingdom of God. "For the residents of San Juan County and Mormon society in general, the Hole-in-the-Rock tale was a powerful tale that provided proof of their divine purpose at a time when the Mormon heroic age was blending into the mundane realities of post-frontier life," Schmieding writes. "The slick rock country provided a forum for continuation of the hero's trial."[23]

The rut marks of the road in that impenetrable country are physical evidence of the Mormons' unquestioning faith in divinely inspired human ingenuity to subdue the land and make it useful to humans. Braving a "wilderness of sand and rock" meant negotiating slick sandstone mountains, canyon gorges, deep sand, and "a treacherous river." The story of the trek is etched tangibly on the land along the trail—at Hole-in-the-Rock, Cottonwood Canyon, Slick Rocks, Comb Ridge, and elsewhere. Another physical sign of the strain the land demanded of the unsuspecting pioneers is the site of Bluff itself. The company stopped short of their intended destination, Montezuma Creek, and founded Bluff at the base of Comb Ridge—not for its desirability but because, in the words of one, "I was so tired and sore that I had no desire to be any place except where I was."[24]

The real danger of the San Juan mission turned out not to be Indians or cattlemen from Colorado, as originally feared. Nature itself proved the most formidable adversary. On the trail, torrential rains mired wagon teams in deep, muddy sand. Broken terrain presented almost insurmountable barriers to movement. Then once in Bluff, the company faced a new set of challenges: perennial flooding of the San Juan River, poor soil, and isolation. In fact, the Mormon pioneers never successfully irrigated and farmed in this country; not until they turned from farming to ranching did they prosper on the land. The settlements they founded were tenuous.

The route forged by the Hole-in-the-Rock crew could hardly be called a road, but that is indeed what the settlers imagined they were making—a permanent two-way road. Incredibly, for more than a year some settlers continued to use that trail. Lewellyn Harris, a Mormon missionary to Mexico, used the route in early 1880. Members of the original company, including Lyman, made a return trip in April 1880, covering in eight days what originally took four months to travel.[25] Surveyors for the Denver & Rio Grande Railroad briefly considered running a line through the San Juan country, along the Hole-in-the-Rock route, but came to their senses, "knowing the country to be impracticable between the San Juan & Colorado."[26] Like the railway, the San Juan settlers looked for new transportation links. Platte Lyman recommended a new road that would cross the river near the Henry Mountains. Not quite a year to the day Bluff was founded, Lyman noted in his diary that "a new road is being made from Escalante Creek to the Colorado River at a point five miles above the mouth of Lake Wash, at which place Brother Hall [Charles Hall] has located his ferry, having moved his boat up from Hole-in-the-Rock, which is an abandonment of that road."[27] The route to Halls Crossing (now Highway 276) became the new east–west link before yet another route farther north at Hite Crossing replaced it.

The original pioneer-carved road is still there to be traversed in parts by foot, horse, jeep, or, for reenactment, wagon. The sweat, fatigue, and wonder of that first journey produced a powerful founding tale that continues to give purpose and direction to San Juan residents. It is a cautionary tale. The story certainly represents the indomitable spirit of industry and sacrifice, of humankind's struggle to tame nature and create a society in a most inhospitable place. No one died on the Hole-in-the-Rock trail except for a stillborn baby, and the new inhabitants did build lasting though tenuous settlements in the San Juan country. That much the settlers could celebrate with pride. Yet they and their descendants could not have mistaken the other lessons of the trek—of coming face-to-face with a harsh land and very nearly being repelled by it. Of his father, Lemuel Redd, who as a young man participated in the Hole-in-the-Rock expedition, prominent San Juan County rancher Charlie Redd said, "My father was a strong man, and reluctant to display emotion; but whenever in later years the full pathos of San Juan Hill was recalled either by himself or by someone else, the memory of such bitter struggles was too much for him and he wept."[28]

The struggle of the trail and of settling an unfamiliar landscape contributed to the Mormons' abiding connection to the land. For most settlers, the San Juan country was disappointing. James Davis wrote, "I very much liked the look of the country, but my wife felt that we were isolated from all civilization and was very down hearted."[29] George W. Decker, at the time a young man of fifteen years, remembered it as "the most rugged gorge, the most tempestuous river, the loneliest and most frightening country I have ever seen." Yet the toil and sheer work involved in settling the country acquainted them and attached them to it, probably in the same way that indigenous people felt a similar knowledge of and attachment to the land. Speaking of the Hole-in-the-Rock, Decker remarked more than sixty years later that "to all that company of pioneers, it certainly is hallowed ground."[30] Perhaps also was the entire road they had built and what it represented—the ability to conquer a most foreboding landscape. For six months, they labored on it. Then they set to work immediately to build a settlement in the desert, transforming with technology, ingenuity, perseverance, and faith the raw natural products of the land to serve human needs.

The work that set the course for the original settlers and generations that followed is also the story that defines the advance of Western culture. Their labor on the land imbued their new home with meaning. The Mormon settlers believed they belonged there. Of course, they were not the first to lay down roots in that region—Native Americans called the San Juan region home long before the Mormons arrived—but the Mormons' conquest theology put them in the center of the narrative.

Hole-in-the-Rock is one story told about the settlement of southeastern Utah. There are, of course, other stories of a very different sort that both converge and sharply diverge from Hole-in-the-Rock, and perhaps none so well as Clyde Kluckhohn's journey to the top of Wild Horse Mesa.[31]

Kluckhohn is best known as a preeminent anthropologist at Harvard University, but his acclaimed academic life was still in the future when as a young man he embarked on several adventures into the backcountry of the American Southwest. Kluckhohn was born in 1905 in Le Mars, Iowa. Still a teenager, he began studies at Princeton University, but ill health compelled him to take a break from formal education and to move to a ranch in New Mexico for recovery. There he first became acquainted with the Navajo culture and language, knowledge of which would later make him famous, and with the broken and wild deserts of the Southwest. For several years, he and his young college companions and Navajo guides journeyed into some of the most uninhabitable terrain on the planet. Kluckhohn successively attempted to penetrate ever deeper into that "enchanted" country. His journeys took him to Navajo Mountain, one of four sacred mountains of the Navajo and described by Charles Bernheimer as "massive and majestic, the commanding, long-distant object of this region. It fascinates, it hypnotizes, for the eye is constantly drawn toward it."[32]

The main attraction in Kluckhohn's imagination, however, was not Navajo Mountain, or even Rainbow Bridge—recently discovered in 1909 and a frequent destination for tourist outback treks, still farther north. Instead, he set his sights on an imposing geologic formation on the opposite side of the Colorado River. It was primarily the mystery and lore associated with a certain mesa and the potential of discovery—not merely the sight or size of it—that attracted Kluckhohn's attention. In 1922, "one of John Wetherill's cowpuncher-guides," pointing off into the distance, told Kluckhohn:

> When you get on top of that little rise where you'll find your last Navajo hogan, look off to the north and west and you'll see a big high mesa stretch' back a hundred miles into Utah. It's way over across the San Juan and Colorado, way beyond Rainbow Bridge, and they say no white man's ever been on it. Zane Grey tried to get there this last year, but the river was too high, and he didn't make it. Some people say he believes there's Mormon villages of "sealed wives" on top of it, but I can tell you there ain't nothing to that. Nobody could ever get on top of that mesa.[33]

A. H. Thompson, the chief assistant to John Wesley Powell on his second expedition on the Colorado River begun in 1871, named it the Kaiparowits Plateau. The Mormons called it simply Fifty-Mile Mountain. Kluckhohn referred to the massive landform that gripped his imagination as Wild Horse Mesa, a name that apparently originated with Grey, the great western novelist. Feeling "an imperative call to adventure" on that "huge tableland," Kluckhohn led several parties between 1927 and 1929 in an attempt to reach its summit. William Gernon, James Hanks, Nelson Hagan, and Lauriston Sharp—all young former college friends—joined Kluckhohn as members of the Kaiparowits Plateau Reconnaissance Expedition in 1928, although Gernon and Hagan later backed out over differences with Kluckhohn's leadership shortly into the expedition. The young compatriots kept a record and took photographs. In the spirit of scientific advancement, they noted the land and Indian artifacts, creating a map and a key to the geography and archaeological sites on the mesa. But above all, the trek was a first-rate adventure. In a letter to his mother written the night before starting out from the Wetherills' trading post, Hanks could not contain his excitement. "All last summer, and so far this summer we have climbed every hill we came to, to get a look of 'the country beyond.' Now that we are really headed for it and will soon be there, where none have ever gone before, I can not tell you how I feel. I suppose it is hard for you to realize, but boys get such a kick out of going."[34]

While Kluckhohn likewise attributed his sense of adventure to his youth, he also believed that the impulse to explore the unknown and the wild was uniquely American. He subscribed to that notion propounded by that "flourishing school of historians" that the "frontier has been the predominant influence in the shaping of American character and culture." Kluckhohn wrote from a Eurocentric viewpoint in flourishes that resembled (maybe even mimicked) Frederick Jackson Turner himself—of "restless, unanchored" Americans moving ever westward, encountering "a sometimes pitiless and terrible land," and of "the terrible struggle for survival against the Indian and against the land itself." This constant process of westward expansion produced in Americans "a certain freedom, a flexibility in our thinking and a vigor and independence in action" that civilized western Europeans no longer possess. "We share, to be sure, in all the splendid achievements of Western Europe because we have a common ancestry alike in blood and in ideas with the men of Western Europe, but we share more distantly, more and more differently." Kluckhohn attributed his own "craving for the distant and unknown" to the larger American tradition.[35]

In a sense, then, Kluckhohn folded his own wilderness adventures into the larger Turnerian conquest narrative. But his story also diverged from the Turnerian narrative in important and crucial ways. Kluckhohn did not share with the Mormons the notion of conquering place, or imposing a certain worldview onto the land. His travels into the canyon country produced some apprehension—in his writings, Kluckhohn refers to the land as "savage," "ruthless," "unfriendly," and "forbidding"—but he also perceived something that perhaps the Mormons did not, or at least did not care to mention. The land was "ruthless," he writes, "as well as magnificent." Kluckhohn's companion James Hanks wrote that far from being something "frightening," it was a "mere pleasure" to trek into that wild and untrammeled landscape.[36] Kluckhohn and his compatriots welcomed the challenges of encountering a wild landscape. In fact, they delighted in it: "We rejoiced that there were yet regions uncrossed by trail where one would be able to travel days or weeks without meeting even a wandering Indian. We rejoiced that the fine isolation of the Mesa was all but impregnably guarded, on the south at least, by the rock-bound courses of two powerful treacherous rivers. All the American blood in us was glad for this fierce landscape, for this land stretched out in utter solitude, for this last considerable frontier."[37]

It may be that, upon reflection, Kluckhohn rejoiced upon entering such wild and isolated lands, but the route that he and his compatriots set out to traverse was daunting. They began from the Red Lake Trading Post on the Navajo Reservation in July 1928, moving north to Navajo Mountain. Circumnavigating the mountain clockwise, they continued north along Nasja Creek to its confluence with the San Juan River but were repulsed. From Rainbow Bridge, the party traveled to Surprise Valley, just north of Navajo Mountain, and then on to Ben Wetherill's trading post in Arizona, the last way station before continuing on to the San Juan River and beyond into a landscape where no trading posts or settlements could be, then or now.[38]

They crossed the San Juan River near where Desha Creek, a tributary from the south, met it. There, the party's horses struggled and nearly sank in the wet sand, soaking the men's supply. A Navajo guide by the name of Hosteen Dogi led the men on the north side of the river, following an Indian trail out of San Juan Canyon, where they then observed "that savage world of rock." They moved in a northwesterly direction toward the Colorado River. Kluckhohn reveled in both the immensity and the intimacy of the landscape. "Its charm lies in its vastness, its very silence, its freedom from human intercourse. Round every corner one hopes to discover a new rock, bridge or a mighty house of the dead." Occasionally, they stumbled upon "a lovely oasis" at the head of a side canyon, where they would lapse into "a pleasant lethargy." About a day's journey from the Colorado River, the men came upon something extraordinary and totally unexpected: Dogi "showed us clear evidence of trail building of a type that Indians would never have done. We faintly remembered a story of Mormons coming down from central Utah and making a bold way over the Colorado to the founding of Bluff and other settlements east on the San Juan." The next morning, the men spotted the walls of Glen Canyon cut by the Colorado and "the rock window which gave Hole-in-the-Rock its name."[39]

In his account, Kluckhohn spends some time describing the river crossings.

Members of the party apparently expected them to be rather uneventful compared to the previous year's attempted crossing of the Colorado River where Bridge Creek flows into it. Hanks had been the unlucky man selected to make the initial crossing and was nearly drowned from the weight of the rope attached to him.[40] This time around, Hanks assured his "anxious" mother prior to setting out on the expedition that an Indian guide would "take us to the Colorado and across," and that "since the river is at present very low, and there is an iron boat to row us across everything is rosy."[41]

Kluckhohn, however, provides a harrowing and perhaps slightly embellished account of the Colorado crossing. Finding the river much swifter than they anticipated, Kluckhohn and Hanks rowed the "tattered, torn, and patched" metal boat furiously to get to the other side. Then, realizing the animals would not swim across without persuasion, they rowed back. The sun and heat, trapped within the canyon walls, were intense. They finally forced the horses and "the even less enthusiastic mules" into the river. At last on the other side, the animals "stood there shivering and motionless, dripping, panting, terrified, exhausted." The next day, the boat made seven more crossings until all the supplies had been moved, but each time the current swept the boat downstream, and each time the men arduously towed it back up the river.[42]

In the ascent up the canyon walls, the men and animals scrabbled up the various grades, essentially following the route forged by the Mormon pioneers from their descent of Hole-in-the-Rock. They even found an old pickax and part of a wagon wheel that had belonged to the earlier party. Kluckhohn notes that along a section of the route, "the footholds chipped in the rock by our Mormon friends" made passage possible. Seeing these markings in the rock again caused Kluckhohn to turn his thoughts to the Hole-in-the-Rock settlers. "Building a 'road' over the rocks was a matter of unending labor with pickaxe and black powder, unending labor over long months. Only the ecstasy of a new religion could have given them the courage to abide in this frightening world, faced always by the possibility of attack from hostile Indians." Kluckhohn seems to have bought into the heroic telling of that journey; to him, as to Bluff residents who told the "tales of heroic men and fearless women," it represented an epic undertaking in a "hostile" world. Yet for all his rhapsodic praise, Kluckhohn did not so much celebrate the settling of the San Juan but admired the incredible trek through what he called "this frightening world." Kluckhohn preferred the country to remain unsettled, unpeopled; it was the isolation that intrigued him most.[43]

Upon reaching the top of the canyon at Hole-in-the-Rock, Wild Horse Mesa came into view, and "our hearts leaped up," Kluckhohn wrote. The young men essentially followed the old Hole-in-the-Rock road from the notch to the base of Fifty-Mile Mountain, but instead of shadowing the road along the mountain's base, they began an ascent to the top. They had no problem reaching the second bench, where they admired the "queer obelisks of clay with huge rock boulders perched on top of them" that from a distance had resembled Stonehenge or Druid altars. The difficulty lay in finding a passage up the mesa's rim. Like the pioneers seeking a break in the canyon walls to descend to the river, Kluckhohn scanned and found a break in the mesa's fortress walls. Kluckhohn was surprised and relieved to find that the route was passable without requiring trail work of any kind. Expecting either to leave the horses and mules behind while the men made a hasty visit to the top or to spend weeks making a trail to the top, instead the party ascended the rim without major incident. Kluckhohn wrote, "At 12:15 p.m. on the 31st day of July we were actually on the top of the Mesa and our six-year-old dream was accomplished."[44]

Relatively few people had ever scaled the plateau's heights, let alone lingered long enough to know the landscape intimately. Kaiparowits is a Paiute word variously translated as "home of the people," and ancient pueblo cliff dwellings and artifacts suggest that people once lived here.[45] But when Herbert E. Gregory and Raymond C. Moore surveyed the greater Kaiparowits region in the early twentieth century, they noted that the Indian remains appeared to be "temporary dwellings, pioneer outposts, or refuges for scattered bands driven out from the better places." In the late nineteenth century, Mormon ranchers grazed their livestock on the plateau's top, but no one would have had the chance to venture very far into the area. By the time Gregory and Moore conducted their surveys, the good grass had been extensively grazed anyway, leaving a deteriorated pastureland. Their surveys were the first of their kind in that place, which has the distinction of being nearly the last area in the contiguous United States to be mapped.[46]

Certainly compared to the desert they had just moved through, Kluckhohn and his companions found at the top an "enchanted island of vegetation in the desert sea." A thick cover of sagebrush, piñon and cedar trees, and tallgrasses blanketed the summit. They enjoyed the cool breeze. "We had expected Inferno," Kluckhohn wrote, "but we found Paradise." If you scale its top, you find not a flat tabletop, as might be expected looking up at the straight-cliff walls, but a series of broken canyons, washes, and crabby redrock extending as far as the eye can take you. Millennia of wind, water, and the uplift of geologic plates below the surface have given shape to the desert forms here. What made it "paradise" most of all was that "here in this quiet valley shut off from all the noise and dirt of the world was rest and comfort, and off beyond the rim lay soul-stirring grandeur."[47] Within eyeshot from the rim, they saw Navajo Mountain. Much farther in the distance to the northeast, they could have seen the snowcapped Henry Mountains, as well as a thousand other features, some familiar perhaps, most not.

The party was also pleased to find evidence of ancient humans. Shortly after reaching the top, they spotted "what was unmistakably a prehistoric trail." Farther on the mesa, they encountered several Indian cliff-dwelling and pictograph sites. But other discoveries on the mesa and alongside those ancient sites disheartened them. There were initials carved on a basswood tree, "Ken Porter" etched on the walls of Pictograph Cave, and "Tillman Felix, Arden Woolsey: February, 1928" carved in a cliff dwelling. Cattle trails crossed the mesa "where it was possible" and "in some places where it wasn't." The evidence of modern humans clearly disappointed, but they tried not to let this spoil the experience. "We had been so long steeped in the Arizona beliefs about the Mesa that the finding of dates, initials, and cattle altered our fundamental attitudes but little. Psychologically, Wild Horse Mesa was still the one virgin outpost of the vanishing frontier," he wrote.[48] Kluckhohn nevertheless learned the hard way that what to him from the Arizona side had seemed so impenetrable was actually quite easily accessible from the north in Utah. Even from the southern end, other men had apparently beaten Kluckhohn to the top. In 1922, six years earlier, a Kanab, Utah, outfitter named Dave Rust led a party from the Crossing of the Fathers to "the crest of the Kaiparowits Plateau," where he ran into Raymond Moore, who was studying the economic geology of the region.[49]

But on the mesa, Kluckhohn thought of none of that. Indeed, his thoughts turned to federal protection of the place. He wanted to extend a proposal by

Charles Bernheimer and John Wetherill and others to create a national park from Rainbow Bridge to Wild Horse Mesa. "It is Mesa Verde on an exaggerated scale," he wrote of the mesa's qualifications. "The panoramas from the rim are more magnificent. Indeed for sublimity of scenery Wild Horse Mesa surpasses even Grand Canyon." But he seemed to reconsider quickly for something more fitting for this wild, unspoiled place: "a national preserve denied to settlement." Did he—could he—imagine a road carrying comfortable tourists to the mesa's top? No, undoubtedly he did not. In essence, he proposed a wilderness preserve that prohibited development of any kind. He emphasized in all caps, "NO ROADS, NO BUILT TRAILS"—penning these words, perhaps coincidentally, around the time of the founding of the Wilderness Society and of the US Forest Service's earliest wild and primitive areas.[50]

In 1931, three years later, Kluckhohn returned to attempt another triumphal trek to the top of Wild Horse Mesa essentially along his 1928 route. The waters at the San Juan were so high that he concluded probably wisely that even if he were to make it to the other side, the Colorado River promised to be even higher, swifter, and more difficult to cross. So he turned back, repelled by "the Mesa's stalwart allies, the San Juan and Colorado." This, however, did not much bother him. "Despite our disappointment, I am a little glad that our last effort was repulsed, that Wild Horse Mesa proved itself still a stronghold not lightly to be taken."[51]

Indeed, Kluckhohn believed that the region bounded by the San Juan and Colorado Rivers represented some of the last vestiges of "unexplored and unsurveyed regions of the world," but he was not so innocent to believe that this "last frontier" would remain untouched. He spent his early adult years in the plateau region during a time when it was beginning to experience the forces of modernity. Kluckhohn recognized this—that efforts were being made to penetrate that country. The federal government was then undertaking construction of a massive dam in Boulder Canyon that would result in the creation of Lake Mead. The year 1929 marked the opening of a bridge near Lee's Ferry over the Colorado River. Fortunately, he felt, the plateau country generally and Wild Horse Mesa specifically presented a formidable "stronghold," a natural defense from development.[52] Kluckhohn would likely be horrified that today the Kaiparowits Plateau is eyed by developers for its vast energy potential. He might protest the roads that penetrate it. What would he think of the San Juan and Colorado Rivers—the swift waters that he so laboriously forded—tamed into a placid reservoir by Glen Canyon Dam? Kluckhohn would undoubtedly be surprised at how much this seemingly vast region has been altered in the eighty-five years since his travels.

Kluckhohn is important, not simply because he provides a delightful and rhapsodic account of a young man's encounter with the Southwest, but because he belongs to and possibly helped to inspire the broader countercultural tradition that gave rise to wilderness activism in the twentieth century. Indeed, his story provides a counternarrative to the Mormon Hole-in-the-Rock expedition. Unlike the Mormon settlers a generation before, Kluckhohn's purpose was not to etch permanent transportation routes and habitations into the land; he would linger briefly and then depart. He had much in common with the next generation of activists who would fiercely defend the region's remaining wildlands from roads and development. He sought, as many have since, in the deep canyons and high mesas an encounter with the sublime, a retreat from modern culture that by the 1920s and '30s had become a matter of concern. Another wilderness itinerant of the canyon country, the better-known Everett Ruess, said it this way in a 1934 letter to his brother:

> As to when I shall return to civilization, it will not be soon, I think. I have not tired of the wilderness; rather I enjoy its beauty and the vagrant life I lead more keenly all the time. I prefer the saddle to the street car, and the star-sprinkled sky to the roof, the obscure and difficult trail leading into the unknown to any paved highway, and the deep peace of the wild to the discontent bred by cities. Do you blame me then for staying here where I feel that I belong and am one with the world about me?[53]

Like Ruess, Kluckhohn also did more than simply wander into the canyons; he wrote about his travels in inspiring and powerful prose. But if his writings seem too romanticized, they are also deeply rooted in a familiarity with and love of the land. To him, the land held an allure and mystery, all the more so because it was roadless, largely unsettled. With each road leading to a destination, he realized, something was being lost. Speaking of Rainbow Bridge, located across the Colorado River from the Kaiparowits Plateau, a contemporary of Kluckhohn, Richard Frothingam, wrote, "If this sublime illustration of the forces of Nature were accessible by a Pullman sleeper or motor car, its name would be on all men's tongues."[54] To Kluckhohn, that would be something to lament. A road leading to the top of Wild Horse Mesa would have reduced his grueling once-in-a-lifetime adventure to a mere weekend excursion.

In this way, Kluckhohn is an ideological progenitor of later twentieth-century writers such as Wallace Stegner, Edward Abbey, T. H. Watkins, and Terry Tempest Williams who have written passionately about the preservation of canyon-county wilderness. His thinking was an ideological antecedent for the countercultural position that the earth's sole purpose is not to serve man, that humans are merely part of nature and not lords over it, and that some crooked paths ought to remain crooked. His was an alternative way of perceiving and acting on the land—one of two contending cultural paradigms that later operated in the conflicts over land use and access in the canyon country.

These particular cultural paradigms are both highly specific to the plateau country and much more widespread. The impulse to perceive the land as either something to domesticate or something to keep wild is not by any means unique to the region, but the combination of unique geological features, cultural influences, and preconceived expectations of the region has given those impulses a particular vitality. The redrock country of southern Utah and northern Arizona had become by the 1920s, according to historian Thomas Harvey, "a particular place within Anglo-American culture," but even to Euro-Americans it was a place that held very different meanings.[55] The people who visited or sought to make the region home certainly recognized it as unique and distinct from other landscapes, yet they brought with them very different cultural ideas and expectations that informed how they would act on the land. If Kluckhohn did not realize this as a young adventurer, he would later understand that how he perceived the landscape was a product of the culture that he carried with him. In 1948 he (with Henry A. Murray) wrote, "Culture directs and often distorts man's perception of the external world.... Culture acts as a set of blinders, or a series of lenses, through which men view their environments."[56] Yet he probably could not have known just how wildly those perceptions, shaped by culture, would diverge later in the twentieth century over the wilderness issues that had concerned him as a young man.

two

Abbey's Road, Black's Highway

Comb Ridge—the last barrier that nearly repelled the Hole-in-the-Rock pioneers—protrudes from the bare desert like a reptilian spine for almost a hundred miles. This remarkable sandstone monocline, which still captivates geologists and archaeologists, divides the lower San Juan region. To the west lies the Sage Plains, a flat, sagebrush-dotted expanse. The Mormon settlers ended up founding towns east of the ridge, either at the base of the Abajo Mountains or along the San Juan River.

To the east, the scene returns to the rock and twisted canyons of the Colorado—the impossible landscape encountered by the Mormons. Writer Edward Abbey approached the ridge for the first time in the 1950s from the southeast and described it like this:

> I hesitate, even now, to call that scene beautiful. To most Americans, to most Europeans, natural beauty means the sylvan—pastoral and green, something productive and pleasant and fruitful—pastures with tame cows, a flowing stream with trout, a cottage or a cabin, a field of corn, a bit of forest, in the background a nice snow-capped mountain range. At a comfortable distance. But from Comb Wash you don't see anything like that. What you see from Comb Wash is mostly red rock, warped and folded and corroded and eroded in various ways, all

> eccentric, with a number of maroon buttes, purple mesas, blue plateaus, and gray dome-shaped mountains in the far-off west. *Except for the thin track of road,* switchbacking down into the wash a thousand feet below our lookout point, and from there climbing up the other side and disappearing over the huge red blister in the earth's surface, we could see no sign of human life. Nor any sign of life, except a few acid-green cottonwoods in the canyon below. In the silence and the heat and the glare we gazed upon a seared wasteland, a sinister and savage desolation. And found it infinitely fascinating.[1]

Abbey's description of "a seared wasteland, a sinister and savage desolation" echoed the Mormons' initial reaction. But in the harsh and barren landscape, he marveled. Abbey shared more in common with Clyde Kluckhohn in celebrating its unique qualities; indeed, explorers, surveyors, settlers, and tourists since the nineteenth century have commonly greeted the canyon country with a similar mixture of repulsion and fascination.

Nature admittedly dominated the scene, but the human presence also had its place. Abbey's "thin track of road" was desired because it allowed passage through the country but also because it resembled the rough land. Its track seemed to blend just right into the desert, affording travelers the experience of moving through primitive and wild country. But at that time, Abbey knew nothing of plans—long in the making—to upgrade it to a paved highway, thus (in his view) irreversibly altering the traveling experience and, indeed, the very landscape itself.

What follows are this road's story and the two ideologically opposite men who collided over its development. The road interwove the life stories of Calvin Black and Edward Abbey, entangling them in provocative ways. Local San Juan resident Calvin Black had helped to build the old, graded State Road 95 and had tirelessly advocated for its improvement into a modern highway; Abbey first gained access to country he grew to love and came to defend via this road. Abbey immortalized Black as the prototype of the antagonist, Bishop Love, in the 1975 novel *The Monkey Wrench Gang.* In a broad sense, the two men came to represent two ways of approaching the canyon country: the one an ideological descendant of Mormon pioneers and tireless advocate for business, industry, and development, the other a prophet of a different sort—perhaps the most influential advocate for natural preservation that this region has ever seen.

Portrayed by Abbey in *The Monkey Wrench Gang* as the Mormon bishop of Blanding, Utah, Calvin Black hailed from the periphery of the Mormon cultural region. The Hole-in-the-Rock expedition and the settlement of the San Juan country in the late nineteenth century had been among the last Mormon efforts to extend their domain. It was originally conceived as just one more site among many future sites of a theopolitical empire that would sweep throughout not only the Intermountain West but also—at least in imagination—the whole of North and South Americas, but political pressure and changing economic and social realities at last ground expansionist plans to a halt. Brigham Young believed that in the deserts and mountains of the West, he was creating a temporal and spiritual homeland where the Saints would assume center stage in the cosmic events of the Last Days.[2] But by the end of the nineteenth century, the Mormon quest for empire had been subsumed into the mainstream body politic. Young's plans to establish a relative autarchy through home industry and manufacture were not to be. Whereas Mormons had established roots in places throughout the West in an effort to develop economically self-sufficient and politically autonomous communities, by the twentieth century their continued isolation was seen as neither possible nor even desirable.[3]

The rocky transition from provincial isolation to national incorporation would play out well into the twentieth century. It would be, in many respects, a slow and tortuous process. The tension between accommodation and retrenchment—a tension perhaps still not fully resolved among Mormons—would characterize the settlers' relationship to religious outsiders as well as to the land. In one sense, the isolating character of the region appealed to their special sense of inhabiting a sacred homeland, but in another it frustrated their yearning to reap the benefits—economic, social, and political—of incorporation into the American mainstream. When the Hole-in-the-Rock party entered the San Juan country, they found themselves at odds with the region's earlier inhabitants, becoming engaged in a land tussle with Ute Indians and cattle outfits such as Edmund and Harold Carlisle's Kansas and New

Mexico Cattle and Land Company, which were already utilizing the region for their own economic enterprises. Yet Mormons also channeled their energies toward carving out a ranching empire that both pitted them against and required close association with the "Gentile" world.[4]

The adoption of ranching as the economic mainstay to a degree jettisoned old Mormonism and traditional notions of Mormon place. Most Mormon settlements in the Great Basin were characterized by the "Plat of Zion"—Joseph Smith's idea of a village's square patterns and wide streets surrounded by farms and pastureland. The design was economic but also, as Samuel Schmieding observes, to provide sacred center points "where spiritual energies concentrated in waiting for the sacred event, the surrounding landscape sustenance for God's chosen people."[5] Indeed, a Mormon village lying at the base of the Wasatch Mountains constituted a powerful image of order, permanence, stateliness, godliness. The image is a variant of a common American motif—the agrarian myth—in which farmers diverted water from streams that originated on snowy mountain peaks and carefully laid out their farms in square sections with straight-lined canals and laterals that gave the appearance of mastery over nature. Technology made the image possible.[6] It was an image that had some representation in southeastern Utah; Bluff residents attempted to follow the Mormon village pattern, as ranchers congregated in town rather than residing on the open range. Even Blanding bore the marks of other Mormon towns with its irrigation canals, sturdy homes, and stately streets laid out on a grid. Established in 1905, twenty-five miles north of Bluff, Blanding may not have been founded on the same communal impulse of Bluff, but it was predominantly (and nearly exclusively for many years) Mormon—what historian Charles Peterson refers to as "the heir of old Bluff," which original settlers had mostly abandoned by 1920.[7]

The agrarian myth was not easy to reproduce on the Colorado Plateau. The original settlers of the San Juan region found out the hard way the difficulties of transforming their new home into an orderly, verdant landscape. Like elsewhere in Utah and the West, it was arid country, but here the redrock, broken canyons, and poor soils made it much more difficult to homestead than the Wasatch Front, where their fellow Saints resided. And it was a poor place to wield the technology of irrigation. Relatively few irrigable acres existed in the county, and most of those lie along the tempestuous and unpredictable San

Juan River, which could (and did) flood at any time—in one instance destroying a season's labor. Although most Mormons impounded and diverted water for irrigation wherever they settled, the great Colorado River and many of its tributaries in the Four Corners region remained largely wild and untapped—partly because the soil was not amenable to agriculture but also because rivers had cut so deeply into the earth that diverting them to fields proved impossible.

While irrigation canals provided the sense of human permanence elsewhere in Mormon country, settlers in San Juan turned to roads to order and stabilize a chaotic landscape. As such, they promised to transform the country from a "wasteland" into a "productive" Eden. Roads took precedence in this country. In pioneer times, far from the centers of power, locals shouldered the burden of constructing them, often to the detriment of education and other public expenditures.[8]

Yet road building and improvement to existing trails progressed slowly. Despite the expenditure of public funds, often at the instigation of boosters hoping to cash in on oil discoveries, the reality of well-built roads remained elusive. Through the first half of the twentieth century, the San Juan region held the deserved reputation as one of the most remote, inaccessible regions in the United States.[9] Even visitors who exulted in the wild qualities of the region found the primitive modes of transportation an annoyance. Reflecting on his 1923 travels in the area, Robert B. Aird wrote that although he had deliberately sought "the untamed ruggedness and the grandeur of extreme nature," that very ruggedness "prevented our even exploring as much as we wished" and "attaining that almost perfect sense of freedom."[10]

For Calvin Black, born in 1929, life in Blanding on the rugged and remote San Juan frontier was similarly confining and economically limiting. He saw his first paved road and his first "colored" person at age twelve, when his family took a trip to Salt Lake City. Not until his teenage years did he stay in a motel or eat at a restaurant. When his family did go on vacation, it was usually to camp on a highway where his father labored on a road project. For Black's generation, and those before him, mobility—or lack thereof—was life defining. Perhaps Black's strongest recollection was of the economic difficulties. His family had virtually no money and little means of support, doing whatever they could to get by. Hyrum Black, Cal's father, held several odd jobs in the county, including state road maintenance foreman. Yet the sorry conditions of Cal Black's youth never concerned him. From a young age, he learned to work long and hard, and the difficult circumstances of his early life no doubt instilled in him a sense of frugality and independence that became hallmarks of his adult life. "One of the most vivid memories of my life was watching my mother and father continually sacrifice and go without so that I and my six siblings had the things we wanted," he would later recall. "I'm afraid I will have to confess that perhaps the most overpowering drive I have is to continually drive myself so I won't have to face what I felt so strongly were Mom and Dad's sacrifices."[11]

Blanding's isolation and limited economic opportunity compelled many of Black's schoolmates to leave the county in search of education or work. College may have been an option for Black, but because his sister's attendance there had placed an excessive financial burden on his parents he decided to start working right away, giving trucking a try. He and his father bought a truck that they used to haul ore over the network of gravel and dirt roads in the county. Then, when there was nothing left for him to haul, Black got into the mining business.[12]

Developed mines require good roads—not necessarily well graded, but at least wide and smooth enough to accommodate large equipment. Because miners stake claims at the location of mineral deposits regardless of proximity to towns or contours of the land, the roads they build resemble a hastily constructed web with threads reaching out to some of the unlikeliest places on the high desert. On a particularly lonely spot lies the uranium Whirlwind Mine, one of Black's earlier claims, on state land within the Navajo Nation's reservation boundaries. Because no road from Oljato—a trading post on the reservation near the Utah-Arizona border—led to the state section, Black and his partners, Merwyn and Burdett Shumway, built the road themselves. Black later called the twenty miles to the mine "flat"; *flat* is, however, a relative term, and in that country roads had to negotiate broken canyons, rock outcrops, and sand. The last few miles wound uphill to the top of a mesa. Using road equipment borrowed from the state, the young men made the road as suitable as possible, but it still took seven hours to travel 110 miles to the mine, "driving as fast as you could [and still] stay in the cab." Black recalled that "she [a Ford truck, the only model he would own] pulled me through, but I vowed to give her something better to run on than the red, rocky terrain of this desolate area."[13]

Black encountered many of the same conditions his father had endured as a road foreman—weeks at a time away from home, no modern conveniences, broken machinery. On the high plateaus, the weather in the winter can turn bitterly cold. While grading the road to the Whirlwind Mine, Black remembered one long and dangerous night without windows in the truck or a blanket to keep out the chill, nor even wood to build a fire. He also recalled being told three times by the Navajo to stay out of the reservation—warnings that went unheeded—and working his mine with a gun at his side in case any of the locals gave him trouble. (Black justified pushing his road through the reservation without permission on the basis that "the Navajos had very poor roads and any improvement was better for them.") Then came the backbreaking process of extracting the ore; after spending about one and a half years of labor and fifteen to twenty thousand dollars, the miners at last made their first shipment of ore. And each load required twenty-two hours on the road—traveling 220 miles at 10 miles an hour.[14]

This onerous operation of locating a mine, building a road, and hauling the ore replayed itself throughout the Four Corners region. At the dawn of the atomic age, post-1945, the Atomic Energy Commission (AEC) offered rock-bottom prices for uranium in ore that could be processed at the mill in nearby Monticello. Later, the AEC leased a mill site in Durango, Colorado, to the Vanadium Corporation of America, and it added a fifty-cent-per-pound bonus on uranium. San Juaners scrambled to locate and file claims on ore mines. Still, small operations barely survived even at that higher price. Yet again the AEC raised prices, setting off a boom in development on the eastern edge of the Colorado Plateau. The uranium boom, coupled with the discovery in 1954 of some of the nation's most important oil fields, had a marked effect on the county. Motels, trailer courts, grocery stores, and even towns sprang up in remote places to cater to the influx of prospectors and miners. But what transformed the land most indelibly were the hundreds of miles of new roads—not unlike the one leading to the Whirlwind Mine—built by miners, prospectors, and engineers. The AEC, under the rationale of national security, funded much of the road building as part of its Access Road Program.[15]

The boom may have produced a few millionaires, but it broke countless others whose mines could not repay the heavy initial investment. Black was one of the lucky few, although he certainly struggled early on. Initially, Black's Oljato Uranium Company produced just enough to keep the business afloat and his family fed. In the lean years, he labored in mines in Cottonwood Canyon west of Blanding and did some prospecting on the side, filing claims and paying the annual assessment fees.[16] Later he changed partnerships and bought up and sold stock to his claims—some shares for many times more than he purchased them. In two decades, Black filed six hundred claims. Most were speculative. He sold or traded many of them, but several materialized into profitable mines. As he told a reporter, "You stake your claim and you take your chances. Come boom or bust, you can't shake the feeling that you're an explorer off on a great adventure." Following his own script, Black ultimately turned his holdings into a working, profitable business.[17]

Given his life's work, it is no surprise that Calvin Black was among the locals in attendance at a ceremony in Hite, Utah, on September 17, 1946, to commemorate southeastern Utah's new, long-awaited State Road 95—the precursor to U-95 thirty years later. He had every reason to celebrate. Hyrum Black, his father, had worked on the road to Natural Bridges National Monument and was the maintenance foreman in charge of extending it to the Colorado River; Cal Black, too, had spent long days and nights helping with the project. At the dedication, Black heard speakers extol the virtues and necessities of roads and praise road builders for carrying on the work of their forebears. He heard Ephraim Pectol of Wayne County tell the crowd, "All who made this trek will go into history as pioneers for the future automobile road and the future development of this great Wonderland."[18]

Developing that part of the country was undoubtedly a slow and onerous process. Well into the mid-twentieth century, San Juan County remained much the same as the Hole-in-the-Rock pioneers found it in the nineteenth. One obstacle was geographical: the region is isolated from major population centers and difficult to access. The county's western section is a twisted maze of canyons, mesas, mountains, and imposing geologic barriers to land travel. East of Comb Ridge, the land levels out to a broken expanse of sage. The few sparsely settled towns—in 1951 the *New York Times* referred to Blanding as a "trading post"—hugged the San Juan River or lay northward to the east of Comb Ridge and the Abajo Mountains.[19] The best road—dirt for most of the way—ran north to Moab, but other roads led east to Colorado and south into Arizona. State Road 95 was the first permanent road in San Juan County to run west.[20]

The road was by all measures primitive, as the road builders had no access to modern bulldozers or graders. The Utah Department of Roads did not forge a new route or barrel through hillsides, but instead followed the route built earlier in the 1930s from Blanding to Natural Bridges National Monument and an old pioneer route the rest of the way to the Colorado River. A ferry at Hite shuttled automobiles and their passengers across the river. The road was circuitous, traversing rough and wild country. As J. M. Adams said at the dedication, State Road 95 would "make it possible to open the way for thousands of acres of land and will make these desert wastes productive of agricultural and mining products. If a region has the finest climate, the best soil and every other natural asset, if it cannot boast of a good road, it is still a waste land."[21]

Constructing State Road 95 in the 1940s was merely the first step in realizing the promise of a conquered landscape. The road builders' task was to find passage over, around, even through the natural barriers that seemed to divinely forbid access. This is not to say they neglected to use the land's contours to their advantage. Early roads in most cases followed the steep grades, curves, and elevations of the land. Yet the task here in southern Utah was to provide passage through impossible places. Early roads cleared the land of vegetation; modern technology enabled builders to dig, blast, grade, and otherwise barrel over and around some of the gnarliest spots on the planet. The task was not merely to subdue nature but to work with it—and in the process complete it. Workers of the land took natural landscapes and transformed them into human landscapes. To do this required technology, but it also demanded knowledge of natural processes and perhaps even an appreciation for the natural world—its limitations and its capabilities. Engineers were best positioned for this work, for they considered themselves to be, as historian Linda Nash pens, "intermediaries between the natural and social worlds, as those most capable of understanding nature and natural laws, and as those best equipped to shape human use of the landscape." If not primarily to conquer nature, engineering became the principal means to reshape it.[22]

That first attempt to construct an east-west route across the Colorado River in southeastern Utah may have animated the locals, but a perfect passage it was not. In fact, State Road 95 in 1953 was quite crude and rough, as Edward Abbey recalled in a 1971 essay in *Slickrock,* providing the best physical description available of it.[23] The road traversed a sea of sand and warped and eroded redrock set against a backdrop of distant buttes, mesas, and laccolithic mountains. Abbey's crew encountered sand pits, potholes, ruts, and a precipitous drop along the harrowing descent down Comb Ridge. The journey required periodic stops to remove barriers to navigability. At one point, the truck got a flat tire. Admittedly, Abbey had no intention to move quickly over the road, but still nearly a full day was required to reach Natural Bridges National Monument—only thirty miles from their starting point.

On the second day, the small group descended toward the river over a "red wasteland" of dust, sand, and sandstone. At Fry Canyon, Abbey remembered driving across "a little wooden bridge that looked like it might have been built by old Cass Hite himself, or even Padre Escalante, centuries before." The trail continued on to more miles of axle-busting ruts and deep sand in the bottom wash of White Canyon. Before the day's end, the little party reached the river and the old settlement of Hite, inhabited by a few families and a handful of "prospectors, miners, bums, exiles, remittance men." From there they rode Art Chaffin's "home-designed ferry," crossed to the other shore, and continued their journey up North Wash.

Abbey mourned that he took for granted that the road would remain primitive. Even as the new dirt road was nearing completion, plans were already in the works to improve it. At the 1946 dedication, speakers spent perhaps as much time reflecting on the need to upgrade the road as they spent praising it. "Today you come down here and you are praising this road. It isn't such a hot road," Utah governor Herbert Maw told the gathering after ironically having arrived late to the dedication due to poor road conditions. "Incidentally let me tell you this: I think it is a disgrace to the state of Utah to, after a hundred years, force the citizens who live in the outlying areas to travel over the kinds of roads some of them travel over (Applause)." The governor insisted not only that State Highway 95 ought to be paved but that "we should never permit a condition to continue, where any town in Utah is not connected to a main highway with an oiled road."[24] Speakers speculated wistfully about the day, perhaps twenty years out, when the crooked path would be made straight. Certain of the righteousness of their work, the celebrants on that September day in 1946 would later be taken aback by Abbey's evocative defense of keeping the roads rough and the remote lands wild and untamed.

Edward Abbey is well known as an iconoclastic writer of the West—a man of contradiction and fire who spoke and wrote passionately about the western landscape and the preservation of open spaces. Few writers are more unmistakably identified with the American Southwest. Unlike Calvin Black, Abbey was a transplant to the West. Born in the town of Indiana, Pennsylvania, and raised on a farm in the backwoods of the Allegheny Mountains near Home, Pennsylvania (which he often erroneously claimed as his birthplace), he gained a reverence and nostalgia for green Appalachia. In later life travels, he reminisced, "I easily remember my home. Yes, yes, I think of home, I think of Home." He would contend that "home" was not the place of your childhood but "where you have found your happiness." Where, then, did Abbey find his happiness? At one time, he said his "home" was in "those mountains, those forests, those wild free lost full-of-wonder places which rise yet (may they always!) above the squalor of the towns."[25]

Abbey later reflected on what he believed was a pivotal event: a 1944 hitchhiking trip at age seventeen to the West. In his essay "Hallelujah, on the Bum," he noted encountering the front range of the Rocky Mountains: "An impossible beauty, like a boy's first sight of an undressed girl, the image of those mountains struck a fundamental chord in my imagination that has sounded ever since."[26]

Other encounters left similarly indelible impressions. He would frequently get in a car and drive wherever the roads took him. Those memorable experiences derived not so much from the destination as the journey, and he savored them. In the essay about his first time driving old State Road 95, he details an unexpected confrontation with a flash flood in North Wash along the Colorado River when he and his compatriots were forced to scramble to higher ground. "From within the flood, under the rolling red waters, you could hear the grating and grumble of big rocks, boulders, as they clashed on one another, a sound like the grinding of molars in a pair of leviathan jaws. The kind of sound, in other words, for which neither imagination nor fantasy can ever really prepare you. The unbelievable reality of the real." With the floodwaters still rushing below them, the crew set up camp. Abbey recalls the ecstasy of listening to the roar of the waters while smelling the juniper fire, tasting the beans and bacon, and enjoying the beauty encompassing him. The next morning, all was serene, though the flood left the road nearly unrecognizable. The day after was spent getting the truck out of North Wash, but he recollects the hard labor "was worth every minute of it."[27]

Abbey's task was to experience nature directly, and he came to know intimately the American West through seasonal park ranger jobs at Organ Pipe Cactus, the north rim of the Grand Canyon, and, most famously, Arches—which inspired his best-known book, *Desert Solitaire: A Season in the Wilderness.* Abbey wrote about preserving wild places, not only because he felt nature had intrinsic value quite aside from humans, but in fact because he reverenced the need for authentic humans to stand in close relationship to the natural world. No free and independent human existence could be achieved without such a connection. To him, nature held an allure, a power to heal, rejuvenate, enliven. In Abbey's writings, you sense his conviction of a deeper meaning to be found in the natural world: the mystery, the charm, the majestic. Environmentalism may indeed be akin to religion in its power to bring purpose to individuals. Like other pursuits with origins in the Enlightenment, environmentalism appealed to reason, but like religion it also "looked beyond knowledge, seeking meaning, and believed each of us needed to form conscious ties to the world."[28] Abbey's was an emotional though not otherworldly experience in nature, for he supposed the earthly enterprise was all that was needed, yet his abiding connection to nature was arguably as strong as another's connection to the supernatural. This underscores his revulsion toward industrial development and the eating away of the nation's wildlands.

Construction of high-speed roads and highways like Utah Highway 95 facilitated that transformation. Abbey was certainly not blind to the economic benefits that roads facilitated, but he bemoaned the road's impact, and he eloquently articulated a need for more roadless places in the canyon country. His was a wistful defense of wildlands. "As you say, we old codgers have had a chance to see the country as it once was, and thank God for that," Virgil Hays of Cheney, Washington, wrote Abbey nostalgically. Hays had spent his childhood on a ranch along the Fremont River in south-central Utah, and upon returning there after a long absence was horrified to discover "a 70 mph highway [State Road 24] right through the middle [of it]."[29]

Abbey also despaired at such development, but he did not stand idly by. At the end of *Desert Solitaire,* despairing of the new road building in Arches, he admits that when nobody was looking, he pulled up stakes put in by road surveyors. Yet his defiance did little to stop road construction. When he first arrived in Arches in 1956, the park was still a primitive backcountry, undiscovered and relatively scarce of travelers. But gradually more visitors poured in, facilitated by the new road, which ultimately drove him out. He would spend a lifetime searching—perhaps futilely—for places to live free from industrial development. Seemingly everywhere he went—even the backcountry of Utah's redrock canyon country—was being changed by development and sliced in two by roads.

State Highway 95 would replace the old dirt road that Abbey recalled with such fondness. The new highway—begun shortly after the dedication of the original road in 1946 but not completed until 1976—would be a twenty-eight-foot-wide bituminous all-weather roadway designed for a speed of fifty miles an hour. State and local officials were calling it the backbone of the Grand Circle—a highway connecting the canyon country's scenic destinations and parks.

The first section to be improved was the stretch from Blanding to near Natural Bridges National Monument. The old dirt road passed well north of present-day U-95. From Blanding it ran west through Big Canyon, Brushy Basin, and Cottonwood Wash, then on to Milk Ranch Point and Elk Ridge on the shoulder of the Abajo Mountains before descending to Natural Bridges. The upside of the route was that it bypassed Comb Ridge altogether, but the downside was that at a higher elevation it was much too long, winding, and expensive to maintain.

Since the uranium industry needed a direct route that could handle large hauling trucks, the Atomic Energy Commission funded the realignment of State Road 95 and the upgrading of the road to Hanksville. The AEC viewed the road—and a slew of other roads constructed during this period—as a matter of national security, so much so that road engineers did not even make preliminary surveys. A history of San Juan County posits that "such extraordinary measures by the Atomic Energy Commission and State Road Commission are strong evidence of the national and state interest finally paid to isolated and remote San Juan County."[30]

To negotiate the formidable Comb Ridge, a route was selected through a break at the ridge that was earlier an ancient indigenous foot trail. A road crew worked its way down from the summit, blasting and drilling through the solid rock, while a second crew worked its way up the sloping ridge on the west side. Once that section was completed, the AEC continued to push the road west toward Natural Bridges, where it merged with the old State Road 95.[31]

Certainly, the new road cut by the AEC was an improvement over the old route in that it shortened the distance to Natural Bridges, but it was still rough and winding—a far cry from a smooth, paved highway. The descent down the ridge was especially harrowing—the very route that Abbey used in 1953—but was still frequented by large uranium trucks on a continual basis. To create an even straighter highway would require yet another cut through the ridge. Bisecting a passage through that seemingly impenetrable wall of sandstone was the engineering feat of the highway. This time there was no attempt to conform the road to the existing landscape; using the muscle of machinery and explosives, road crews in the early 1970s blasted out a huge hunk of the rock. The dugway leading up to the cut was possibly bolstered by the rock that had been cut loose from the summit. Today, motorists can speed by without knowing that at one time the ridge had been practically impassable.[32]

Like the section of road through the ridge, the remaining highway took form in phases over several decades. In the 1950s the AEC built an improved route to Natural Bridges and graded the rest, and beginning in the 1960s road crews realigned and paved various sections. The Utah Department of Transportation divided the new highway into manageable sections, while the Bureau of Land Management (BLM) granted rights-of-way and ensured compliance of construction requirements.

The first funding cycle, secured in 1964, would be used to build the bridges. Unlike the old days, there could be no simple crossing at Hite. The site of the ferry that shuttled passengers and automobiles across the perpetually moving

Colorado River would soon become the upper end of Lake Powell—what Abbey referred to as "a motionless body of murky green effluent, dead, stagnant, dull, a scum of oil floating on the surface."[33] Where the old road snaked down Farley Canyon and crossed the Colorado River at Hite, the new highway would arc around the north end of the reservoir and cross not just the Colorado but the Dirty Devil River as well. A third bridge was also planned where the road crossed to the north side of straight-walled White Canyon. Completed in 1965–66, costing nearly two million dollars, they created the only road crossing of the Colorado River between Glen Canyon Dam in Arizona and Moab, Utah.[34] In each case, the steel-arch modern bridges contrasted sharply against the twisted, rugged landscape, although they were beautifully—even artistically—designed. In a 1970 US Senate hearing to consider extending Canyonlands and Glen Canyon National Recreation Area, Harry Helland, Utah State Road Commission director of highways, touted the bridges' design and function. To him, these three man-made steel bridges were every bit as impressive as the three sandstone natural bridges in their namesake monument forty miles east.[35]

Some believed that the highway engineers were creating a road to complement the desert aesthetic. Where visible from the new highway, the old road was to be obliterated and seeded for a natural appearance, but where not visible, no restoration or landscaping was required. The BLM carefully considered which grasses to use in reseeding the highway's shoulders. Native plants like four-wing saltbush, sand drop seed, black brush, or sagebrush offered a more natural appearance than exotics.[36] Since the highway would pass through rangeland used by deer as well as domestic livestock, road designers were challenged to determine the best way to build a road and fencing for winter range cattle without harming deer migration. Three-strand barbed-wired fences were utilized to keep cattle off the highway while still allowing wildlife passage. The BLM also recommended no blasting in a section of the highway between Atomic Rock to Fry Canyon during bighorn sheep lambing season, May through June. In general, the BLM had instructed road crews to use nonintrusive road-building methods to minimize road scars and adverse impacts to land and water resources.[37]

Still, road construction is, by nature, a highly environmentally disturbing act. Constructing U-95 entailed significant impacts to the land and cultural resources. In one section of the highway, construction crews inadvertently damaged several key archaeological sites west of Mule Canyon and entirely destroyed several others, including one containing important late Basketmaker and Pueblo pit structures and dwellings. Only one pit structure and artifactual trash at the last site could be salvaged.[38]

Road cuts had further impacts on the landscape. In some sections of the highway, such as up Elk Ridge and to Cedar Mesa, engineers forged brand-new routes instead of overlaying the new highway over the existing road alignment. Creating a new alignment engraved an entirely new path through the ragged country, resulting in additional damage to the land, soil, and vegetation. It was violent work, despite attempts by engineers to design the construction to be as unobtrusive as possible. Of particular concern was a section of highway from Atomic Rock to White Canyon, a stretch that adheres mostly to the old alignment. Still, the impact to the landscape was tremendous. Since the new road would straighten out and eliminate sharp curves and dangerous dips in the road, even where following the old alignment, this would take the highway off the old road by up to 150 yards.[39]

The BLM feared that a highway culvert might cause irreparable damage in Fry Canyon, a deep, narrow gorge adjacent to White Canyon a few miles west of Natural Bridges. Instead, they proposed building a new bridge across the canyon, not unlike the old road's previous bridge. Although the Scenic Highway Group had lobbied to keep the old bridge, the Utah State Department of Highways argued it would be a liability. Bob Brock of the BLM had proposed the new bridge with a walkway for those hoping to view the canyon. Again, the Utah State Department of Highways ruled that the walkway would be a liability, and one was never built.[40]

Throughout 1976 road crews blasted, cut, filled, graded, and paved segments of U-95. Completion of each section became a cause for celebration. On November 2, 1974, San Juan resident C. Alfred Frost blessed the road, Mormon style. He began by thanking "our Heavenly Father" for the men and women who worked on the road, then asked that it be blessed "for the beneficial use of man—that it be used for commercy [*sic*] and industry in transporting the necessary goods and materials necessary for mankind to pursue his livelihood here on earth" and that man would "travel this graceful road" to "get away from the strife and hustle and bustle of his life" and "have his soul renewed."[41]

Who would benefit from the new highway, and how would it be used? Seldom Seen Smith, portrayed as a Jack Mormon outfitter in Abbey's *Monkey Wrench Gang*, assured his companions, "The only folks [who] want this road are the mining companies and the oil companies and people like Bishop Love. And the Highway Department, which their religion is building roads. Nobody else ever heard of it."[42] That description fits the original purposes of the road as funded by the AEC: to provide access for prospectors and haulers moving ore to the processing plants. But when the waters of Lake Powell reached Hite, the circle of benefactors widened. Now the road would benefit the marinas, hotels, and stores that would cater to the boaters and sightseers, but road boosters also recognized its broader impact on tourism in southern Utah. Calvin Black had debated earnestly during the highway's construction that the road would "not only provide for local needs" but also tie together the scenic wonders of the canyon country "for the use and enjoyment of all Americans."[43]

What Black did not state explicitly, but what would have been apparent to anyone who knew him, was that he also stood to gain from the highway's construction. Since the dedication of the original road in 1946, he had dreamed of and prepared for its expansion. After making his start in the mines, Black had become a successful entrepreneur with businesses and real estate properties so numerous they read like a directory.[44] Among his many developments in the late 1950s and early 1960s, the largest and easily his favorite, was the recreational development at Halls Crossing on Lake Powell. Black's son remembers going to the site-which would soon boast a marina, stores, facilities, and a ferry—"while there was still a river there and Dad was trying to explain to me the development that was going to take place there." The ferry notion germinated while Black was stationed in the army in New York and rode the Staten Island Ferry. When he returned home in 1957, not long after passage of the Colorado River Storage Project Act, he conceived that a "water highway" on the lake could connect the two sides of the lake, transporting tourists up and down, as far south as Wahweap and north to Hite, and maybe even up the San Juan River. By working *with* nature, he reckoned, a new water road would be the easiest ever built in the canyon country.[45]

Through the 1960s, Black put his energies into the developments at the future site of the lake marina. Partnering with J. Frank Wright, a former river runner who had worked with Norman Nevills, he formed the Lake Powell Ferry Service, Inc., having been granted a concession permit from the National Park Service (NPS) for a marina, trailer court, and ferry. In October 1963, the company operated a small barge on the river and a boat dock—"a small wooden platform with a barrel of gas and a hand pump"—a trailer court, an office, and a store.[46] To expand the marina would require an adequate road connecting the reservoir to U-95, then under construction, so Black went to work championing its upgrade. "When there is an oiled road into Halls Crossing," he predicted, "there will be need for at least 40 motel rooms, a restaurant of 60 seats, slip, buoy and dry storage facilities for 200 boats, a trailer court of at least 50 spaces, and, of course, employee housing, a school, service station, and other related facilities."[47]

Pushed by Black, construction of Highway 276 to Halls Crossing would prove a major undertaking. The NPS allocated several million dollars for road construction within the Glen Canyon National Recreation Area, and half a million on facilities in the Bullfrog Basin area across the bay. When completed in 1969, Highway 276 provided direct access to Halls Crossing and from the east to Bullfrog Marina and the bay from the north.[48] At length Halls Crossing expanded to include a floating gas barge, pumps, service station, office, trailer court, repair shop, and dry storage yard, but the city Black had envisioned with schools, a golf course, swimming pools (to accommodate those too timid to brave the lake), and parks failed to materialize. But part of Black's original vision was realized in 1984 with the dedication of the long-sought ferry connecting Halls Crossing and Bullfrog.[49]

To Edward Abbey, construction of U-95 and its offshoots like Highway 276 defamed a landscape he idolized. He detested that the highway would provide a route for industry and big business, which had grown even bigger since the dammed waters of Lake Powell reached Hite. Moab native and wilderness advocate Ken Sleight blamed this on "local people, starting with Calvin Black," and "the prevailing culture" in Utah. "[Black] wanted to build roads and he did build roads and it was very hard," Sleight said in an interview several decades after completion of Glen Canyon Dam. "U-95, right after Lake Powell, well, after the filling, here comes roads...and off those roads come more roads, hooking up all the various concession sites that they decided on. And now...they still want to make more roads."[50]

It was the composite development and industrialization of the canyon country that so irritated Sleight and fired Abbey up to pen *The Monkey Wrench Gang.* Sleight suspects that Abbey conceived the idea for the novel in 1967 after the two men met at Lee's Ferry, fifteen river miles downstream of Glen Canyon Dam. Sleight, who had made a living as a river guide since 1953, knew of Abbey through his writings, but they met when Abbey, who was working as a park ranger at Lee's Ferry, approached Sleight to inspect his outfit. They sat at the edge of a boat and trash-talked Lake "Foul" (Powell) until two or three in the morning. "We spoke with derision about the Glen Canyon Dam. That god-awful dam was destined to become the object of many discussions." A few hours after Sleight launched his boat on the river, Abbey pulled alongside in his ranger powerboat and called to him, "Ken, we'll take that god-damned dam down yet."[51]

Abbey began writing the novel in earnest in the early 1970s. He wrote in his journal on February 28, 1971, that it was "time to be thinkin' of work, man. Time for the Wild bunch to ride again, the wooden shoe mob, THE MONKEY WRENCH GANG! Strikes! Again!"[52] He believed that people were ready for the political and social message of his book. In the foreword to a 1970 edition of *The Brave Cowboy,* Abbey wrote that the nation had become more receptive to anarchism and defending wilderness. "Now both ideas are flourishing in the fiery heads of the boldest of the young. For which I say, Praise Be."[53]

Ed Abbey's foremost beef was with the builders and developers bent on taming the nation's wild, primitive areas. Calvin Black—with his strong persona, economic empire, and unflinching commitment to road building—likely seemed a good model for the Gang's principal antagonist. Abbey may have heard about Black during his stint as a ranger in Arches National Park. More likely he came to know Black in the 1960s after returning to southeastern Utah to work as a ranger at Canyonlands. Abbey would later move back to Tucson, Arizona, in the early 1970s, but while writing *The Monkey Wrench Gang* he kept close tabs on affairs in the Four Corners area by periodically asking Ken Sleight, "What damn thing is Cal Black up to now?"[54] Though it is doubtful Abbey knew the full extent of Black's economic empire, he apparently knew enough to construct a composite though exaggerated portrait of Black as Bishop Love. Black was easily cast as a profit-motivated capitalist. And with Black's business connections tied to construction of roads, critics liked to point out that Black's support for U-95, Highway 276, and others was self-serving. As Abbey's monkey wrencher Seldom Seen Smith (based loosely on Ken Sleight) scoffed, the road was "to help out the poor fellas that own the uranium mines and the truck fleets and the marinas on Lake Powell, that's what it's for. They gotta eat too."[55]

The fictional Bishop Love was not simply a developer but an ecclesiastical leader of a Mormon congregation. If readers remember much about the antagonist, it is likely that he was a jeep-revving, power-hungry Mormon bishop. One of the Gang says of Bishop Love, "We got plenty like him in Utah. They run things as best they can for God and Jesus and what them two don't want, why, fellas like Bishop Love pick up."[56]

That Abbey made the leader of the posse a Mormon, and a bishop at that, is not surprising given that a majority in southeastern Utah belong to that religion. This was on Abbey's part a broader critique of the Mormon Church. He cared little for Mormonism's founder, Joseph Smith, or Smith's claims of a "golden bible," although Abbey's disdain was probably no more for Mormonism than for any other organized religion. Still, as he wrote in his journal, he respected their "agrarian socialism, communal feeling, healthy and sane way of life. A good way of life." Mormons exhibited a kind of social behavior that—paradoxically, in light of today's Mormon culture—flourished for a time on the cooperation of egalitarianism, not the competition of capitalism. In *Desert Solitaire,* he praised Mormons for building "coherent, self-sustaining communities with a vigorous common life in which all could participate, free of any great disparities in wealth, small enough to make each member important." Abbey had a fairly idealized view of the earlier Mormon pioneer period, but like his disdain for the various reincarnations of State Road 95 he lamented the "evil institution" that he perceived the church had become. "Like all institutions, they think they're doing good. The Mormon church has sold out completely to the capitalist system. They are one hundred percent in favor of industrial development and profit making—damn the consequences.... They made a religion out of money making!" That seemed to be complaint number one. Then he rattled off a few more—among them the crackdown on dissidents, narrow-mindedness, and treatment of women as "breeding machines."[57]

If there was ever something to admire about Mormons, according to Abbey, it had been abandoned in the pursuit of a better, more comfortable life. The problem for Abbey and other environmentalists was that as a bloc, Mormons in general opposed wilderness protection. Whether this stance stemmed from their theological belief that the earth had been created for the use of man or because their isolation and independence created a fierce resistance to government oversight of the land—or both—Mormons in southern Utah are among the most conservative individuals in the country. Abbey portrayed rural Mormons as two-dimensional, simple-minded, and power-hungry, not unlike earlier popular characterizations in novels like Zane Grey's *Riders of the Purple Sage.*

Where Mormons placed their trust in capitalistic individualism, Abbey put his faith in nature. Historian Thomas Dunlap has characterized environmentalism as its own kind of secular religion that challenges popular ideas in Western culture, and indeed *The Monkey Wrench Gang* is both product and sacred text of that movement. The novel belonged to the postwar counterculture generation of cynics, anarchists, and antimodernists who had become disillusioned with technology thanks to the specter of nuclear war, distrustful of the industrial machine that polluted the planet, and skeptical of a government that catered to warmongers and capitalists. Like others of this generation who lived during the Vietnam War, Abbey believed it imperative to make major structural changes to Western civilization by dismantling the industrial economy and starting over. In nature he and others of his generation sought refuge, and perhaps the underpinnings of a new society and culture. Abbey's novel laid out a vision and a strategy in its defense. The Monkey Wrench Gang's war against the "the advance of Technocracy, the growth of Growth, the spread of the ideology of the cancer cells" was Abbey's war, too.[58]

If the Gang's ultimate fantasy bull's-eye was the ever-present yet untouchable Glen Canyon Dam, they settled for smaller targets: machinery used to build bridges and the roads that spread like spidery veins in and out of the desert country, many constructed or upgraded since the dam's erection. So the motley group would take their stand on Utah Highway 95. In an opening scene, Abbey positions his characters—led by the Vietnam vet George

Hayduke—atop Comb Ridge with the San Juan country in southeastern Utah spread out before them. From the northern summit, they see "a turmoil of dust and activity" generated by a parade of road equipment hard at work on the highway. Their eyes follow the machinery and men at work on the road. The bulldozers have left piñon pine and cedar "smashed and bleeding, into heaps of brush, where they would be left to die and decompose." A second wave of bulldozers has ripped up loose rock; drill rigs have blasted into bedrock, and dump trucks have carried the rubble to the fill sites. "Powdered stone floated on the air as the engines roared. Resonant vibrations shuddered through the bone structure of the earth. More mute suffering.... Cut and fill, cut and fill, all afternoon the work went on. The object in mind was a modern high-speed highway for the convenience of the trucking industry, with grades no greater than 8 percent. That was the immediate object. The ideal lay still farther on. The engineer's dream is a model of perfect sphericity, the planet Earth with all irregularities removed, highways merely painted on a surface smooth as glass."[59]

That scene was in fact a blending of fact and fiction, a product of Abbey's mind and, no doubt, experience. Abbey would have in person observed machinery then at work on the highway in the 1960s and 1970s, and, like the Gang, it was likely in a similar setting that he too began to envision its destruction. Abbey wrote of what he knew, and he also lived some of what he wrote. For instance, Abbey later admitted tongue in cheek to doing a bit of "field research" for the novel. In April 1975, he and a friend sneaked into White Canyon on U-95 and, reminiscent of the mischievous monkey wrenchers in his not yet published novel, damaged the road equipment to the tune of twenty thousand dollars by pouring sand or sugar in fuel tanks and shooting holes through machinery tires at the construction site. Above all, Abbey fantasized driving a bulldozer off a cliff like Hayduke, but since he could not get one machine's engine to start, perhaps that's why he settled for smaller acts of sabotage. He may have also been complicit the next year when a perpetrator put 110 pounds of sugar in the gas tanks of twenty vehicles used to construct U-95, causing fifty thousand dollars in damages. Such acts, Abbey later acknowledged, "made me feel good temporarily," but the feeling did not last. While the damage was expensive and certainly an impediment to construction, it did not long delay the twenty-three-million-dollar highway project.[60]

Authorities responded to the ecotage (sabotage performed on behalf of the environment) by going after a handful of suspects known to oppose the highway. Ken Sleight became a suspect, and he claims Cal Black instigated the search against him. Black even publicly accused Sleight of carrying out the sabotage, though Black had no evidence to back it up. "I was about to sue the bastard," Sleight later huffed. "It got kind of nasty after a while."[61] No evidence turned up against Sleight or anyone else; the miscreants so well hid their tracks that the investigation uncovered nothing, nor was anyone ever charged. At that time, Black must have been clueless that his man was Abbey or that Abbey's novel would soon provide added fuel to the smoldering fire. Not until after the novel's publication in 1975 did Abbey become a marked man in southeastern Utah. Abbey's critics would get some satisfaction after someone reportedly filled his gas tank with dirt while Abbey and Black—who by then shared a cordial relationship, although their personal interactions were few—dined together in a Blanding café.[62]

The covert monkey wrenching was one of a handful of confrontations that occurred when the highway's completion was close at hand. Black's diary briefly notes in January 1976 a physical confrontation with those who belonged to what he called the "Sahara Club" over U-95's construction, but little else is known about the exchange. The altercation probably stemmed from the Sierra Club's protest of gravel removal from Glen Canyon National Recreation Area for construction of the highway.[63] Neither the monkey wrenching nor the protest, however, put a halt to the highway project. In 1976, U-95—the Trail of the Ancients Scenic Byway—was completed and dedicated, promising to lay bare southeastern Utah's scenic and mineral riches.

The life stories of Black and Abbey are reflections of and contributions to dominant Euro-American ideologies at work in an American desert. Each man articulated and represented a compelling model of how to act on the land. Abbey's environmental ethic dipped into ideas with deep roots in American culture. Before Abbey's time, intellectuals had begun to esteem nature, but environmentalism did not coalesce into a mainstream political philosophy until the 1970s. Although the environmental movement incorporated a diverse collection of ideologies, some essential points were common throughout all green philosophies: the fundamental value of nature, the reality of natural limits, and a rejection of the capitalistic development mode. Any green ideology required restructuring the human relationship to the nonhuman world and acknowledging the human connection to and interdependence with nature rather than sole dominion or lordship over it. The environmental movement widely rejected the modern industrial machine that equates "progress" with economic growth.[64]

From one standpoint, these ideas suggest an ecocentrism that is decidedly ambivalent when it comes to humans' place in the natural world. Critics of the green philosophy deride environmentalists for caring more about any other species than their own. It is a charge often leveled in the conservative rural West, suggesting a necessary choice between eco-friendly practices and the well-being of human beings. The bumper sticker sported during the spotted-owl controversy in the Northwest—"Are You an Environmentalist or Do You Work for a Living?"—was a clever way of characterizing environmentalists as elitist and out of touch. Yet though environmentalists certainly value the nonhuman world, the green philosophies could also be anthropocentric in the sense that living in sustainable harmony with nature would liberate humans to live authentic, happy lives.[65] Abbey speculated that not only did industrial development wreck the environment but it ultimately did a disservice to the communities it aimed to help. Although to Abbey the natural world existed and operated perfectly independent from human need, he believed that humans could also play an integral moral role in it. Abbey's environmentalism was tied up in his conviction that people ought to live individual and free lives.

Black's ideology, meanwhile, wove strands of religious and secular ideas into notions of land and nature. His was a faith in economic growth, in the power of technology to mold the natural world into a commodity, and in man's preeminent role in this undertaking. Each of these ideas derives in part from the mainstream American intellectual tradition, but also holds particular prominence in Mormon religious doctrines. Black's concept of "creating"—that is, turning raw materials into usable, consumable products (like desert into irrigated farmland or trees into two-by-fours)—is more closely aligned with Mormon theology than mainstream Christian doctrine. To most of Christendom, when God created the earth he did so ex nihilo. Mormons do not share this belief that God created the earth and humans out of nothing but that he (always male) organized "intelligences" and matter from preexistent forms.[66] The idea of organizing a chaotic mess from raw materials into an organized, usable form had theological precedence for Black. By so creating, humans were copartners with God.

Other notions of land use advanced by Black also paralleled Mormon theology. His rhetoric that the land and its bounties were entitlements derived widely from the Mormon (and Christian) belief that God created the earth for humans' use and dominion. *Homo sapiens,* designed in God's image, sit atop the food chain as the capstone of God's creation, heirs of celestial glory. In Mormonism's theology, this point is especially emphasized. Joseph Smith and other early Mormons spoke of humans not merely as "angels" of God but as literal inheritors to his glory and possessions.[67] Taken to the logical (some might say heretical) extreme, Mormons consider themselves gods in embryo, destined, in fact, to become possessors of their own worlds and humanoid populations. Such anthropocentrism easily suggests the sense of entitlement to land and resources that many Mormons in southern Utah claimed. The idea of eternal increase finds satisfying expression on earth to Mormons who accumulate large property, homes, cars, and families as physical expressions of divine favor.

Historians and scholars disagree, however, over how Christian conceptions of land, God, and creation contribute to the ways people perceive and transform nature. Lynn White Jr. and Roderick Nash have argued that Judeo-Christian religious culture is responsible to a large degree for many of the world's ecological challenges because, in the words of White, it "not only established a dualism of man and nature but also insisted that it is God's will that man exploit nature for his proper ends." Some Judeo-Christians interpreted the biblical creation story as God setting man above the rest of creation, thus giving them dominion over the earth and its resources.[68] Mark Maryboy, a Navajo who served with Black on the San Juan County commission, recognized this type of thinking among his Mormon colleagues. Referring to Mormon leader Brigham Young's injunction to "build cities, adorn your habitations, make gardens, orchards, and vineyards, and render the earth so pleasant that when you look upon your labors, you may do so with pleasure, and that angels may delight to come and visit your beautiful locations,"

Maryboy added, "It is an interesting religious notion that angels would not be willing to visit God's creation until man had improved upon it."[69]

Nevertheless, another interpretation of the Genesis story may be gleaned—one not of dominion but of stewardship. Wendell Berry, historian Thomas G. Alexander, Mormon apologist Hugh W. Nibley, and others have argued that Christian scripture points to a relationship between humans and earth that, if not akin to modern-day environmental thinking, is at least in line with the view that humans are more participants in a larger ecological system than lords over the earth. In this interpretation of scripture, God demanded that humans be good stewards of his creations, and early Mormons who settled the West often spoke in these terms.[70] Indeed, early Mormons embraced a communalistic ideology that is at utter odds with the individualistic, capitalistic attitudes of today. Brigham Young and other early church leaders at times spoke out against private landownership and excessive timber cutting or destructive grazing practices. Yet their notion of a steward was generally understood as a gardener or improver. Although they often spoke of caring for the land, the idea was not so much to live in harmony with nature as it was to bring nature harmoniously into the ideals of a human-inhabited celestial place.

Modern-day Mormons living in San Juan County would not disavow these ideas. They, too, articulate a land ethic that, if not ecocentric, at least acknowledges the need to manage wisely the land and its resources. It is not uncommon to hear ranchers with deep roots in the region claim to be the "true environmentalists." Black's preference for the built environment was both practical and sentimental. He spoke of providing high economic yields (for example, at a congressional hearing on the proposed Trans-Escalante Highway, he spoke of a private housing development on the northwest shore of Lake Powell that would include "water and sewer systems, paved roadways, golf course, riding stables, country club, and recreation area including swimming pool"), while speaking of the value of living in the rural West away from the industry and pollution of the big cities (at the same hearing he hoped development would allow residents "to stay [in San Juan County] instead of moving to the congestion and pollution of the big city"). He apparently saw no contradiction advocating for industrial development in his home county and decrying its presence in the city.[71] It was a sentiment not incompatible with his religious forebears who sought to pattern settlement in southeastern Utah after the religious injunction to make the desert blossom as the rose. The garden motif implied neither overwhelming industry nor an uncultivated, unused landscape. One might imagine that even someone like Black would have stopped short of industrializing had he felt it threatened his sacred sense of space.

Still, Black and other ideological descendants of the region's original Mormon settlers perceive the land and its resources in primarily anthropocentric terms. Some of this is certainly driven by religious tenets. Consider the words of scientist and Mormon apostle John Widtsoe, who unapologetically attempted to convey the spirit in the biblical book of Genesis: "The destiny of man is to possess the whole earth; the destiny of the earth is to be subject to man. There can be no full conquest of the earth, and no real satisfaction to humanity, if large portions of the earth remain beyond his highest control."[72] Nonetheless, to attribute this statement solely to religious dogma would be a mistake, since it so plainly blends the religious and secular notions of land that have been historically dominant in American culture. Mormons today espouse what writer and activist Stephen Trimble calls "the sanctity of industrious hard work" as zealously as they had once embraced communal ownership of resources—in other words, "secular entrepreneurial energy replaced sacred stewardship."[73] Religious ideas now dovetail neatly into the dominant thinking of the American mainstream.

Both Abbey's and Black's worldviews had developed primarily through lived experiences in the Southwest. The land gave form to their visions. To Black, the country was big enough for as many roads as could be built to service developments along the lake. "You could honestly say that when we build these roads, because of the vastness and nature of the area, it will make little more of a mark than to plow the ocean!" he declared to a congressional subcommittee in 1970.[74] Paved roads like those built to Halls Crossing or into Arches National Park and the Needles District in Canyonlands National Park "opened" nature's wonders to the public while still retaining the natural feel and appearance of the place. Building roads was just the first act of creation. Like old State Road 95, roads might be improved, made faster, slicker, and straighter. Then the lakeside marinas, gas stations, visitor centers, and more roads extending like limbs to the outer hinterlands would surely follow.

Yet as a young man, Black affirmed that building roads was infeasible in that broken canyon country. "After I started prospecting and saw how rough that country was, it just did not ever seem possible—building a road," he had said of upgrading the dirt road to a modern paved highway. By the time Calvin Black reached adulthood, he had begun to appreciate the power of machines to transform the land—or at least his perception of it. At age twenty-five, he took his first airplane ride. "When I saw that country from the air for the first time, it did not look as big and formidable as it had." He would come to appreciate modern Cat tractors and graders for their ability to cut and grade and fill in a way his father as road foreman had never known. As an independent miner, Black built his own access roads to his mines, became a strong advocate of road building (including U-95), and later as San Juan County commissioner secured state and federal funds to pave other poorly maintained dirt roads. Roads were essential; they belonged on the landscape and provided the means to extract wealth and security from the land. Undoubtedly, no other man was more responsible for the network of modern roads in the county.[75] His infatuation with roads was such that BLM veterans recall how Black thought the phrase "black is beautiful" referred to asphalt.[76]

In his lifetime, Black would witness the powerful impact of road building in the desert. With completion of Glen Canyon Dam, U-95, and the promise of new oil and gas wells or mines, marinas, hotels, and gas stations, at last—it seemed—San Juan County was becoming a destination. Part of this new promise stemmed from a heightened sense of a newfound power over the land—that where once the broken terrain set the limits, now technology and human ingenuity proved the greater forces. Faith in progress likely transformed attitudes about the land and nature. Now that the county could be crossed by high-speed vehicles, the land did not seem so forbidding, vast, or untouchable. Now that bulldozers and graders tore through the east-west length of the county paving new roads, now that the lake allowed boaters to weave effortlessly in and out of the Colorado River side canyons, the physical barriers to travel were not so great. Once technology allowed human access to some of the remotest places on the planet, tourists' perceptions of place shifted from fear to awed appreciation of beauty. And for the residents of southeastern Utah, the mental inertia based on the land's perceived limits gave way to a new kind of faith in human power over nature.

Edward Abbey would not have denied the power of technology to overwhelm nature, but this he did not celebrate. Whereas Black descended from a tradition that viewed the lived-in landscape as paramount, Abbey believed that the spirit of the desert demanded apartness from people. Abbey recalls the story in *Desert Solitaire* of driving the old Flint Trail, built by uranium miners like Black but subsequently abandoned by them. He reveled in taking that trail in a four-wheel-drive jeep, "up and down hills, in and out of washes and along the spines of ridges." Each traveled mile was rougher than the last until finally he reached the end of the road, about as far away from "civilization" as was possible. To Abbey, the road was an irresistible lure into the backcountry.[77]

Still, in his view, it would not be possible to linger and stay. Abbey writes that "this sweet virginal primitive land will be grateful for my departure and the absence of the tourists." To him, the paradox was that while the desert—"desolate and still and strange"—called to him and roads provided passage, the desert could not be inhabited. Arches National Park was one of those places that to him stood apart from the rest of industrialized modern America. And even Abbey longed to return to "this new America of concrete and iron" that he found repulsive and welcome at the same time. But he expressed ambivalence about whether the desert could survive the impending onslaught of cars and tourists and modern development. Abbey could not know whether the desert he was leaving, perhaps for good, would ever be the same again. A new main road into Arches would be forged, and more branching out to nearly every scenic attraction in the park, propelling people in and out of the park at a pace that would deny visitors the kind of intimate experience of the place that Abbey craved and wrote about so movingly.[78]

In other words, Edward Abbey was increasingly skeptical that the "middle" landscape described by American studies scholar Leo Marx could be preserved.[79] In his mind, roads like old State Road 95 represented the ideal; rough and used by locals for so many years, they had almost blended into the landscape. Abbey referred to the original dirt road as "primitive," which evokes the image of wilderness untrammeled by man. Not so with the new modern high-speed highway. There was something about paving over, about erasing the natural contours of the land, about the audacity of cutting through natural barriers instead of going around them, about new steel bridges spanning previously unspannable gorges and canyons. There was something sinister about speeding by without considering the character of the terrain, without feeling the place. The loss was not only nature's, but a deeply felt human loss.

In his essay recalling old State Road 95 before the lake submerged the old trail and the modern highway bridged the canyons and carved deep scars into the ridges, Abbey wrote,

> All of this [the new road], the engineers and politicians and bankers will tell you, makes the region easily accessible to everybody, no matter how fat, feeble or flaccid. That is a lie.
>
> It is a lie. For those who go there now, smooth, comfortable, quick and easy, sliding through as slick as grease, will never be able to see what we saw. They will never feel what we felt. They will never know what we knew, or understand what we cannot forget.[80]

In lamenting the loss of the old road, Abbey did not reflect on time primeval before people had permanently scarred the landscape. He emphasized preindustrialization, not prehuman contact, and wrote about a primitive backcountry, not a pristine, untouched wilderness. In a way, he was contrasting a romanticized view of the pioneer period with the profoundly more cynical view of a destructive and transformative modern era. But it was also recognition that the canyon country has a profound human history that should be acknowledged, if not celebrated. A reviewer from the National Park Service criticized Abbey for referring to the Escalante River region as a "clean and pristine wilderness" in an unpublished essay originally intended for *American Heritage.* The country, the reviewer noted, had a history of mining and grazing and even then was being drilled for oil. "Of course the Escalante area is not an *untouched* wilderness—but what is?" Abbey responded. "The old corrals and cabins do not detract from the land's primitive quality; and as for that oil-drilling near Davis Gulch, the last I heard it was a dry hole. Anyway, all the more reason to have the area made official wilderness, quick. Before they *do* muck it up."[81]

Machines and technology do provide the difference between a primitive landscape and a fully domesticated one. Of course, it is all a matter of perspective. What to some is degradation to others is progress. What to some is loss, to others, gain. Where to some construction means overwhelming nature, others see it as improving on nature or at least using the fruits of what nature so generously endows.

Perhaps it is unfair to characterize Black and Abbey as Manichaean opposites. In a sense, neither man fits squarely in the boxes popular perceptions put them in. Abbey never felt entirely comfortable with the self-styled environmental crowd. If progress is development, and development brings ecological ruin, Abbey's monkey wrenchers do not entirely represent the antithesis to progress. Hayduke and Seldom Seen Smith drove big cars and tossed their beer cans out the window like the rest of them. In "The Second Rape of the West," Abbey famously confessed, "Of course I litter the public highway. Every chance I get. After all, it's not the beer cans that are ugly; it's the highway that is ugly."[82] For Black, despite his reputation as a hardheaded moneymaker, people who knew him speak nearly unanimously of his magnanimity and good nature. Although his opponents have said that having an argument with Black was like "riding a bull," he disarmed his critics by his command of the issues and facts, not through personal attacks or insults. Moreover, while Black made no apologies for his drive to develop and conquer the land, he also spoke of having a regard for the environment and styled himself as one of the "true environmentalists." Calling Abbey an environmentalist and Black a developer is a good method of characterizing positions or ideologies but not necessarily true to life.

Still, I am not the first to point out the contest between these two warring factions. Abbey received at the tail end of his life an interesting letter from Tom Austin, the chief of police in Blanding, Utah, who had grown up on a midwestern farm, then "migrated to Utah to keep from starving to death." He said that while in college, his professors had introduced him to Abbey's work, which spoke to him as someone who had fallen in love with the Southwest. Later, after joining the police department, he read *The Monkey Wrench Gang* at the behest of his colleagues "so I would know what to watch for if any of 'those long-haired-hippie-bastards' showed up in my town." As a cop, he "highly resented the tactics" of the Gang but admitted that he enjoyed the story.

Austin told Abbey that in a college paper, he represented Abbey as "the figurehead of the radical environmental movement in the United States" and Calvin Black as a "leader among the radical materialistic factions in the state of Utah and certainly San Juan County." The representations probably seemed natural to Austin. In his writings, Abbey had been a persistent "voice in the wilderness" urging direct action to defend the earth. *The Monkey Wrench Gang* in particular helped inspire the creation of Earth First![83] Austin undoubtedly knew and worked with Black. By the mid-1980s, Black had a reputation in the state and even beyond its borders—and especially among environmentalists—for being a determined and successful developer.[84]

The Monkey Wrench Gang itself helps to establish the bifurcation. In a sense, the novel characterizes to the point of exaggeration. Abbey's novel is purposefully irreverent and provocative but, according to him, "though fictional in form, is based strictly on historical fact. Everything in it is real or actually happened. And it all began just one year from today." He was not just referring to the sand in the gas tanks or the chases by quasi-official local vigilantes. He meant the engineers who would stop at nothing to achieve "perfect sphericity" and men like Bishop Love who could "hear a dollar bill drop on a shag rug." Abbey was also sure that the wheels of "progress" would roll on, and he was equally sure that people would come to the defense of Mother Earth. The novel is a reflection of a contemporary situation and a projection for the future. The two stories—the one of industrial progress, the other of environmental defense—had already begun to diverge and branch apart as the two groups dug in and claimed their positions.

And so these two contending stories may be personified by Black and Abbey. Both men were more than champions of contrary ideologies at work in the canyon country: they came to represent, in life and still in death, a distinct way of thinking about and acting on the land. Black, San Juan county developer and commissioner, was a self-made millionaire with an extensive career championing limited government, state ownership of federal lands, and maximum economic development of natural resources. Although Abbey's depiction of Black as the human face of the technocrats was perhaps exaggerated—calculating, armed, jeep revving, yellow toothed, leading a sheriff's posse to apprehend the four lawless renegades—Black was larger than life in his own right. So, too, was Edward Abbey. Through Abbey's writings—chiefly *The Monkey Wrench Gang*—he created a conception that stuck as the antithesis of development and "progress" in the West. The life stories of Abbey and Black became intermeshed in an expansive clash over development and preservation in the Southwest.

Rarely did the two men directly cross paths, but the antagonism on both sides was always present. At a speech given at the University of Utah in 1988, Abbey half joked, "It may be true that Utah has the world's worst county commissioners. I'm thinking primarily of San Juan, Grand, and Garfield counties." Making special reference to "my old friend Calvin Black from Blanding" as being among that group, he paused to ask, "Hey Cal, are you out there? Got any new plots for sale?" to the delight of his audience. Despite these jabs in public statements, Abbey did say he respected Black "as a person." Late in 1988, in a letter of condolence upon learning his old nemesis had contracted cancer, Abbey wrote to Black:

> Dear Cal—
>
> I hear rumors that you've come down with a serious illness. If true, I hope you beat it. Although you and I probably disagree about almost everything, you should know that I have never felt the slightest ill-will toward you as a person. Furthermore, you still owe me an airplane ride. Good luck & best wishes, Ed Abbey

Sadly, Abbey died unexpectedly a few months after he penned the note, a year before Black succumbed to cancer.[85]

Both men likely embraced their role as figureheads of ideologies at work in the West. In life they crafted their personas, and in death their adherents continue the causes for which they fought. Each man articulated a compelling vision of the best way to act on the land. In the 1970s over construction of U-95, these ideologies had begun to come into conflict. It was, for people who welcomed it, the long-awaited east-west route across the Colorado River. For Abbey and like-minded, it was a lamentable scar on the land and—like Glen Canyon Dam—a call to action. The road, then, forged a new path, a beginning. Abbey and Black had helped to set the trajectory of that path.

three

Roadless in Negro Bill Canyon

In the canyon reaches just north of Moab, Utah, the Colorado River jogs around the northwest point of Porcupine Rim and then turns around Big Bend before briefly emerging from the deep canyons into Spanish Valley north of Moab. About midway along this stretch between Big Bend and the river's confluence with Highway 191, a small creek has split open the rock cliff on the south side of the mighty Colorado. The place is Negro Bill Canyon. At its base, Navajo sandstone walls streaked with black desert varnish rise like sentinels. In the canyon bottoms, a perennial unnamed trickle of water laps gently over rock and sand. A trail follows the creek, then, after less than two miles, negotiates higher ground to reach Morning Glory Natural Bridge, one of the largest natural arches in the world. If you know where to look, an outline is scarcely visible of an old road, now closed, that enters the canyon from the west, follows the high ground for a time, then descends, crossing the creek several times for about a mile and a half up the canyon.

That road once stood as the centerpiece of a volatile conflict over designated wilderness. In statute and in the public's eye, wilderness equated roadlessness, suggesting that the old motorized road like that in Negro Bill Canyon would preclude wilderness designation. But what constituted a road? When it began reviewing lands qualifying for wilderness status, the Bureau of Land Management adopted a nuanced definition that classified each vehicle route according to whether it had been built by machinery or by hand tools, whether it had been used and maintained on a regular basis, and whether it was considered a "public thoroughfare" under the nineteenth-century mining law Revised Statute 2477. The BLM ultimately distinguished a road from a "way," with the latter defined as a temporary road maintained solely by the passage of vehicles that did not impinge on the wilderness characteristics of a particular area.

Yet defining roads in wild places is fraught with complexities, not least because how one defines a road hinges on how one sees the landscape. To many locals in Grand County, Utah, living a stone's throw from Negro Bill Canyon, the route signified this was a lived-in, working landscape. The proposed wilderness area hardly fitted their preconceived ideas about wilderness: wild, remote, unused; places without history. Negro Bill Canyon's history was undeniably inscribed on the land.

Negro Bill Canyon derives its name from William Granstaff, its earliest inhabitant. Legend has it that in 1881, Granstaff hid in the canyon to evade angry Moabites who sought his blood, but details of this incident or even of Granstaff's life remain scant. John Riis in *Ranger Trails* postulates Granstaff must have had a rough past because of his multiple gunshot scars.[1] Granstaff reportedly ran a homestead and grazed cattle in the canyon and likely forged the first trail there. It was not until about 1940 that a short segment of the trail was widened to allow motorized access. Over time it became a two-track road that extended into the canyon, providing access to the occasional rancher and prospector. At the time of the BLM's wilderness inventory, D. H. Shields and Mike Shumway had staked two hundred mining claims there.[2]

Trails like this are not difficult to identify, especially from the upper tablelands above the canyon. There was no logical order to the trails except to those who first forged them. They developed like many other roads in this country, first as stock trails, then seismograph roads for oil and gas exploration, mining roads, and jeep roads. As one mining company moved out and another moved in, new routes appeared. "Sometimes you'd have a road here and another hundred yards you'd have another road parallel to it, because they didn't care," Moab resident Ray Tibbetts explained. "The bulldozer operator got more money by putting in a new road."[3]

Negro Bill Canyon was not unlike other canyons, mesas, and valleys now managed by the Bureau of Land Management. For generations, homesteaders, explorers and adventurers, treasure seekers, ranchers, miners, and itinerant travelers had crisscrossed the public lands. Here in the arid desert country, their marks linger, creating an almost cumulative effect, layer upon layer of human history.

Officially designated wilderness areas would have to contend with this deep human history. The modern wilderness movement was designed to counteract the forces of modernity and industry that produced many of the marks in the first place. Technological "progress" had its place, but increasingly in the twentieth century it also came to represent many of the problems of modern society. Human beings, growing in number, possessed the technology to alter the landscape to a greater extent than ever before. The Wilderness Act of 1964 framed wilderness preservation as a means to ensure that "an increasing population, accompanied by expanding settlement and growing mechanization, does not occupy and modify all areas within the United States."[4]

The Forest Service had been experimenting with the idea of wilderness for decades before Congress passed the Wilderness Act of 1964, thanks in part to the efforts of Aldo Leopold, Arthur Carhart, and Bob Marshall. The agency had set aside "primitive" areas since the 1920s, but these were administrative designations not protected under federal law. The 1964 act established a national wilderness system and immediately designated 9.1 million acres of national forest wilderness that was to remain "unimpaired" and retain "its primeval character and influence." The initial act to establish wilderness was merely a prelude; the wilderness system would be organic and expanding. Section (3)(b) of the act mandated the Forest Service to initiate a review of its remaining "primitive" areas for wilderness designation. Any land deemed to be wilderness worthy would remain "unimpaired" until Congress took action.[5]

The architects of the wilderness bill made concessions: they permitted language allowing grazing, existing mining uses, and even water development if deemed appropriate by the US president.[6] But for critics, wilderness was by definition area outside history, and in fact much of what Congress designated conformed to that notion. Wayne Aspinall of Colorado, perhaps the most persistent and effective opponent of the Wilderness Act in Congress, backed the final compromise version of the bill in large part because it clearly demarcated those areas to be managed for economic uses and those that would be protected. In one place roads and development would be allowed. In another they would be off-limits. Put another way, designating one area for wilderness essentially meant permanently opening another for commercial use. "If we stop mining and stop grazing and stop water development and stop lumber harvesting in an area, we have stopped maximum use," Aspinall rejoined. "I am not afraid to stop maximum use in some areas" lacking high commercial value.[7]

Among the acres designed as wilderness in 1964 were forestlands considered of little economic worth. Congress had deliberately omitted BLM-managed lands like those in Negro Bill Canyon from the wilderness system, for inclusion of these would have killed the bill. The reason for this can be understood with some background into how the BLM was originally created. Congress established the BLM in 1946 by merging the General Land Office and the US Grazing Service. The new agency inherited from the former the tradition of disposal and from the latter the government's desire to promote commercial use of the public lands. The 1952 BLM emblem featured a miner, a rancher, an engineer, a logger, and a surveyor against the backdrop of covered wagons, train tracks, and industrial development. Under the early leadership of Marion Clawson and Edward Woozley, the agency became committed to the principle of multiple use and to the classification of lands for their "best" and "highest" use, which, by BLM standards, tended to be either grazing or mining. Wilderness simply did not figure into the agency's image. (This despite the fact that Congress had essentially affirmed in Section 2 of the 1960 Multiple-Use Sustained-Yield Act that preservation belonged at the table of multiple use.) Besides, it would have been hard to sell to the public and even some conservationists at the time that relatively unknown, low-elevation, vegetatively monotonous desert lands deserved inclusion in a national wilderness preservation system.[8]

But this narrow view of the public lands slowly shifted. The same mechanization that invited economic exploitation also led an industrial society to identify in the West's open lands ecological and aesthetic values quite apart from commercial uses. Gradually, more conservationists recognized the value of desert lands and the need to protect some from industry and private gain. This epiphany was subtle but profound. Although people had been using the land for generations, only slowly did perceptions shift of the land as wastelands that nobody wanted to threatened, fragile places in need of protection.

Ever so slowly, the BLM took to task a reinvention of itself. Its current emblem, released in 1964, simply depicts a mountain, a tree, and a river valley. Agency officials came to see the BLM's role as a conservationist of natural resources on par with the national park and forest systems. The most significant legislative sea change occurred with passage of the Federal Land Policy and Management Act (FLPMA) in 1976. Sometimes referred to as BLM's "Organic Act," FLPMA established policies and guidelines for managing its lands. Notably, it stated that the federal government would retain the public lands in perpetuity unless "it is determined that disposal of a particular parcel will serve the national interest." Management was to be based on principles of sustained yield, multiple use, and conservation "in a manner that will protect the quality of scientific, scenic, historical, ecological, environmental, air and atmospheric, water resource, and archeological values."[9] At last, the BLM had its management directive.

Section 603 of FLPMA mandated, upon the recommendation of the Public Land Law Review Commission's report, a wilderness review of BLM lands and established criteria for identifying areas with wilderness characteristics. The Wilderness Policy and Review Procedures dated February 1978 set the guidelines for conducting the review. The process was to begin with an initial inventory to identify areas exhibiting wilderness values. Then a more intensive review would be made, followed by a study. Those areas formerly designated as natural or primitive prior to November 1, 1975, were to be reported to the president by July 1, 1980. Otherwise, the law gave the Interior Department until October 21, 1991, to report recommendations to the president. The Carter administration, however, fast-tracked the process by requiring BLM state directors to report their recommendations by September 30, 1980, "or sooner, if possible within limits of man power and funding." The fast-approaching deadlines meant rapid-fire review and evaluation of vast sections of the public lands held by the BLM. The directive was for the state BLM director to evaluate the public lands all at once, with the option of conducting smaller regional reviews if resources were not available.[10]

The public lands managed by the BLM would be evaluated based on four criteria established in the 1964 legislation: size, roadlessness, naturalness, and outstanding opportunities for solitude or primitive and unconfined recreation, or both. The question of size was the most objective. The area had to be at least five thousand contiguous acres, not including private or state holdings within the unit's boundaries. Smaller areas could be considered if they met specific characteristics. If size criterion was straightforward, proving evidence of outstanding opportunities for solitude or a primitive and unconfined type of recreation was trickier. Indeed, what affords a solitary experience for one individual may be quite different for another. Still, the criteria did not make or break the initial inventory; an area not meeting standards might yet move on to intensive review.[11]

The meat of the matter was roadlessness and naturalness, qualities that might on the surface appear to be clear-cut. It would seem simple to determine whether a road existed or if a human "intrusion" had made a substantial impact, thus detracting from an area's naturalness. In truth, assessing wilderness integrity was intricately complicated. If the review had stipulated assessing the "natural integrity" of a place, it may have been easier. Instead, the standard was "apparent naturalness," which according to the handbook "refers to whether or not an area looks natural to the average visitor who is not familiar with the biological composition of natural ecosystems versus man-affected ecosystems in a given area." Indeed, given that a large percentage of BLM lands had been heavily grazed, virtually nothing could be called *ecologically* untouched by humans (or livestock). This is a key reason "apparent naturalness" remained the judging criterion. The concern was not the human impact itself so much as the noticeability of its imprint. Even conspicuous impacts might be mitigated, because for potential wilderness areas the BLM guidebook permitted returning human developments to a natural condition "by natural processes or by hand labor."[12]

In one sense, the criteria embraced an expansive definition of wilderness that more closely aligned with what many believed was the original intent of the 1964 Wilderness Act. It was deceptively simple to assume that when the act referred to wilderness as "an area of undeveloped Federal land retaining its primeval character and influence, without permanent improvements or human habitation," and "where the earth and its community of life are untrammeled by man," this imparted a definitive wilderness definition. But to so assume would be a mistake. Howard Zahniser, an architect of the Wilderness Act, had selected the term *untrammeled* deliberately: a trammel is a net used to catch fish or birds, so *untrammeled,* as Zahniser understood it, meant "free, unbound, unhampered, unchecked."[13] That is, it meant unworked areas, not those completely devoid of the human presence, as one might infer.

Many areas up for wilderness designation since passage of the 1964 act had been worked—in some cases intensively. It is not uncommon to encounter a barbed-wire fence, old corral, line shack, or the outline of an old road within wilderness areas. However, by the standards applied to wilderness designation, these did not constitute permanent human markings because *permanent* referred to structures intentionally maintained for current and future use. Thus, the 1964 act used qualifying language to define wilderness, stating that an area of wilderness "*generally* appears to have been affected *primarily* by the forces of nature, with the imprint of man's work *substantially* unnoticeable."[14] Wilderness was not to stand outside the human experience; rather, it would enclose marks of its presence.

These criteria seemed a departure from traditional notions of wilderness as "pristine" or entirely untouched by humans. According to the "purity doctrine," as wilderness advocates derisively called it, wilderness should contain no trace of the human imprint. Wilderness opponents often favored a purer definition as a place where humans had never been, could not go, or would have no intention to visit. "There is [*sic*] only one or two places in this country [Grand County, Utah] that would fit the description of wilderness, and one is that big stand of rocks on that rim [west of Moab]—you can't walk them, let alone make a road through them," said Ray Tibbetts. "They're there because they're there, and that makes it a wilderness. Another one, there's a big island out by Dead Horse Point. I don't know if it's got five thousand acres, but on top of that mesa is wilderness because there are no roads. You get up there and it gives you the attitude that that's what it is."[15]

Defining wilderness as a place untouched by humans might be seen as a tactic opponents used to keep more land in the multiple-use framework. The presence of trails, stock ponds, and mining claims made it difficult to convince wilderness opponents that the area's highest use was to protect it and leave it untrammeled. Many felt that if a place had been grazed or accessed for mining, then it belonged to the ranchers and miners. Otherwise, if it had seen no human intrusion or was largely inaccessible, then the highest use might be wilderness. This line of reasoning had been applied by the Forest Service in its early wilderness evaluations—to clearly distinguish "pristine" areas in the high country from more accessible forest areas in the lowlands that might better serve the commercial timber industry. Moreover, with passage of FLPMA some believed wilderness designation of the public domain was unnecessary; as John F. Tanner of the Association of Counties wrote in 1978, the 1976 law already contained "adequate provision for the protection of wilderness values" by the BLM without formal congressional designation of wilderness areas.[16]

In the years after passage of the Wilderness Act, Congress would pointedly reject the purity doctrine. Over time it passed legislation adding lands in the eastern states—many with long histories of human use and habitation—to the wilderness system. When in 1968 Congress designated the thirty-seven-hundred-acre Great Swamp Wilderness in New Jersey, the area's roadbed and utility lines had to be removed.[17] In debates preceding passage of the Endangered American Wilderness Act of 1978, Congress expressly addressed the purity doctrine and determined not only that areas might still be considered for wilderness where the human imprint was "minor" or at least not "substantially noticeable," but also that a wide range of recreation would be permitted in wilderness areas. As Idaho senator Frank Church put it in 1973, "Nothing could be more contrary to the meaning and intent of the Wilderness Act. The effect of such an interpretation would be to automatically disqualify almost everything, for few if any lands on this continent—or any other—have escaped man's imprint to some degree."[18]

The statutory dismantling of the purity doctrine meant that areas like Negro Bill Canyon, which were close to towns, might still be considered for wilderness designation. The BLM wilderness review proceeded on the same assumption—that places previously inhabited and worked by humans ought to still be considered as long as human impacts were "substantially unnoticeable." The initial review of Negro Bill Canyon counted twenty-four miles of motorized routes, but since BLM staff reasoned that the routes impinged very little on the area's naturalness, they were instead considered mere "ways." The piñon-juniper cover largely concealed the tracks from view except along one high-ground area between the canyon and Porcupine Rim. The canyon itself had "little evidence of human activity and still appear[ed] very natural" and was "deep and winding so that sights and sounds of other people would be easily avoided." Notably, the canyon contained "outstanding opportunities for solitude in the sandstone," "basically retaining" what the staffer considered the canyon's "natural appearance."[19]

The local BLM staff concluded that the Negro Bill West unit located between Negro Bill and Moab did not merit wilderness consideration because it was smaller than the minimum 5,000 acres and lacked sandstone formations and a canyon like the main Negro Bill unit.[20] But they did recommend designation of 27,600 acres in the main stem of Negro Bill Canyon and the upper benchlands as a Wilderness Study Area (WSA). It would be among the more than 6.3 million acres identified by the BLM in the statewide initial inventory for wilderness consideration.

Not unlike the Forest Service's first wilderness review (RARE I), the BLM's initial wilderness inventory pleased few. Wilderness proponents derided it in the same way they criticized RARE I for underrepresenting the amount of land that qualified as wilderness. Critics claimed that the BLM did not adequately involve the public or apply wilderness criteria consistently and that the process was hasty and shoddy. Janet Ross confirmed these deficiencies in the Moab district, where she worked on the review as a wilderness specialist but later quit in disgust over the process. She recalls asking the wilderness coordinator, Diana Webb, how to do a proper wilderness inventory and being told, "Oh, it doesn't matter. Just make it up as you go along." According to Ross, the initial wilderness review of Mancos Mesa in San Juan County was rushed in just one day and was a "frustrating experience" and "a total political boondoggle."[21]

Perhaps even more frustrated were local Moab residents opposed to designating so much wilderness close to home. At wilderness study open houses hosted by the Moab District in San Juan County, locals were not shy to voice their alarm. Nearly all opposed wilderness of any kind, though a few favored it in Grand Gulch or Dark Canyon. At a meeting in Blanding, Utah, according to a staff report written by Ross, county commissioner Cal Black burst into the room and yelled at BLM staffers Bob Turri and Paul Happel for proposing wilderness in areas with roads. "We've had enough of you guys telling us what to do," Black declared, gaining steam. "I'm not a violent man, but I'm getting to the point where I'll blow up bridges, ruins, and vehicles. We're going to start a revolution. We're going to get back our lands. We're going to sabotage your vehicles. You had better start going out in two's and three's, because we're going to take care of you BLMers." BLM wilderness inventory team leader Paul Happel replied, "Mr. Black, I hope you are not threatening me." Black retorted, "I'm not threatening you, I'm promising you." Local resident Devar Shumway then piped up, "If Cal will be our leader, I'll be the first to follow him."[22]

The menacing atmosphere continued into an evening meeting where more citizens arrived to express their contempt for wilderness, government oversight, and a BLM supposedly run by "bureaucrats, over-educated, and outsiders." After the meeting Black denigrated the service work of BLM employees, referring to them as "parasites" on society. "All things in life come from the earth, and you've never produced anything," he purportedly told BLM staffer Bonnie Neumann.[23]

Navajo Mark Maryboy, who served with Black on the San Juan County Commission, has remarked that arguing with Cal Black was like riding a bull, but it was the force of his personality and the weight of his argument that bucked you off the saddle, not the threatening nature of his words.[24] Black's style was certainly aggressive, but it was more posturing and showmanship than anything. A few weeks later, a contrite Black walked into the Moab office with a copy of the staff report in his hands. San Juan County would cooperate with the BLM through the inventory, he promised.[25] Although he likely had personal reasons to be critical of the review, given that some of his mining claims might be impacted by the designation, Black claimed he played the role of messenger at the wilderness meetings. "I feared that talk might turn into action," he later wrote, implying that his was a benign role in escalating the tension.[26]

Indeed, talk in southeastern Utah was unsettling. Men in trucks threatened Dick Carter of the Utah Wilderness Association (UWA) at an overlook near Hanksville. BLM district manager S. Gene Day endured all kinds of threats and lawsuits. "Some of [Black's] townspeople, their marbles already loosened, their fears incited by Black, is where the problem lies," penned BLM employee Bill Haase. "Put a gun in their hands and someone will get blown away. After last Thursday's meeting, we all go to bed with this fear. It's hard to sleep when friends and their families are potential targets."[27]

The threats of violence reflected a sentiment and growing political movement among those who objected to wilderness designation, environmental regulations, and federal ownership of public lands. All of these concerns would come to rest under the cloak of a movement known as the Sagebrush Rebellion. But the rebels were simply pouring new wine into old bottles. Many westerners had long resented a federal presence in the West, although writer and historian Bernard DeVoto has observed the irony of western attitudes toward the federal government, summed up in the phrase "Get out and give us more money."[28] Anger and mistrust—usually over perceived rights and sovereignty to exercise jurisdiction over land and resources—rarely boiled far from the surface. Rebels spoke of the West as being on "unequal footing" with the East, since the majority of public lands were in the West.

Although the Sagebrush Rebellion, which began in Nevada, was mostly political theater, the movement to transfer ownership of the public lands to the western states received quite a bit of support from westerners of all stripes, particularly politicians. It was both a rural and an urban movement given lip service by congressional delegates, state legislatures, and western state governors and embraced according to public opinion polls by a slight majority of citizens of the Rocky Mountain states. Orrin Hatch was joined by Jake Garn (Utah's other senator), Dennis DeConcini and Barry Goldwater of Arizona, Alan Simpson and Malcolm Wallop of Wyoming, and Paul Laxalt and Howard Cannon of Nevada when he introduced Senate Bill 1680 on August 3, 1979, calling for the "return" of "rightful title" to public lands and national forests in the West.[29] Utah legislators also expressed antigovernment sentiment; for example, during a special session, some wore insignias that read, "Welcome to the West: Property, U.S. Government."[30]

Part of the problem was that rural westerners like those in Moab felt shackled by increasing federal restrictions and powerless to advance their own agendas. The Sagebrush Rebellion offered a regional forum to resist environmental legislation and federal intrusion into local autonomy. Other organizations like the Western Association of Land Users (WALU), organized and headed by Moabite Ray Tibbetts, had similar objectives. According to Tibbetts, some groups sympathetic to the objectives of WALU were afraid to speak out. A rancher was reluctant to criticize federal land management for fear of getting hit with a notice of trespass or being harassed by the BLM. A group of river runners supposedly refused to join the group because the BLM controlled permits to the rivers.[31] But probably only a few hesitated to join for fear of reprisal. WALU had a strong following among those who objected to the BLM's direction of managing lands under FLPMA.

For Sagebrush Rebels, the wilderness study designation in Negro Bill Canyon seemed the ideal opportunity to translate frustration into action. About a year before the Sagebrush Rebellion caught national attention, prospector Mike Shumway had driven his bulldozer a mile and a half into the canyon to access D. H. Shields's mining claims. A few months later, as the BLM prepared to initiate its wilderness review, they worked out an agreement with Shields that kept access open to the mining claims but closed the road to the public. The BLM then dug a trench and placed boulders at the mouth of the road. According to Shields, after the initial wilderness review had been finalized by mid-1979, the BLM sent him a letter with instructions to discontinue work at the mine or face fines or even a jail sentence for noncompliance. Shields was understandably upset. "I don't understand the reason why they all of a sudden have this absolute authority over mining prospectors and developers, when they said that the area was open to multiple use when I decided to stake the open area several years ago," he mourned. "I just know that I must be allowed to at least complete the minimum work or I will lose my claims."[32]

Although we do not have the other side of the story, several details from Shields's version seem off. The BLM had waived a provision in the 1872 mining act requiring miners to complete one hundred dollars' worth of assessment each year on their claim. Whereas Shields asserted the BLM denied him access to his claim, in fact the BLM did not have authority to do so, even in a designated wilderness area. The BLM could restrict only motorized access and certain kinds of surface disturbances, which is likely what they were mandating in his case.

In the meantime, Grand County commissioners decided to call attention to the BLM's management of Negro Bill Canyon by opening up the road and putting it on the county's Class D road system. On July 7, 1979, Mike Shumway removed the boulders and again drove his bulldozer partway up the canyon.[33] Ray Tibbetts remembers standing next to Jim McPherson of the county commission when the dozer started its slow ascent. McPherson questioned whether they were in the right for opening the road. "Jim, you know damn well we are," Tibbetts rejoined.[34]

The BLM responded by replacing the barrier. Again, with the apparent blessing of Grand County commissioners, Shumway removed the boulders. The federal government issued a cease-and-desist order for Shumway and demanded a court order to request an assessment of damages and prevent removing of future barricades. The BLM had no intention of replacing the boulders a third time, but in late August it installed a cable across the road about a quarter of a mile up the canyon. The commission subsequently had the cable cut. After an unidentified party rolled rocks onto the road from the cliff above, the county once again removed the boulders.[35]

Running a dozer up the road and oiling and graveling a short portion of it were intended as much to assert county control of the road and make the canyon ineligible for wilderness designation as they were to provide vehicular access to Shields's mining claims. To the county, the issue was public access to the public lands, for Shields and anyone else who wanted canyon access. Though the road was still rough, the week after the county removed the boulders the first time, about fifty locals managed it in four-wheel-drive trucks and held a picnic. The outing was a flagrant display of contempt for the BLM's wilderness policy and rebellion against its authority. The road, they hoped to show, existed and served a public purpose. Tibbetts clearly presumed that the human markings in the canyon disqualified the area for wilderness consideration. "You can't take a place with a road on it and call it roadless," Tibbetts declared on the day of the outing. "Once the roads are in, that bed will be here forever. And, as you can see, there are cement foundations here and there where people have tried to put cabins or parts of the road."[36]

Yet no one had any delusions that the area was pristine wilderness. The rebels' purpose was not merely to reveal the human presence in the canyon; opening the road was a direct call to action, an assertion of road ownership in Negro Bill Canyon and, by extension, elsewhere in the county. And it was almost certainly a deliberate strategy to sabotage the wilderness process by improving or maintaining a road in a proposed "roadless" area.

The man making the decisions in Negro Bill Canyon and responsible for the wilderness inventory in southeastern Utah was S. Gene Day. As head of the BLM district office, Day occupied a powerful seat in southeastern Utah. He had the final say in that local BLM office to determine management of public lands and to sign off on the wilderness inventory. It did not help matters that Day projected obstinacy and some arrogance. That, at least, was the perspective of his largely conservative constituency, some of whom threatened him and treated him with contempt. Although Day was a self-described environmentalist, wilderness and environmental allies also found him difficult to work with and reprimanded his every move. When in early 1980 Day scheduled, rescheduled, and finally canceled a field trip with environmental reps to witness firsthand off-highway-vehicle damage to the environment and archaeological sites in Comb Wash, Brian Beard of the Utah Chapter of the Sierra Club fired off a livid letter. "This action is becoming all to[o] famil[i]ar with your office, its lack of responsibility and concern for our natural environment." Rocco Dodson of the Sierra Club Legal Defense Fund, Inc., chided Beard for being "too angry": "I guess what I'm saying is that an underhanded, uncooperative, incompetant [*sic*] district manager is bad enough; we don't want an an[g]ry under-handed, uncooperative, incompetent district manager."[37]

Given the tension over Negro Bill Canyon, Day was no doubt eager to appease both sides, but especially wilderness opponents. Not long after the "musical bulldozers" incidents, he quietly reduced the Wilderness Study Area in Negro Bill Canyon by more than two-thirds. The proposed 8,406-acre WSA now encompassed primarily the canyon and much of the high land situated between the canyon and Porcupine Rim. Deleted from the study area were those places "intruded by roads" and lacking "primitive recreation" like Porcupine Rim and the Slickrock bike trail.[38]

But the concession did not have the desired effect. Drama at Negro Bill only escalated. The following year, the commissioners planned a large public rally there. They hoped to make a big show of it by inviting neighboring counties (who chose not to take part) and the media and by staging the event on July 4. When, exactly, Day and his staff learned of more protests in Negro Bill Canyon is unclear, but they seemed eager to extend a second olive branch. On June 23, 1980, Del Backus of the BLM reported in a county commission meeting that the "BLM was ready to put the picnic area in Negro Bill Canyon if the county wants to take over maintenance of the road." No mention was made whether the BLM would drop the area from the wilderness review, but a picnic site and improved canyon road would certainly have been a nonconforming use in a wilderness area. Probably because the commission was interested in seeing the protest through, however, Ray Tibbetts on behalf of the commission soundly rejected the offer until he could see "more positive signs of BLM cooperation with the county."[39]

The original scheme to take a bulldozer up the canyon changed when Utah governor Scott Matheson suggested moving the demonstration "to another location" and grading a road "that's already on state land"—though no one would have to know this latter detail. The protest would still serve its symbolic purpose to call attention to federal landownership and management without the threat of reprisal. On July 1, 1980, the county commissioners convened a public meeting to announce the planned protest and justified the action as "protecting the Health & Welfare of the Citizens."[40]

But no one informed the BLM that the protest had been moved to a section of state land within the proposed Mill Creek WSA just to the south of the proposed Negro Bill Canyon wilderness area. BLM officials and federal marshals planning to make arrests showed up at the mouth of the canyon; everybody else—250 to 300 people—gathered at the Moab City Park and caravanned in eighty four-wheel-drive vehicles and a few cars over dirt roads to the site in Mill Creek Canyon. Once on the Sand Flats, brief speeches, mostly from the commissioners, welcomed the crowd. Harvey Merrell criticized "the cancerous growth of the [federal] bureaucracy" and promised to "take control of our destiny in Southeastern Utah." Larry Jacobs, also a commissioner, reportedly proclaimed in religious parlance, "We have prayed we are doing the right thing, and at this point I think we are doing the right thing." After the speeches, a bulldozer displaying a US flag and flashing a "I'm a Sagebrush Rebel" sticker lowered its blade and drove a few hundred yards.[41]

A "big old tough environmentalist" stepped defiantly in front of the dozer and strewed himself across the dirt road. When the dozer lunged forward, spitting dirt, the man sprang up and jumped out of the way. A couple of "husky miner boys" determined to "get that son of a bitch" and "whop him good" later confronted the man at a local pub and broke his nose in a brawl. After the victim filed a complaint, a cousin of the perpetrators reportedly broke the man's nose again after he left the hospital.[42]

The commissioners maintained that the county owned the road and many others by authority of R.S. 2477. Ronald L. Rencher, US attorney for the District of Utah, called the action of July 4 "intentional, deliberate, and in violation of the laws of the United States," and demanded that the county commission restore the area, within ten days, to the condition it was "prior to July 4, 1980." If they failed to comply, the restoration would nevertheless occur and Grand County would be charged with the bill. Aldine J. Coffman Jr. considered it absurd to restore the area and sardonically responded to Rencher that "prior to July 4, 1980, the road was a road.... [To] demand that the road be restored to a road is really a concurrence with the acts of maintenance conducted by the Grand County Commission."[43]

Records do not show what eventually became of the exchange, but in the end the county commissioners got the better deal. By the end of the year, at the behest of BLM director Frank Gregg and his instructions to investigate BLM's Moab office, more than half of the units in the Moab area including Negro Bill Canyon, were redlined from the intensive wilderness review. The WSAs remaining on the map dated November 1980 were mere remnants of larger contiguous roadless areas proposed in April 1979.[44]

The decision to eliminate these potential wilderness areas devastated wilderness proponents. Of the more than 5 million roadless acres reviewed in Utah, the BLM identified only 1.9 million that they felt met the wilderness criteria.

Together with Instant Study Areas (which automatically qualified for wilderness study because of their pre-FLPMA status as primitive or outstanding natural areas) and previously identified WSAs, it raised the total roadless acres considered suitable for wilderness to 2.46 million.[45]

Negro Bill had been dropped from the final inventory based on the rationale that "the remaining natural area in this unit is less than 5,000 acres and the pattern of non-Federal lands adversely affects opportunities for solitude and primitive and unconfined recreation." The BLM further announced that it would drop the original lawsuit over the illegal August 1979 barricade removal. In a memorandum outlining the agreement "to preserve the beauty of Negro Bill Canyon and at the same time make it available for public use," the county agreed to remove the road up the canyon from the state's Class D system. The BLM in turn would maintain the quarter-mile section of road and permit the county to construct a parking and picnic area at its head. The agreement gave the county what it wanted—road access to the canyon and its elimination from wilderness consideration—while it still retained federal oversight over motorized use in the canyon.[46]

Here was a clear case of local influence in the wilderness decision process. The outcry and the demonstrations of civil disobedience had seemingly worked. Before year's end, a BLM staffer quit over how the inventory was being carried out, district manager S. Gene Day was transferred at the behest of some locals, and the BLM published an inventory that seemed designed to satisfy wilderness opponents. The lessons learned by both opponents and proponents of wilderness were important: they reinforced a local tradition of radical dissent. Locals opposed to wilderness saw that emotional outbursts, threats, and uncompromising demands would get the desired response. The BLM could be cowed into submission.

Environmentalists learned that lesson, too. Dave Foreman, who on July 5 held a rally to protest the demonstration as part of the first annual Round River Rendezvous near Moab, later observed that the bulldozing episode had been the "last straw" in his gradual realization that moderate, mainstream environmentalism was not enough to counter "the howling, impassioned, extreme stand set forth by off-road-vehicle (ORV) zealots, many ranchers, local boosters, loggers, and miners." That same year Foreman would match "zealots" with zealots by creating the "radical" environmental group Earth First![47]

Several environmental organizations led by the Utah Wilderness Association banded together to file an appeal to the Interior Department's Board of Land Appeals (IBLA), alleging deep flaws in the BLM's statewide inventory process. The fourteen-hundred-page appeal—the largest wilderness appeal ever filed before the IBLA[48]—disputed BLM decisions on 925,000 acres in twenty-nine units. The appeal not merely protested the exclusion of individual units but also pointed to chronic structural problems that could conceivably disqualify the review entirely. The complaint against exclusion of the Negro Bill Canyon WSA, led by the Utah Chapter of the Sierra Club, was a compendium of BLM failure to comply with FLPMA and wilderness review policy. The BLM improperly deleted from the inventory large areas of roadless lands that met wilderness criteria (areas "completely natural and other areas with imprints that are substantially unnoticeable") and modified the inventory record to support their decision to delete the unit. These violations were intentional, the plaintiffs contended; district manager Day had been quoted by a staffer as stating, "When in doubt, throw it out and give the public and private interests a chance to promote its inclusion."[49]

A Department of the Interior solicitor upheld the Sierra Club's complaint that in the case of the Negro Bill Canyon WSA, the BLM had failed to follow wilderness review policy, wrongly altered the record without proper documentation, and incorrectly assessed the area's solitude and recreation potential. The IBLA directed the BLM to reconsider areas with potential wilderness characteristics. The same person who made the initial field report at Negro Bill—Diana Webb—returned to the area to comply with the court decision. Unlike its previous review, this time the BLM used roads as the boundaries for the Wilderness Study Area. To resolve the problem of access to state land sections, the BLM now proposed "cherry stemming" a road (in essence, drawing the wilderness boundary around the road) by closing a narrow portion of land on the northern portion of the unit that connected state land and the unit boundary.[50] On the other hand, mineral exploration roads made it into the WSA, partly to enable prospectors to access legitimate claims.[51]

But James Catlin of the Utah Chapter of the Sierra Club would contest Diana Webb's assessment of roads on the benchlands. The Porcupine Rim Trail forming the proposed eastern boundary of the unit, he argued, received infrequent travel and was difficult to see as it wound up and over rocks. And the old mail trail to Miner's Basin had a cover of regrowth. Catlin maintained that the cherry-stemmed seismograph routes and the "constructed access routes" defining the northern recommended boundary were insignificant and hardly qualified as roads at all. He proposed, therefore, extending the unit north to encompass Drinks Canyon. Catlin argued that although the upper benchlands were not as well vegetated as the canyon and possessed a few road scars, they ought not be disqualified due to superb wilderness qualities with amazing vistas—the view of Arches National Park to the north, Manti–La Sal Mountains to the east, and deep canyons of the Colorado to the west.[52]

While the high bench routes were debated, the crux of the court suit centered on the road up the canyon. The post-IBLA decision summary evaluation noted that "about ½ mile of the road existed pre-FLPMA." There seems to have been some question about the road's length; Catlin pointed to a statement from acting BLM manager C. Delano Backus that sometime "between 1935 and 1966," a road one-quarter-mile long had been constructed but was closed due to traffic concerns on Highway 128. "The road was abandoned and allowed to revegetate. There does not appear to have been any maintenance work done after this period." Not until Shumway reopened the road in 1978 was the route again accessed. Catlin thus contended that because it had been constructed illegally after FLPMA, the road did not qualify under R.S. 2477 and in no way impeded wilderness designation of the canyon.[53]

In July 1982, the BLM once again reversed its decision at Negro Bill Canyon and reinstated a 7,620-acre WSA. While the BLM recognized that a portion of the unit possessed wilderness characteristics, it did not agree that roads on northern boundaries were unnoticeable or sufficiently unused. The proposed WSA excluded some seismographic routes on the upper benchlands and cherry-stemmed the road up the canyon on the grounds that since the mining claims had been staked and accessed prior to passage of FLPMA, "the claimant has the right by law to construct roads to these claims and drill on them."[54] Nevertheless, prowilderness groups were pleased the unit was reinstated. "It was a victory—a small one—for us, in that it reversed the BLM's earlier stand to throw out the entire area," said Rob Smith of the Sierra Club and the Wilderness Society in Salt Lake City.[55]

The court decision left some of the original protesters considering action once more at Negro Bill. Ray Tibbetts mulled over staging another protest; D. H. Shields wanted to drill a uranium hole in the canyon.[56] The issue, however, became one for the courts. The Red Rock 4-Wheelers Club of Moab stepped up to appeal the reinstatement of the WSA.[57] For another half year, the Sierra Club and the Red Rock 4-Wheelers Club led by George Schultz (who also worked for a uranium mining business, and who, interestingly, was married to the BLM's wilderness coordinator in the Moab District, Diana Webb) continued to protest wilderness designation in Negro Bill Canyon. On January 10, 1983, the Utah Chapter of the Sierra Club filed a petition to block the appeal of the Red Rock 4-Wheelers. The IBLA eventually affirmed the BLM's decision to classify the unit as a WSA but not to bring the deleted 1,800 acres back into the unit.[58] Later in the year, the Utah BLM made its final decision by designating 538,000 acres (twelve units) as WSAs, of which the Negro Bill Canyon unit was a part.[59]

In 1991 the State of Utah recommended wilderness designation on BLM lands, but Congress never acted on these or any other proposals to designate BLM wilderness on a large scale in Utah. The Moab Field Office, which is part of the Canyon Country District, contains approximately 1.8 million acres, of which approximately 355,000 acres are WSAs, and another 5,000 acres are designated wilderness.[60] The WSAs are presently managed to preserve and protect their wilderness characteristics. At Negro Bill Canyon, that means the old road up the canyon has been closed to motorized vehicles and nearly reclaimed by nature.

Why did the hoped-for process of sorting out conflicting land uses under FLPMA not work in Utah? Who is to blame for what became a highly polarized and ultimately unresolved wilderness inventory? In the first place, BLM officials in the Moab district could have more firmly upheld the original decision to designate Negro Bill Canyon as a Wilderness Study Area without repeatedly caving to local antiwilderness interests, thus enraging wilderness advocates. Wilderness was then and is now a highly polarizing issue, but it became more so when the BLM did not tackle the issue head-on when it had the chance. Recourse to the courts on both sides may be an indication of failure on the BLM's part to settle the issue.

The troubles at Negro Bill Canyon also stemmed from structural problems with FLPMA and the regulations governing BLM wilderness designation. FLPMA, passed in 1976, certainly was landmark legislation, providing comprehensive authority and guidelines for management of the public lands. But the act did not repeal earlier statutes governing BLM lands, and it did not contain provisions, in the words of historian James Skillen, that "might have genuinely reshaped the property rights regimes and the goals of public lands management." FLPMA merely reflected and acknowledged rather than resolved the plurality of BLM land use. The directives governing wilderness designation on the nation's BLM lands were open-ended and potentially inconclusive. FLPMA limited the secretary's discretion to prohibit existing uses that were inconsistent or threatening to the wildness of the potential study area, even as it provided that existing uses not damage the WSA from further wilderness consideration.[61]

Some BLM officials curiously believed that selecting wilderness-qualifying areas from the public domain would be relatively straightforward. "A thorough and professional inventory process should insure that there will be no valid basis for questioning the inventory results," Arnold Petty had conjectured in June 1979.[62] Obviously, he could not have been more wrong. Petty might have been correct had the BLM worked with firm, unambiguous definitions of wilderness. But in contrast to the Forest Service's RARE reviews, the BLM wilderness review process had been set up at least tacitly to acknowledge the ambiguities of designating wilderness areas and the inherent problems of assessing their qualities. The BLM employed a flexible definition of wilderness in part because finding pristine land completely untouched by humans is nearly impossible, but also because it subscribed to the view that eliminating permanent human impacts on the land is neither possible nor desirable, a point suggested by the Wilderness Act and FLPMA.

Far from being straightforward or definitive, defining wilderness characteristics is a subjective process of seeing what one wants to see. Permanent markings are to some temporary, and vice versa. What is wild and natural to some is domesticated to others. It was in part this subjectivity that made designation so highly controversial. Setting aside areas for wilderness consideration is not merely a matter of locating clearly demarcated natural areas and calling it wilderness. It is, rather, a process that integrates the culture, biases, and perceptions of the people who create them, manage them, and recreate on them.

At Negro Bill Canyon, wilderness opponents insisted on a strict definition of wilderness that precluded any human markings at all and any human impacts to the land as permanent. In court they repeatedly pointed out those places where human imprints still remained after many years. "The road is a physical thing," read the Red Rock 4-Wheelers' Statement of Reasons protesting the Negro Bill Canyon WSA. "It can be seen, felt, and photographed. It exists upon the face of the earth. It is reality." And especially on the dry benchlands above the canyon, road scars still remain.[63]

Yet today the road up Negro Bill Canyon, once so clearly visible, can hardly be seen at all. The idea of permanence is a construct. Nature changes constantly; nothing is truly permanent on the land. The dirt road was no more permanent than any of the natural canyon features like vegetation or the course of the stream.

The broader question is what do these human markings mean? Some may have a long-lasting presence on the land; others will disappear relatively quickly from sight. What does it matter that the imprint of an old road or the foundation of an old mining cabin remains in wilderness? The case could be made that lingering scars notwithstanding, human impacts like roads do not necessarily damage the ecological condition of wilderness or in some way render it useless as a place of renewal. Roderick Nash has upheld that how the wilderness area is used by modern humans threatens the wilderness quality of an area more than the mere presence of a road, mine, or even a dam.[64]

Wilderness proponents sometimes make the case that extant human imprints in wilderness should not be erased from the landscape but are a worthy feature of it. George Wuerthner of the Montana Wilderness Alliance, in keeping with a bioregional approach to wilderness designation, proposed creating wilderness areas that encompass not only mountain peaks but low-lying valley areas as well. To get around the problem of roads that "bisect otherwise roadless country," he proposed closing them to motorized traffic and allowing them to "remain open for horse drawn wagons"—a proposal he specifically made for the Burr Trail. This would help satisfy wilderness opponents who believed that wilderness discriminates against people who cannot walk or otherwise enjoy wilderness without the aid of a motorized vehicle. When potential wilderness areas contain private inholdings like ranches, Wuerthner proposed turning these places into dude ranches that could be used by wilderness "explorers." These "wagon wilderness" areas, as Wuerthner called them, would "alter the view of many people that wild places are only for the young and fit." Roads, then, would serve wilderness rather than merely be a case against it.[65]

It may be hard for some wilderness proponents to conceive of a road—or what used to be a road but is now a "trail" or wagon route—in wilderness. Roads, after all, have become powerful cultural symbols as facilitators of exploitation. Defining wilderness as roadless was essentially a means to keep vehicles (and thus development) outside of these areas. Further, although certain human impacts on the land may not physically threaten the wildness of an area, they may still invade the spirit of wilderness. The idea to keep man-made objects out of nature is more to satisfy some human desire or need than to protect ecological systems or keep the land undefiled. It serves as a reminder, in the words of Edward Abbey, "that *out there* is a different world, older and greater and deeper by far than ours, a world which surrounds and sustains the little world of men as sea and sky surround and sustain a ship."[66] It is the sense that human "intrusions" in wilderness areas distract the mind that nature exists separate and independent of human need.

Nevertheless, even demarcated wilderness presents opportunities to explore humanity's place in nature. "There are among environmentalists a sentimental fringe, people who respond...with blind preservationism in all circumstances," penned Wallace Stegner on the place of humans in wilderness. "But you can't do that. You manifestly can't go that far, though it would be nice, visually and in other ways; people do have to live too. Some kind of compromise has to be made." His essay, a history of Dinosaur in eastern Utah, referred to the monument as "a palimpsest of human history, speculation, rumor, fantasy, ambition, science, controversy, and conflicting plans for use." To him the human marks belonged on the landscape; the Anasazi petroglyphs, Spanish carvings on a huge cottonwood, William Henry Ashley's name on a rock—they were what he referred to as "marks of human passage."[67]

Stegner is an apt commentator on the meaning of human marks on the land, since in the debates over the original passage of the Wilderness Act in 1964 he was an eloquent spokesperson for designating areas that had been "wounded" by the works of men. In his famous 1960 "Wilderness Letter,"

Stegner argued that even if the land had been "deflowered," that did not mean that it might as well be "harvested." The western deserts had been "scarred somewhat by prospectors," he wrote. "In that desert climate the dozer and jeep tracks will not soon melt back into the earth, but the country has a way of making the scars insignificant." It did not matter that the marks of humans remained on the land. Stegner appropriated the argument sometimes attributed to locals opposed to wilderness: that the land is large enough to absorb the human footprint. The track of an off-road vehicle or the tailing of a mine did not despoil. These "wounds," as he called them, did not destroy the central essence or character of the desert. The damage was a matter of degree. As of 1960, the land had been merely wounded.[68]

Writing twenty years later during the BLM's wilderness inventory, Stegner argued that the human impact on the Colorado Plateau had become more lasting. He now argued that the region's vistas and landscape were being threatened by developed mines, power plants, and water projects. "We are 20 years closer to showdown," he penned in 1980. The need for wilderness protection was as necessary then as it ever had been. Stegner "spoke with some feeling about the deserts of southern Utah," recognizing the need to protect this landscape before industrial development changed it for good.[69]

In Negro Bill Canyon, the question remains whether the human markings overwhelm the wilderness characteristics of the place or blend into or even add to them. The mere presence of jeep marks, mine holes, old cabins, or cows ought not to confuse the issue. Negro Bill Canyon is a reminder that wilderness has been and ought to be still considered in places close to home that yet bear the human imprint.

four

Posturing on the Burr Trail

Unfurling nearly a hundred miles north to south, the Waterpocket Fold's tilted, bare rocks protrude, exposing a geologic conglomeration of layers and hues. Lyndon Johnson, in 1969 on his last day in office, increased the size of Capitol Reef National Park by six times just to include the entire length of the massive geologic landform—a move that infuriated stockmen who worried the designation would curtail their grazing privileges.[1] From Navajo Knob on the north end of Capitol Reef, the view south is dizzying. The Waterpocket Fold angles downward, shifting the land and water eastward toward the Colorado River. Indeed, the Colorado Plateau begins here. The interplay between geologic and climate forces is made plain as the eye pans eastward from Dixie National Forest to the fold and beyond.

This perspective of the Waterpocket Fold—Capitol Reef's spine—is typically all motorists glimpse. Like Comb Ridge, the Waterpocket Fold is a nearly impenetrable barricade to land travel. The few exceptions include the Fremont River, which slices a crack in the otherwise impassable rock wall, and Highway 24, which piggybacks along the river's course. In this northern section of the park lie a rich human history of land use, a showcase of ancient and modern human artifacts, as well as spectacular rock formations. The Fremont Indians were the area's first inhabitants, and petroglyphs inscribed on the rock walls are reminders of their bygone presence. In 1878 the Mormons settled a town, Fruita, which lasted until the park's establishment in 1937; all that remains now is an old schoolhouse and orchards still maintained by the National Park Service. This sole paved road through the fold presents a scenic tour of this outstanding landscape. The other motorized route is a dirt road, the Burr Trail to the south, where in the nineteenth century John Atlantic Burr had followed an Indian trail down the precipitous east face of the Waterpocket Fold. Later upgraded by the Atomic Energy Commission to a crude road to haul uranium ore to the mills from the Circle Cliffs, the route descends down a zigzag of hairpin switchbacks.

That was merely a section of a sixty-six-mile road connecting the tiny town of Boulder with the Bullfrog Marina on Lake Powell. For many years, the trail was little used. As the postwar generation discovered the canyons, mesas, and rivers of the region, the road attracted more attention—not merely for facilitating access but as an attraction itself. Driving the road was an experience, an adventure, a risk—especially descending the fold. The Burr Trail would transform beyond a mere means of passage to a powerful icon of wildness. When state and county officials proposed a plan in the early 1980s to pave the length of it, the conservation community organized to defend the dirt route, concerned about not only despoliation of the Boulder backcountry but also intrusion on the area's primitive qualities. Paving the road would disrupt the aesthetic balance. As might be expected, the two sides locked into rigid positions, one insistent on a paved road based on county-claimed R.S. 2477 rights, the other just as determined to keep the region primitive. A local power struggle over the fate of a backcountry road became a national discussion over preservation of wild spaces and about perceiving, remembering, using, and contesting place. The conflict thrust into the public sphere conflicting viewpoints of a place that was among the most isolated in the country, dotted by a few tiny, mostly Mormon, towns.

The town of Boulder is situated squarely within the Escalante River basin. The region is now well known for the maze of sandstone canyons drained by the Escalante River and its tributaries, although it is a diverse topography that includes a multilayered collection of canyons, high-elevation mountains, forested plateaus, and desert expanses. The Boulder, Escalante, and

Henry Mountains loom along the outer edges of the basin. To the west and the south, the land descends into dry desert country—broken and uneven, sculpted over millions of years by wind and water patterning a labyrinth of swaths in the sandstone. "The Sun shining down on this vast red plain almost dazzled our eyes by the reflection as it was thrown back from the fiery surface," wrote Mormon rancher Franklin B. Woolley in 1866 from a perch at Bowns Point on the Aquarius Plateau. The stark contrasts of color and form presented an unmatched spectacle.[2]

Although the unique combination of high mountain terrain and low canyon gorges makes this one of the most isolated regions in the lower forty-eight states, evidence of ancient human habitation abounds. Over centuries peoples have passed through, and some have called it home. In the first millennium, the Escalante region was part of a larger cultural site inhabited by Archaic, Anasazi, Fremont, and Numic peoples. The town of Boulder at the Burr Trail's western terminus overlays a large Kayenta Anasazi village abandoned circa 1275 CE; an early Mormon settler, Amasa Lyman, extended an ancient ditch to divert water for irrigation.[3] Evidence of indigenous habitation is scattered elsewhere—sometimes in the most unlikely places—in deep canyon gorges or on lonely mesa tops. One wonders whether these peoples felt as isolated and disconnected as the Euro-American visitors and settlers who would later follow.[4]

Almon H. Thompson and members of the Powell survey party encountered a band of Ute Indians in the area when they passed through in 1872. On errand to retrieve a boat cached the year before at the mouth of the Dirty Devil River and to survey what was then unknown territory, the men set off from Kanab. They eventually reached the upper headwaters of the Paria River and, further on, the Escalante River, which they initially mistook for the Dirty Devil. They then skirted the southern edge of the Aquarius Plateau and the western edge of Boulder Mountain. Assessing the country standing between them and the Henry Mountains, Jack Hillers viewed "gulches and canons for miles...a dry country and almost impossible" to travel through. Following Pleasant Creek along an Indian trail over what Frederick S. Dellenbaugh, a young oarsman for the Powell expedition, called "strange country," the party encountered a band of Red Lake Ute. The Indians directed the men to a route through the Waterpocket Fold (so named for the "water pockets" they found there), probably in the vicinity of Notum, Utah. Thompson and Powell's men went on to scale the Henry Mountains and locate the object of their travels.[5]

Powell and Thompson's surveys helped open this region to the public eye. The Henry Mountains were the last major mountain range in the lower forty-eight states to be mapped, the Escalante the last major river to be discovered. This was isolated country. It hardly conformed to the notion of land that Powell had hoped to locate for settlement. In his *Report on the Lands of the Arid Region of the United States*, published in 1879, Powell had warned of the limitations of irrigated agriculture in the West, especially in the high-plateau region like the Escalante. "Agriculture is there [in Utah] dependent upon irrigation," he wrote. Only a small part of the territory, however, can be redeemed, as high, rugged mountains and elevated plateaus occupy much of its area." Powell referred principally to southeastern Utah. "The Colorado River runs through the southeastern portion of the Territory and carries a great volume of water," he observed, "but no portion of it can be utilized within the Territory from the fact that its channel is so much below the adjacent lands."[6] The terrain was better suited to timber cutting and grazing than irrigated agriculture.

Yet Mormon settlers seemed intent on proving Powell wrong. They applied the agrarian model of orderly town sites and farms relatively well in the Fremont and Sevier River valleys. Even the town of Escalante in what was originally called Potato Valley was patterned after the typical Mormon farm-village plat. Powell had been correct that the land was limiting—farmers even in well-watered valleys in south-central Utah contended with short growing seasons, harsh winters, and low-value crops like grains and forage—but the typical Mormon farm-village model here seemed to work well enough.

Boulder's pedigree was different in that Mormon settlers depended not on farming but on cattle ranching. Hillers, a member of Powell's 1871–72 party, identified "the finest pasture I saw in Utah" when passing through, perhaps glimpsing the grasses that blossom on the well-watered slopes of Boulder Mountain.[7] Ranchers permanently moved into these pasturelands in the late 1880s, but it was a rough place to establish a community. Isolated on the edge of the Aquarius Plateau and the canyons of the Colorado River, Boulder was mostly self-sustaining. Although the area was not suited for agriculture, settlers grew their own food by diverting water from Boulder and Deer Creeks and ran their cattle herds on public lands free of government control. Well into the twentieth century, the US government delivered mail using pack mules, and Boulder was one of the last communities in the United States to gain automobile access. The town's main road to Escalante was not built until 1935 and not fully paved until 1971.[8]

In a region of limited mobility, Boulder residents traditionally relied on an economic practice that is, in fact, highly mobile. Ranchers depend on a large land base for grazing and on the capability of moving cattle from one place to another. This is true even in an area requiring extensive hay farming to feed cattle in the spring and summer. Even today this is accomplished by horse over rough terrain, but ranchers still require a good route. This suggests the origins of the Burr Trail. John Atlantic Burr forged the trail to range his cattle to the Burr Desert east of the Henry Mountains. At summer's end, area ranchers commonly drove their cattle from Boulder Mountain east to the lower, warmer, elevations. The trek was no gently sloping journey. Like steps, the trail drops from the upper white-and-red rock cliffs to the relatively flat plateau in the shadow of the Circle Cliffs. Long Canyon connects the two, presenting the most scenic, pleasant prospect: cottonwoods and lush vegetation in many spots—ideal for cattle, no doubt—and imposing cliff and rock formations eroded by the elements.

Beyond Long Canyon, which climbs gradually to the east culminating in a spectacular overlook, the road dips down to a mostly barren plateau varnished with a thin layer of red topsoil. The vegetation is sparse, with an intermix of juniper and piñon pine. Continuing on, the road enters what is now Capitol Reef National Park and drops down the face of the Waterpocket Fold—a route reportedly used prior to the mid-twentieth century to haul grain up by mule train for sheep in the Circle Cliffs.[9] At the base of the fold, the road swings south and essentially follows Halls Creek. But it is not an easy section; at one half-mile stretch, the road crosses the creek no fewer than six times, making the route impassable during periods of flood. Farther on, the road cleaves to Middle Point, descends and crosses Bullfrog Creek, and eventually persists to Bullfrog Marina at Lake Powell, although ranchers would not have taken their cattle that far.

On a wet day, the soil turns to a deep clay mud, but even in dry weather the sandy soil is not easily traversed. If the route was onerous for an animal to negotiate, for a vehicle it proved practically impassable. Boulder resident Lincoln Lyman noted that along a portion of the route, the sand was "bad enough" that all motorists could do was to take a run at the sand, back up, and try again. Eventually, the automobile made it by "crawl[ing] up right out of there."[10]

In this rugged country with poor roads and dispersed populations, herding cattle from mountains to ranches taxed even the experienced cowhand. Cattle on the open range tend to scatter, and without fences or plots they cannot congregate. This made rescue efforts problematic, and dropping hay into centralized locations was not an option. Roads provided the only manageable way to rescue cattle, especially more recently since ranchers no longer actively herd their cattle. For instance, when deep snows hit the range area southeast of Tropic in late January 1979, local ranchers and the State of Utah cooperated in locating cattle by airplane and grading a road using CAT tractors. Some cattle died of exposure, but rescue efforts saved nearly a thousand head. In the Loa-Bicknell area, ranchers were not as fortunate. The cattle were lost in the Henry Mountains, and although planes and bulldozers helped ranchers locate five hundred head, some six hundred cattle remained missing.[11]

Sections of the Burr Trail might have originated as an Indian route and then used by ranchers and uranium miners, but county officials would later have a much different purpose in mind for it. The creation of Lake Powell and the Glen Canyon National Recreation Area in 1972 convinced local boosters that they finally had something to showcase, a destination that promised to attract thousands if not millions of tourists to southeastern Utah. A paved Burr Trail would directly connect Garfield County to the marina at Bullfrog from the west, as well as induce travelers to drive through county towns. Officials in Garfield County had no plans to miss out on potential business opportunities otherwise diverted to Lake Powell border towns and Wayne County. By 1983 Utah politicians were actively courting federal and state funds to study and construct a "Burr Trail Highway."

Paved roads, it appeared, were crucial to unlock the region's wonders, market its scenery, and attract tourists. By the mid-twentieth century, many local boosters and state politicians believed that parks and the roads leading to them would provide a significant economic boost to southern Utah. But making this vision a reality would entail developments on a grand scale. The original plan for Canyonlands National Park had been to outfit the Needles District—a collection of colorful spires of Cedar Mesa Sandstone—with roads, hotels, and other services, not unlike the Grand Canyon's North Rim. Engineers working for the State Department of Highways sketched maps of highways designed to take motorists to every conceivable canyon country destination. The Trans-Escalante Highway would parallel the western edge of Lake Powell and continue north even through the roughest parts of Canyonlands National Park. Hotels, restaurants, marinas, and stores would greet tourists at major stops along the way: at Castle Butte, Halls Crossing, Bullfrog Basin, Hole-in-the-Rock, Crossing of the Fathers, Warm Creek, and Wahweap Basin. The plans were fanciful, if not foolhardy. But the purpose was to open southern Utah's scenic wonders to the world to help generate revenue for local economies.[12]

The full realization of these proposals never materialized. The proposed route from Glen Canyon City that would run northwesterly along the west edge of Lake Powell—the Trans-Escalante Highway—succumbed not long after congressional hearings were held in Washington, DC, in 1972.[13]

Utah senator Jake Garn clearly recognized the connection between turnout of recreational visitations in southern Utah and appropriate development of the national parks and public lands. Creating an economy based on tourism in southern Utah was not ideal, yet he saw no other choice than to push for roads and the infrastructure to support tourist populations. In a letter addressed to Senator Howard Metzenbaum (D–OH), Garn claimed that national environmental regulations had consistently shut out industrial development in the region, contributing to the withdrawal of three coal power plants and two major proposed coal-mining operations. The largest project was a proposal to build four massive open-pit coal mines and a coal-burning power plant on the Kaiparowits Plateau (Kluckhohn's Wild Horse Mesa), south of Escalante. "If southern Utah is going to be forever denied the opportunity to develop itself industrially, then I for one can not sit back and just watch it happen," he wrote. "I am going to do everything I can to develop its economic base centered around tourism."[14] It was hoped that a paved Burr Trail would attract not just any tourists, but wealthy ones. "[The visitors now] come in here in a Volkswagen and their backpacks. They buy a dollar gas and a dollar groceries, and they're gone for a week. You can't blame them, but paving the road would open this end of the county up to the people who stay at the motels and eat at the cafes and spend some bucks in the county," postulated Boulder resident Dell LeFevre.[15]

Senator Garn, Utah's other congressional delegates, and Governor Scott Matheson all agreed that if tourism was to become "the natural foundation of our state's rural economy," the top priority would be to complete or upgrade the unfinished road corridors connecting the state's parks and scenic destinations. U-95 had been the "backbone" of the Grand Circle, but other roads also supplied vital links. Aside from some fanciful routes planned but never constructed, nearly all roads deemed essential had already been paved. Only the road over Boulder Mountain connecting Boulder to Highway 12 remained unfinished, and if completed would essentially round out the Grand Circle. Road boosters were now touting the Burr Trail as the "proposed Central link" to the Grand Circle Adventure. It would provide a two-way route joining the county to the marinas at Halls Crossing where the state planned to build a ferry (dedicated in 1985 and named for John Atlantic Burr), bridging both sides of the reservoir. State funds had been used to build the ferry there; an improved Burr Trail would usher more tourists to it. The road would also enable more folks to experience the wild Escalante outback.[16]

More than a decade earlier during the Trans-Escalante Highway hearings, as a bargaining chip conservationists had testified in opposition to the highway by recommending an "upgrade" to some existing dirt roads—like the Burr Trail—instead. They had vied that built roadways ought to take advantage of existing routes and connect local communities instead of forging new paths.[17] But when the Burr Trail came to the chopping block, Ruth Frear of the Burr Trail Committee backpedaled that the earlier stance was merely to create a "fine dirt road," nothing more, and that a paved road would change the character of the country.[18] Backers of a paved Burr Trail, however, pounced on this, labeling the position of wilderness groups as duplicitous. As Governor Matheson and the entire Utah congressional delegation noted in a letter, "While today we are certain some 'hard liners' will argue that upgrading the present dirt track was not meant to imply actual paving of the road, we believe any reasonable interpretation of the 1972 testimony would conclude that a safe, all-weather scenic road was exactly what was intended."[19]

It may have been that in the 1960s and early 1970s, some conservationists did indeed support an upgraded—even paved—Burr Trail. But times had changed in the subsequent ten-plus years. The impulse to protect what portions of "wild" Utah remained derived in part from a sense of nostalgia, as conservationist Jim Catlin observed in the *Utah Sierran*: "As recently as our childhood much more of Utah was truly wild and untouched." In opposing a paved Burr Trail, Catlin reflected:

> There was no road across the San Rafael Swell, no road down the Fremont river through what is now Capitol Reef National Park. A very rough track was the route to Glen Canyon. Now we have U95 which covers the drowning of the lower Dirty Devil and the Colorado River. White Canyon by natural Bridges was serviced by a rough dirt road. All the roads into Canyonlands and Arches National Park areas were either nonexistent or dirt. The potash plant near Dead Horse Point, the power plant plumes south of Price, and the Navajo power plant plumes didn't exist.

A newly paved Burr Trail would further threaten a section of Utah's backcountry with "increasing mechanized use of this very fragile area." Catlin did not expect this pressure to pave roads to relent, but he did demonstrate that new roads often divert business away from communities and provide little boost to their economies.[20]

A handful of local conservationists organized a defense. Gordon Anderson and Lucy Wallingford, both of Moab, Utah, and Grant Johnson of Boulder organized the Save the Burr Trail Committee to campaign against federal appropriations to improve the road. Johnson, Clive Kincaid, and Robert Weed's Southern Utah Wilderness Alliance had been formed, in part, to contest the proposal. For Kincaid, Burr Trail country was as close to primeval wilderness as could be found in the United States. Here was a chance to memorialize what he called "another Utah—as close to time warp as one can find."[21] Terri Martin of the National Parks and Conservation Association observed that the "battle to protect the Burr Trail as a rural, scenic, backcountry road is a battle for the Escalante Canyons."[22]

Conservationists were certain that a paved road would result in ecological damage. They distrusted the findings of a jointly produced BLM and NPS draft environmental assessment (EA), released in May 1985, that downplayed the environmental impact of the Garn proposal in areas like the Waterpocket Fold, even as it acknowledged that new cuts through the fold would have to be made.[23] They even dismissed National Park Service director William Penn Mott Jr.'s middle-of-the-road recommendation to upgrade the Burr Trail to an "all weather gravel surface" with pavement on only "the most critical portions of the road." Critics quipped that the "critical portions" just happened to be environmentally sensitive areas like Long Canyon and the switchbacks down the Waterpocket Fold.[24]

For several years, the plan was stalled with no federal or state money made available. Then in early 1987, the State Community Impact Board, which distributes mineral leasing revenues to local governments, awarded Garfield County two million dollars to commence paving the road's first twenty-eight miles. The decision to fund an "improved" Burr Trail had not come easily for state lawmakers. Many questioned the benefit of paving a rural road that the Utah Department of Transportation had estimated might ultimately cost as much as eighty million dollars in public funds. Opponents of the paved road had merely assumed that the high cost of the project would be the best defense against it.[25]

A coalition of environmental groups threatened an action of injunctive relief against Garfield County, whose representatives had awarded a contract to Harper Excavating, Inc.[26] When the county refused to stand down, Lori Potter of the Sierra Club Legal Defense Fund, Inc., and Wayne Petty of Moyle and Draper sought a temporary restraining order against the county in district court to prevent construction. The county, the complaint alleged, would have to comply with an environmental review (including impacts to adjacent Wilderness Study Areas) before making any major changes to the road.[27]

The larger legal question of Sierra Club v. Hodel centered on the validity and scope of the county's claim to right-of-way. Invoking the nineteenth-century mining law granting rights-of-way for "highways" over public lands, the county countered that the long history of travel and use on the Burr Trail unmistakably proved their legal rights. The plaintiffs cited precedence that R.S. 2477 roads were to be used "for the purpose originally granted," referring to 1984 correspondence from BLM state director Roland Robison stating that although "Garfield County does have a right-of-way for this road," it did not have a right to make a "substantial deviation or realignment from the existing right-of-way." However, in another letter from Robison to Petty on February 13, 1987, no mention was made of any realignment restrictions; he simply held that the county "is entitled to carry out improvement and maintenance activities on the roadway within it," and intimated that the BLM had no intention of interfering with that right—a point the county capitalized on in court. Since FLPMA—the legislation governing rights-of-way on BLM lands—made no mention of the scope of allowable maintenance on an R.S. 2477 claim, the county advanced its right to expand the roadway and alignment to "accommodate increased tourism activity in the region."[28]

In court testimony to establish the origins and evolution of the road, defendants held that the road had been in use since the late nineteenth century and continually upgraded since the 1930s as "an important link between the east part of Garfield County and the west part," thus proving right-of-way. But it was a tightrope walk, because while insisting the county had regularly maintained the road, they had to simultaneously show how it was in serious need of upgrade. A local, Margie Spence of Ticcabo, testified that the road was well maintained since 1946—as long as she had lived in the Escalante region—and had been used widely by "farmers and ranchers, by oil and gas people, by school people, by health people, and sheriff's," among others. She and other locals characterized it as "a pretty good country road" in need of an upgrade. For most of the year, Spence traveled the road two times a week for work in an LTD Ford or a Chevy Celebrity. But wet conditions made travel treacherous, and she could not "remember how many times" she had skidded off.[29]

John S. Williams, another witness for the defense, supposed that the road had been "created for the desire to uncover or discover the natural resource—the potentials of Garfield County," and that it would still play an important role in future developments, benefiting Kirkwood Oil and Gas Company and others. Besides, locals, hikers, backpackers, boaters, and sightseers all traversed it. Road use would surely increase in the coming years, Williams posited, pointing to a spike in use over the past two years due to the publicity of the Burr Trail.[30]

In March 1987 district judge Aldon J. Anderson ruled that the proposed upgrades were "of a substantial nature" to warrant further study before construction could begin. He ordered the county to produce an environmental assessment of how road improvements might impact adjoining BLM Wilderness Study Areas. Anderson personally believed the county had right-of-way to a through road but questioned its right to widen and realign it for the sake of attracting tourists. His ruling gave both sides the impression that the battle was "a long way from being over."[31]

Rather abruptly, the court stalemate ended just nine months later in December 1987, when the district judge cleared the way for improvements to the Burr Trail, citing "overwhelming evidence" that the county held the right-of-way. In earnest, county officials moved immediately to conduct the roadwork without obtaining a federal permit and conducting botanical and archaeological studies as the judge required.[32] "Only 3 days after the federal district court injunction was lifted," read the SUWA bulletin, "Garfield County assembled every piece of heavy machinery at its disposal and began moving earth" in Long Canyon's steep-walled riparian environment. The machinery thrummed an entire day. While the plaintiff's legal team labored to put a stop to it, environmentalists called in the media to document damage to soil, water, and vegetative resources. The next day, with reporters and cameras poised, county officials signaled to rev the bulldozers. But the machines failed to start. The story of the day pivoted from the potential destruction of a canyon to suspected sabotage of road machinery.[33]

Proponents of a paved Burr Trail had feared that opponents would resort to sabotage or other harassment to hinder road building. The same month conservation groups filed a lawsuit in district court, SUWA had distributed a flier with a drawing by artist R. Crumb depicting people engaged in monkey-wrenching activities under the heading, "Save—Don't Pave—The Burr Trail." But the plaintiffs immediately distanced themselves from the provocative flier. SUWA volunteer Fred Swanson, who wrote the text to the flier, asserted, "The drawing was added to the flier without our knowledge, without our consent," adding that SUWA in no way condoned "equipment sabotage or other acts of monkey-wrenching." Earlier, SUWA attorney Wayne Petty had assured the county that he was "instructing my clients that under no circumstances are they to engage in any activity which constitutes threat, harassment, intimidation or attempts to do any of the foregoing."[34]

Convinced of willful vandalism nonetheless, county officials immediately pinned the suspected crime on Boulder resident Grant Johnson. They believed they had every reason to suspect Johnson, who had none of the genealogy of most Boulder residents. A job as a uranium miner drew him into the area in 1975, but the wildness and isolation induced him to stay. After mining, he worked for a contractor repairing ancient Indian ruins and with his wife gathered and sold seeds of desert wildflowers. The country suited his interests as a lover of wildlands, and Johnson spent his spare time exploring the outback and defending it from despoilment. A founding member of the Save the Burr Trail Committee and SUWA, he sometimes took lone stands against the Burr Trail paving plan at public meetings. Locals in Escalante burned in effigy this mild-mannered man and Clive Kincaid, another Boulder resident, just as they had done to Robert Redford a decade earlier for publicly opposing a proposed coal mine and power plant on the Kaiparowits Plateau.[35] Based on evidence reportedly linking Johnson's shoe print to the scene of the crime, the county sheriff hauled him to jail (insulting him all the while, according to Johnson, by calling him "an animal living in a rat-infested trailer") on an original bail of $250,000, higher than famed Mormon document forger and murderer Mark Hofmann's bail at the same time.[36]

Johnson attributes the hostility to the "political side" and not to local ranchers in Boulder with whom he had "worked out personal relationships." He maintains that two old-timers that he knew well, Doyle Mooseman and Max Behunin, did not support a paved Burr Trail, but that some of the younger residents, such as Dell LeFevre, did.[37] County officials hatched and orchestrated the scheme, Johnson alleged, "to take my land and throw me out of the county." He was over time acquitted of all charges connected to the supposed vandalism, but the affair came at a high price to him personally. While the case was being investigated, he and his wife endured intimidation and threats. Boulder resident Larry Davis had suggested they leave town because of rumors that they might be shot from the road. Johnson faced public humiliation and two and a half years of costly legal expenses. The media also misrepresented his character. In a five-minute clip on *The Today Show*, a phrase spoken by Johnson—"Man created God to give him the Earth to do whatever he wants"—was altered as "God created the earth so man could do what he wanted with it," which made him sound like a fundamentalist Christian.[38]

Johnson was also ostracized by his own. He had become alienated from Clive Kincaid and SUWA two years earlier, but the charges of vandalism further distanced him from the organization that he had a role in creating. Due to the negative press from the apparent machinery ecotage, other environmental organizations also condemned Johnson's alleged actions and dissociated themselves from his perceived brand of extreme environmentalism. Darrell Knuffke of the Wilderness Society derogatorily referred to him as "a tattered relic of the Sixties who is suspected of sabotaging road-building equipment on the trail, which is felonious, and who told a national audience that he talks to rocks and they to him, which is merely ridiculous."[39] Although Edward Abbey in a 1988 speech at the University of Utah publicly defended Johnson, Abbey, too, assumed Johnson was the monkey wrencher. "They charge this poor guy with vandalism when these county commissioners in Garfield are doing their best to destroy one of the most beautiful primitive areas left in the whole state of Utah. Who are the true criminals in Garfield County?" he questioned. "Well, not the fellow who tried to save the Burr Trail from final destruction, but that little gang of county commissioners and BLM bureaucrats who have been conspiring together for years to vandalize, industrialize, and pollute the land that is the rightful property of all Americans."[40]

The hostility toward Grant Johnson was emblematic of the infighting between environmental groups over the appropriate strategy to resist paving of the Burr Trail. From the beginning, the Sierra Club, Wilderness Society, and the newly organized SUWA had formulated a "no compromise" position on the basis that the road would, in the words of Doug Scott of the Sierra Club, "inevitably lead to exactly the kind of heavy industrial development in that entire region of Utah which the Club has strenuously opposed, legally and politically, for a generation."[41]

The parties conspiring against paving also recognized the virtues of compromise, if the terms were right. In late 1985, some environmentalists urged compromise as long as "[we] get something for it in terms of protection of the land." One such proposal was to allow the county to pave a portion of the road—twelve miles under NPS director Mott's proposal—and gravel the rest if the environmentalists got right-of-way, wilderness designation, and other key provisions, such as no commercial hauling. Specifically, they insisted on "minimal improvements," federal right-of-way, trade-out of state sections bordering the road, and wilderness designation of 350,000 acres adjacent to the Burr Trail. They apparently agreed to settle on a full paved road "if [we] get 1.1 million acre wilderness designation," meaning the 350,000 acres under the Utah Wilderness Coalition proposal in addition to wilderness in NPS areas.[42]

To Garfield County proponents of a paved Burr Trail, this last provision may have seemed more like a slap in the face than a compromise—not far from what Edward Abbey sardonically proposed at a public hearing for the Trans-Escalante Highway: "Give us back our river [Colorado] and our canyon [Glen Canyon], as they used to be and as they always should be, and you can have your new highway."[43] Still, these cases illustrate that even the most ardent activists might have been willing to compromise if the terms were right. Indeed, environmental protection is a game of compromise. To survive in the arena of multi-interest group politics, environmentalists had to adjust to the realities of the political system—a system that large, national environmental groups understood well. So they hired lobbyists and lawyers and negotiators. They wrangled in courts and in the halls of Congress, but they also sat down across from their opponents to hammer out deals. In the process, they made hard decisions, compromised, and sometimes gave up cherished positions in exchange for a gain of higher priority.

Radical environmentalism, as it is derisively called by some, in part developed to respond to what some perceived as excessive appeasement by mainstream environmental organizations. Dave Foreman, who lobbied for the Wilderness Society in Washington, DC, in the 1970s, thought some mainstream environmental groups bartered away too many wilderness areas, critical wildlife habitats, and open spaces in the name of compromise. He cofounded Earth First! in 1980, an environmental organization influenced by such nineteenth-century conservation stalwarts as Henry David Thoreau and John Muir and by the writings of Aldo Leopold, Rachel Carson, and Edward Abbey in formulating the ecocentric position that human beings merely belonged to the web of life and were not lords over it. Earth First!ers adopted the slogan "No Compromise in Defense of Mother Earth!," and Foreman penned *Ecodefense: A Field Guide to Monkeywrenching* (1985), giving would-be saboteurs techniques to take out road equipment and stall development.[44] On the Burr Trail, Foreman made perhaps the most uncompromising proposal of all: to completely close the Burr Trail (along with the Hole-in-the-Rock road) to "unite slickrock canyon country north and south of this road into one huge Wilderness."[45]

SUWA was ideologically a close kin to Earth First! Articles published in the *Earth First!* journal praised the leaders of the new grassroots organization for being "a couple of self-righteous royal pains in the opposition's ass" that deserved support.[46] Not unlike Earth First! SUWA founders were fed up and disillusioned and arose, in part, out of frustration with the Utah Wilderness Association's role in the 1984 designation of wilderness on Utah national forestland. Grant Johnson of SUWA would later allege that Dick Carter of UWA had bartered away qualifying wilderness on nearby Boulder Mountain for wilderness in the Uinta Mountains. Using the Save the Burr Trail Committee mailing list, Johnson, Kincaid, and Weed formed the grassroots advocacy group.[47] SUWA subsequently helped to coordinate the formation of the Utah Wilderness Coalition and the drafting of a 5.1-million-acre (later increased to a 5.7-million-acre) wilderness proposal in Utah, significantly more than the 3.8-million-acre proposal of the Utah Wilderness Association. The proposal was considered so extreme by some (though not nearly so as Earth First!'s 16-million-acre BLM wilderness proposal) that Senator Jake Garn dismissively called it "ridiculous" and that any chance of it becoming reality would be "over his dead body."[48]

The Utah Wilderness Coalition had clearly been organized to counter the Utah Wilderness Association's more conciliatory influence in the Utah wilderness debate. During the Burr Trail contest, Dick Carter remained convinced that "it is far more important to focus the battle of preserving roadless lands as wilderness than diverging into piecemeal opposition of already constructed roadways such as the Burr Trail." He insisted that "the 'Glen Canyon Dam' issue of the 80's is not the Burr Trail."[49] But that position proved an unpopular one. "You know some very nasty and unnecessary things have been said over the last few months about UWA & me," he wrote Terri Martin of the National Parks and Conservation Association in May 1985. Disappointed at "how little reconciliation is going on," he relayed how hurt he was "when I saw the Burr Trail alert signed by everybody but us."[50] Meanwhile, Doug Scott of the Sierra Club proposed sidelining "Dick Carter and his followers who are too willing to compromise" by "taking a hard, no compromise line" on the Burr Trail. In Scott's estimation, such an approach would "be very positive for our longer-term agenda in Utah," since it would "give us a continuing press hook for the Coalition and SUWA" and "further solidify the collaboration between all of us, building an ever firmer base on which to proceed with the Utah wilderness fight in the years (probably quite a few of them) ahead."[51]

Yet the Sierra Club's Lawson LeGate had come to agree with Carter that reaching a compromise with Garfield County officials would be better than prolonging a costly and bitter lawsuit. In a letter to Carter, LeGate acknowledged that their positions were, in essence, similar. He indicated that plaintiffs in the court case had opened closed-door discussions with the county "for many weeks about reaching a negotiated settlement." Notes from these meetings show that environmentalists agreed to pave the road with a red surface as long as commercial hauling, utility lines, roadside development, and shoulders at cliff sides were prohibited. In exchange, the county would give up claims to right-of-way. Environmentalists also lobbied the county to support wilderness designation for the Escalante River Canyons and Mount Pennell areas (which county officials "really balked at"). The county reportedly agreed that no construction would begin on sections of roads as long as conservationists remained committed to the negotiations. Nevertheless, it was a precarious agreement; environmentalists knew any understanding between the groups was "so preliminary and sufficiently vague as to allow them [the county] to raise the stakes on us in this manner."[52]

And still, a deal with the county would put an end to expensive court battles while enabling the environmental community to maintain some leverage. The idea was to allow the county to pave the road in exchange for its claim to R.S. 2477 rights. That issue in particular was important, because obtaining R.S. 2477 rights to the Burr Trail could serve as precedence on other state road claims. LeGate believed that a compromise would be "good publicity" and convince the public that environmentalists were willing to work with rural county officials on the opposite side of the ideological divide.

And he thought a compromise would suit the needs of the county as well, since officials wanted an end to the expensive legal proceedings but needed something to show their constituents after a long court battle.[53]

Still, where LeGate and others saw an opportunity to protect the land along the Burr Trail and prevent commercial use of the road, the trade-off was tremendous. Agreeing to the paved road would leave conservationists in a tough position; their support might require testimony before Congress in favor of paving through a section of Capitol Reef National Park. Then there was the question of jurisdiction. SUWA and the Sierra Club supported a BLM road over an NPS road because it would generate less use, but the NPCA would accept that scenario only "with kicks and screams." Environmentalists reached no consensus on these issues.[54]

In a confidential letter addressed to certain members of the environmental community, SUWA's new executive director, Brant Calkin, reasoned:

> Why negotiate with the county? The shorthand theory is that we can get a better road, one that is less damaging to the land and the traveler than if the county went ahead on its own. I have never been persuaded that the difference for the land is significant or worth conceding. And I frankly don't care much for what happens in the minds of the drivers of a paved road. The most essential point, I feel, is that paving the Burr Trail in any color or configuration is death to the wildness that remains in the area of the road. I do not contemplate negotiating the diameter and hue of the rope that hangs me.

Calkin questioned the usefulness of a compromise to secure passage of wilderness areas; furthermore, he doubted much would come from these discussions beyond resolution of just the Burr Trail anyway. "The Burr Trail discussions came about as a result of conflict, not cooperation. The cooperation will continue only as long as the conflicts and ability of each side to serve its needs continue," he explained. A "shot-gun marriage on the Burr Trail" would not likely lead to better relations between sides.[55]

Calkin held no illusions that it would be easy or cheap, but fighting to protect the wildness of the land and to preserve the "unique and worthwhile experience" of driving the dirt road was worth it. Although the lawsuit had drained their budget and resources, he made a plea to continue the fight, to raise additional funds, and to sink the county's credibility. "It is time to declare the county's position as unilateral and uncompromising, and for us to put the blame for the destruction of the road where it belongs—on the county."[56]

By December 1988, it had become clear that Garfield County had no intentions of compromising anyway. No doubt emboldened by the Utah legislature's sudden act of appropriating another two million dollars in mineral royalties on federal lands for road paving, county officials abruptly broke off the talks. Although the plaintiffs had hoped the county would hold off on construction to ensure road work was done properly, not deviating from the alignment, the county insisted that it would begin work immediately after the BLM released its EA. The plaintiffs knew the county's insistence put the tentative agreement "in serious jeopardy," but they were utterly blind-sided when on December 3 the county once again called out bulldozers to upgrade the road.[57]

Technically, the county would break no laws by commencing construction. Hearings in November had persuaded the court that to issue an "order partially dissolving injunction" was acceptable for certain sections of the road that did not adversely impact the WSAs. The sections adjoining the WSAs would still be governed by the injunction and were subject to National Environmental Policy Act compliance. Long Canyon belonged to a stretch not protected by the injunction, so construction there could commence. Notwithstanding, Judge Aldon J. Anderson indicated that proceeding without notifying the plaintiffs was in "bad faith," and he "requested" the county cease construction until both parties agreed on proceedings; otherwise, he would issue a restraining order.[58]

In March 1989, the defendants petitioned the judge for complete dissolution of the injunction, a move that the plaintiffs promptly appealed. Meanwhile, the plaintiffs lost another appeal to prevent the county from using a gravel site near the road. Throughout different phases of the case, the plaintiffs continued to challenge the county on seemingly insignificant points just to keep construction at bay—on boundary issues, width of the proposed road, and possible impact on spotted owls, which may not have nested near the road anyway.[59] On May 16, 1990, the district court dissolved the injunction, and the plaintiffs, once again, appealed. "The environmental groups have undertaken every activity, whether or not reasonably justified, to make each step as drawn out, complicated and expensive as possible," Grand County commissioner Louise Liston criticized. "I believe there is no doubt that this is part of their strategy and that anyone attempting to carry out a project which they want to stop will be faced with the same tactics."[60]

Just as environmental groups chose to continue the lawsuit on the basis that the Burr Trail was part of a larger battle over preserving wild places in southern Utah, Liston insisted the lawsuit would prove precedent setting in the larger battle over R.S. 2477 claims in the West. She and fellow colleague Thomas Hatch trusted the time, money, and energy invested in the case would be worth it. "Every single governmental entity in Utah which relies upon R.S. 2477 for rights-of-way has benefited immeasurably by the efforts which Garfield County had undertaken in this case," Liston penned.[61]

Liston was right that the Burr Trail case had already made a material impact on R.S. 2477 claims. In 1988 Interior Department secretary Donald Hodel, responding to the Burr Trail case, signed a new department policy to "recognize with some certainty the existence, or lack thereof, of public grants obtained under R.S.-2477." The policy showed land agencies how to resolve R.S. 2477 disputes by outlining rights-of-way criteria. To the term construction, Hodel applied a loose definition: "a physical act of creating the highway." This could mean an act as simple as clearing away vegetation or large rocks. And "construction" could stretch out over several years. Significantly, Hodel ruled that "the passage of vehicles by users over time may equal actual construction" and that a "public highway" could be "a pedestrian or pack animal trail." Because earlier Interior regulations in 1938 stated that "the grant becomes effective upon the construction or establishing of highways," the new policy confirmed R.S. 2477 claims to be self-executing. No action from government agencies was necessary to make the claims valid.[62]

This generous definition of R.S. 2477 emboldened county governments in southern Utah to ensure nearly every dirt track within their political borders had R.S. 2477 rights. Not long after the Hodel policy, the BLM issued an invitation to Garfield and other counties to compile a list of R.S. 2477 roads within their borders. Indeed, FLPMA mandated the identification of such roads. Brian Bremner, Garfield County engineer, subsequently submitted the lists of claims, which numbered 76. Neighboring Wayne County identified 116—enough in these two counties alone to "blanket the public lands," as William Lockhart, an attorney representing environmental groups in the lawsuit, noted.[63]

The Hodel policy would be overturned by the Clinton administration, but it contributed to the divisions in the Burr Trail controversy from the start. Certainly, the policy legitimized the county's legal and political claims to roads within their borders. This sense of entitlement would spill over to more contemporary battles over roads on the public lands as in the Grand Staircase–Escalante National Monument.

On the Burr Trail, the courts sided with the county's claim to a valid right-of-way on the road's western end. Despite attempts by environmental groups to appeal the decision and delay construction, the Board of Land Appeals not only recognized the county's R.S. 2477 claim to the road but also granted under the so-called Harper contract the right to grade and gravel the segment from Boulder to the west boundary of Capitol Reef National Park, including those areas not adjacent to the WSAs.[64] Not long after this ruling, the county would successfully call out road crews to pave the western section of the Burr Trail. The outcome of Sierra Club v. Hodel did not, however, settle the matter or set precedence for other R.S. 2477 claims. The court refused to resolve the responsibility of parties in establishing valid claims. The absence of clear guidelines guaranteed that issue would continue to move slowly through the courts, which it has.[65]

In the two decades since the court decision, the ultimate fate of the Burr Trail remains unresolved. The courts established the county claim to the right-of-way to the first twenty-eight miles on the western side, but ownership of the remaining length has yet to be determined. Those twenty-eight miles up to Capitol Reef National Park are paved and maintained by Garfield County, while the rest remains dirt. Scars from the controversy are visibly imprinted on the land. Even more marks have been made since 1991—as when Garfield County bulldozed a hillside within the park boundaries without the NPS's permission—which Terri Martin called "a deliberate act of destruction, vandalism and arrogance."[66]

The Burr Trail controversy stamped its mark on Utah's environmental movement as well. Although it attracted national attention, the episode signaled the emergence of local environmental activism in southern Utah, giving rise to SUWA and the short-lived Save the Burr Trail Committee. SUWA arose as a grassroots environmental organization in much the same way that a handful of discontents organized Earth First! Although some locals accused Clive Kincaid and others of siding with national environmental groups unconcerned with local issues, the Burr Trail was in fact mostly fought by Utah-based activists (albeit most living in the Salt Lake City area) who cared deeply about the future of the canyon country. But the conflict also unearthed fissures within the Utah environmental community, marking the demise of Dick Carter's moderate, compromise-driven Utah Wilderness Association and the emergence of more hard-line organizations like SUWA.

Frustrated environmentalists opposed to taking the Burr Trail issue to the courts pointed to the wasted years debating the merit of a highway when the real issue was over wilderness. For years the Escalante region had been a key target of Utah wilderness advocacy groups; in fact, a few years after passage of the Wilderness Act of 1964, the Escalante Wilderness Committee considered the Escalante region, for all its inaccessibility and beauty, to be "one of the last areas of desert canyon country that can qualify as wilderness."[67] Some environmentalists insisted that efforts would have been better spent fighting for designation of the nearly one million acres—or one-third of the county—identified as Wilderness Study Areas by the BLM. They may have been right. Although some activists had wanted the Burr Trail lawsuit to be a "forerunner of how wilderness would be pursued through the courts," Garfield County ended up retaining R.S. 2477 rights to a portion of the road. By essentially taking the Burr Trail debate out of public hands and turning it over to lawyers, the long-drawn-out court battle may have actually deadened enthusiasm for the effort to save the road from being paved.[68]

The pragmatism of wilderness advocates like Dick Carter was an obvious attempt to forge connections, common ground, and compromise among locals for a specific purpose: to protect as much land as possible. The benefits of compromise are unmistakable. Trading a paved road for adjacent wilderness may have been a good deal if it had been possible to orchestrate. Some wondered why a few environmentalists chose to pursue a course that de-emphasized—in fact, abandoned—the political discourse of compromise even when it may have served their better interest. "They seem to enjoy a fight to the death even if they lose!" wrote one frustrated local environmentalist who trumpeted a compromise-driven strategy over an uncompromising approach on the Burr Trail.[69]

Whereas some conservation leaders may have presupposed their strong legal case would triumph, the ultimate strategy to contest the Burr Trail in the courts derived primarily from the prevailing cultural and political winds in rural Utah. County commissioners leading the fight took a hard-line approach, at once defending a paved road while proclaiming the righteousness of their cause and the venality of their opponents. Demanding full privileges of public land use for economic purposes, they held enduring resentments against environmentalists and federal land managers who sought an alternative management framework on those lands. And Earth First! and SUWA wilderness proponents knew that playing nice yielded little benefit unless the other side was willing to play nice, too. In the rural West dominated by radical libertarians in the 1980s, Earth First! argued that the environmental movement needed a few uncompromising groups to counter the uncompromising positions of their opponents—to fight fire with fire.

These staunch positions contributed to harsh and violent rhetoric and an unwillingness to discern value in the standpoint of the other. Ideology figured prominently. Both sides demonized and reduced the other to caricatures or two-faced hypocrites. Perhaps inevitably, then, perceptions and memories became negative. A local storekeeper in Boulder recalls a day during the Burr Trail stalemate when Clive Kincaid walked into her store to buy shotgun shells to put out a noisy robin, which to her underscored his duplicitous relationship to nature. Regardless of her conclusions, it is revealing that she chose to remember and tell the story at all. The same ideological fervor drove some to perceive Grant Johnson as a violent saboteur. What is probably unknown to most is that several years after the accusations, Johnson gave to Harper Construction at no charge the excess of his 1.5 cubic feet of water rights to Deer Creek for construction purposes.[70]

This all suggests that at its core, the Burr Trail conflict was more an ideological contest than a debate about the virtues of a paved road. Both sides dug in even when compromise might have served their better interests. Environmentalists may have pointed to a victory in preventing the remaining trail from being paved, but that came at a high cost and erosion of goodwill and possible future alliances with locals in a larger fight over wilderness that has yet to conclude. Likewise, the county successfully negotiated a court ruling to allow a portion of the road to be paved, but at what cost to local relationships? The very road that the county ardently defended—perhaps to some degree just to chagrin their opponents—continues to drain their budget; the chip-seal surface used on the road is less expensive than asphalt but requires more maintenance. Dell LeFevre, a once vocal proponent of the paved road, now laments that any was paved at all. Not only is the hard surface costly to maintain, but the traffic it has attracted also disrupts his cattle drives. Perhaps after realizing that a paved Burr Trail changed the isolation and character of Boulder, LeFevre remarked in 1996, "We wanted it for us, not tourists."[71]

LeFevre's sentiments spotlight the real dilemma that rural places like Boulder confront. To some degree, the quest was to build trails and roads to make the country accessible. Yet the very inaccessibility created a kind of nostalgic attachment to the land's character and a fierce pride in the ability to survive there. Tales are retold of living in isolation with grit and ingenuity. Visitors reveled in the same qualities so admired by locals. "People are attracted to Boulder and Escalante precisely because they are at the end of the paved road," noted Russ Henrie of Panguitch during the Burr Trail debate. "This could be capitalized on without being destroyed. People come here for adventure, excitement, and for recreation, a renewal of traditional values and ties to the natural beauty of the earth. People can get an 'easy trip thru' anywhere."[72]

Few places in the West remain as Boulder once was. Paved roads lead everywhere, it seems, even to rural outposts at the edge of the world. The onward march of growth threatens the very characteristics that make rural places unique. Even obdurate proponents of a paved Burr Trail probably shared the impulse to maintain the traditional even as they labored to bring modern comforts, industry, and tourist dollars to their towns. And even Grant Johnson can recognize the benefits of the Burr Trail as it is today. The road serves his ecotourism into the backcountry, a business he began in 1991, not long after a portion of the road had been paved. It would have been much more difficult to run his trips to the Waterpocket Fold and the Little Rockies if the road had never been improved. Paving the Burr Trail afforded a kind of devil's bargain, a lure that was difficult to pass up and to swallow at the same time.[73]

five

Abundance and Scarcity in the Book Cliffs

Fortresslike sedimentary walls form a long downward arc across the northeastern corner of Utah, marking the canyon country's northernmost boundary. The ashen-hued Book Cliffs are so named for their uncanny resemblance to books on a bookcase. Within eyeshot of Interstate 70, the Book Cliffs and neighboring Tavaputs Plateau beckon the traveler, but their foreboding landscape is customarily passed over for the more iconic redrock destinations due south. Aesthetically, the cliffs are not immediately striking. The overwhelmingly grayish shale is drab and the broken-sand cliffs less visually stunning than the stark copper-red assortment located elsewhere in the region. Nineteenth-century visitors, considering the region strange, barren, and unproductive, avoided it. Even today the Book Cliffs can hardly be regarded as a tourist destination.

It was here that in the late 1980s, commissioners in Grand and Uintah Counties devised a plan to build a road straight through the 190-mile citadel. And not just any road—a north-south high-speed freeway connecting I-70 and Vernal, Utah, that would in effect bisect the Book Cliffs. But the road proposal came just as people were beginning to recognize the region for its potential economic as well as aesthetic and ecological worth. Indeed, comparable geologic formations cannot be found anywhere in the world. The Book Cliffs feature diverse ecosystems supporting an array of wildlife:

from numerous species of small mammals, birds, fish, amphibians, and reptiles to large game such as antelope, Rocky Mountain elk, bighorn sheep, mountain lion, black bear—even bison and moose. At the same time, the region presented economic promise that belied its rather austere appearance. Energy companies straightaway eyed it for the vast oil and gas reserves dormant beneath the surface. The debate that would inescapably ensue over the proposed road turned to what was unseen: infinite stores of energy resources below the surface, which conservationists paralleled to potential death to the wildness, diversity, and pristine characteristics of the region.

The clash would hinge on dual perceptions of land. Was this region a valueless expanse or profitable real estate? Was it to be prized principally for its wilderness qualities, geologic formations, and biological diversity, or for its below-surface stores of hydrocarbon fuel? What was the land's highest use? Highway advocates supposed that the highway set the appropriate course, a physical and symbolic mark pointing to the land's best use. Conservationists feared that the web of roads would greatly increase private development. Hunting interests, which typically supported increased vehicular access to backcountry, lined up in opposition due to the perceived impacts on wildlife resources. All sides converged in the early 1990s, the proposed highway the linchpin that would largely determine the future of land use in the Book Cliffs.

Historically, Utah's northeastern corner was just as wild and isolated as the southeastern corner. The northern boundary of the northeastern region is flanked by the high Uintas, the only major Rocky Mountain range to run east-to-west. The mountain rivers drain the Uinta Basin and converge in the Green River, a Colorado River tributary. The basin is a place of extremes: of searing heat in summer and plummeting temperatures in winter. The Ute Indians considered the region part of their traditional homeland, but they used the basin more for hunting than habitation. Mormon church president Brigham Young set his settlement sights on the basin in 1861, lured in part from reports that the region contained "fertile vales, extensive meadows, and wide pasture-ranges." But Young called off the enterprise after an exploring party reported that the region was "one vast 'contiguity of waste,'" fit only for "nomadic purposes, hunting grounds for Indians and to hold the world together."[1]

This repulsion was not an uncommon initial reaction for visitors, particularly those merely interested in the land's potential economic benefits. Millenarian-minded Mormons could not fathom why God would create these "waste" places for no immediately recognizable purpose to satisfy human need. When in 1848 Mormon Lawyer Pratt set eyes on the San Rafael Swell in central Utah, he later wrote that "if there is no mineral wealth in these mountains I can hardly conceive of what earthly use a large proportion of this country was designed for!"[2] Indeed, the lands in eastern Utah—including the Book Cliffs region—possessed the qualities of the other: the opposite of flat and fertile. The scripture "every mountain and hill shall be made low" (Isa. 40:4) was not merely allegorical but to them represented the impulse to inhabit useful spaces.

In 1865 the Uintah Valley Reservation was established for several bands of Ute Indians. Not until 1872, more than a decade after the exploring expedition, did Mormons establish a settlement in the basin's Ashley Valley. The town of Vernal followed five years later. After 1905, when portions of the Ute Indian reservation were opened to white settlement, Mormon communities sprouted up in Duchesne County. Meanwhile, homesteaders, ranchers, and cowboys from Colorado had also trickled into the area, seeking the promise of cheap land and profitable enterprise. In time, the basin became a mixing ground where Mormon and "Gentile" settlers planted small towns and homesteads on the high valley soils drained by cold mountain rivers. The Ute Indians who had considered the basin as their homeland were relegated to the Uintah and Ouray Indian Reservation spread out over portions of the Uinta Basin and Book Cliffs region.

At least those settlements were located in the relatively arable sections of the basin drained by the Strawberry and White Rivers. To the south, the land was even drier and more undesirable than the northern portion. Outlining the southern rim of the Uinta Basin, the Book Cliffs and the Roan Cliffs are the major geologic features, protruding walls of sedimentary sandstone. Portions of the greater Book Cliffs region are forested and mountainous, reaching as high as eight thousand feet. And the proposed highway would extend into the heart of this remote region.

We know little of what early explorers and settlers thought of the Book Cliffs region, because in large part they avoided it. Incidentally, the corridor of the proposed highway had been a migration route since before the arrival of Euro-Americans. The Uinta-ats (Uinta), a band of Ute, reportedly used the route to move between summer and winter hunting areas. Trappers may have also followed Westwater Creek through the Book and Roan Cliffs into the Uinta Basin. The early French fur trader Antoine Robidoux likely traveled at least a portion of the route, as evidenced from his inscription at the confluence of East Canyon and Middle Canyon and also near P. R. Springs. Historian Doc Marston has suggested that the Robidoux inscription was an advertisement of sorts, alerting Indians to trading post(s) that he had established in the Uinta Basin. These Indian and trapper routes were clearly visible. When Lieutenant John W. Gunnison conducted railroad surveys in the 1850s, he noted "heavy Indian trails" leading to the Westwater Creek area as well as following the Dolores River north.[3]

Over the past hundred years, oil and gas development has transformed a large portion of the Uinta Basin and parts of the Book Cliffs region from a mostly untrammeled landscape to a domesticated one. The first mineral exploration and subsequent development in the Uinta Basin dated to the early twentieth century, near P. R. Springs. A road connected Ouray on the Uintah and Ouray Indian Reservation to P. R. Springs and then to Watson, a small town that mined gilsonite, a substance that resembles asphalt found only in the Uinta Basin. Later in the 1940s, mining companies dug wells for oil and gas and for the next half century created a web of roads to reach claims.[4] These areas remain major petroleum producers. Topographic maps published by the Bureau of Land Management in the 1990s labeled in large print the southern portion of Uintah County as "Oil Shale Reserve." Other place-names underscore the dominant economic activity in the region: San Arroyo Gas Field, Cisco Dome Oil Field, and Buck Canyon Gas Field.[5]

It is easy to envision the energy potential of the Book Cliffs region. Eastern Utah and western Colorado contain vast stores of oil, gas, gilsonite, oil shale, tar sands, sand, gravel, and other mineral resources. Some scientists hypothesize the region contains among the largest reserves of oil and natural gas in the world.[6] The oil dates back to the Eocene when a lake covered much of the area, and the organic matter that settled in the lake's bottom was enclosed in mud and sediment. These layers eventually hardened. Intense pressure and heat transformed organic matter into a form of oil or natural gas, which settled in pockets within the rock layers or porous rock such as sandstone. But in eastern Utah, the oil and natural gas reserves are embedded quite deep within the sedimentary rock or shale, and are therefore difficult and expensive to extract. The rock first needs to be mined from large pits or, if the shale resides deep within the earth, underground shafts. Converting oil shale and tar sands to refined oil is highly water intensive, requiring an estimated three to four barrels of water for each barrel of oil produced. Where the oil is deposited in shale or surrounds rock in an oily film, no cost-effective mining method yet exists.[7]

The proposed highway would cut through this enormous region with underlying oil, shale, and tar-sand reserves. It would complement other roads reaching out to the energy resources that were well built and wide enough to move equipment into the backcountry since mining companies typically constructed roads to lead to drilling locations. Sometimes roads connected to other roads, but more often than not they dead-ended at the well sites, spreading out like branches of a tree. In addition to requiring road building, oil and gas development entails other extensive infrastructure like pipelines, electric distribution lines, compressor sites, well sites, and gas-collecting plants.

For a brief stint in the 1970s, voices would quicken when speaking of the basin's envisioned role in solving the nation's energy shortages. Dreams of the bounteous energy potential cached underground in eastern Utah and in large sections of Wyoming and Colorado became subsumed in the larger narrative of energy production. Richard Nixon had originally articulated a plan centered on nuclear power production, but Jimmy Carter later shifted the focus to coal, which also exists abundantly in the Uinta Basin. Many predicted a boom in energy resource development here and elsewhere in the West. The U-tar division of the Bighorn Oil Company operated a pilot plant in the P. R. Springs vicinity. Several oil companies explored tar-sand development projects in the area, although nothing came of their proposals.[8]

But oil and natural gas extraction yet remained viable. From 1985 to 1990, natural gas production increased 18 percent in Uintah County. Uintah and Grand Counties reportedly contained a combined 4,028 oil and gas wells, with more than half producing. And the potential energy stores that could be tapped were extensive. According to a 1992 US Geological Survey report, oil shale in the Green River Formation contained an estimated 321 billion barrels of oil. This did not account, however, for recoverable quantities under existing economic and operating conditions. Recoverable oil reserves worldwide, according to the 2007 BP *Statistical Review,* approximate 1,239 billion barrels—with more than 755 billion barrels located in the Middle East, compared to about 30 billion in the United States. Recoverable natural gas reserves totaled nearly 238 trillion cubic feet in the United States and approximately 6,290 trillion cubic feet worldwide.[9] Economic boosters in northeastern Utah anticipated a time when the technology existed to unleash the region's energy potential and the price of petroleum rose high enough to pay for its costly extraction.

Bryon Merrell, in a 1985 Uintah County Commission meeting, proposed "surfacing" a fifty-three-mile stretch of the Seep Ridge Road, "thereby deterring major users from going to Grand Junction, Co." But the justification had little to do with funneling tourism through eastern Utah. Merrell had in mind an energy development corridor benefiting Mobil, Kirkwood, Duncan, Getty, Texaco, Intercorp, Geo Kinetics, Northwest, TXO, Bradshaw, and other oil companies. Commissioner Neal Domgaard gave a nod to the proposal if mineral lease payments funded it.[10]

Prior to 1988, the federal government returned a portion of mineral-lease royalties collected from mineral development to western states where those royalties originated. The money went into a state slush fund to be used primarily for road construction. Grand and San Juan County commissioners worked to change Utah's allocation method to return a percentage of royalties not to the state, but to the counties on the basis of mineral production. The new system of mineral lease–funding allocation prompted the formation of special transportation districts. As Ray Tibbetts of Moab recalls: "Someone at the [state of Utah] attorney general's office said they needed to come up with a new district to hold [the county's royalties]. 'Have you got any idea?' [Jimmie Walker of the Grand County Commission] said, 'Yeah, the most important thing we have that needs help is roads. Not only San Juan but Grand County, all of them—these roads, there is always a perpetual need, new equipment and so forth.' So they provided a new service district based on roads."[11]

In November 1988, a few days after Grand County commissioners Jimmie Walker and Dutch Zimmerman lost reelection primarily due to their support of a proposed toxic-waste incinerator in Cisco, Utah, the outbound commissioners announced the new transportation district's formation that would direct the use of mineral-lease payments for road building within the county. Remarkably, Walker, Zimmerman, and David Knutson appointed Zimmerman, Robert Shumway, and Ollie Knutson (David Knutson's father) to the district's governing board and Walker as the district's new paid director. While Moab resident Jim Stiles had penned that many citizens of Grand County believed the 1988 election reflected a "New Day" for county politics—"a new found environmental awareness and a movement away from the promotion of industries that could threaten the beauty of the canyon country and the health of the people who live here"—they soon discovered to their dismay that the outgoing commissioners' hands would still be in the county coffers.[12]

If the staffing of this new district was not controversial enough, the district's first matter of business was none other than to propose a highway through the Book Cliffs. "We always wanted to improve access between here [Moab] and there [Vernal]," Walker recalls. "We got the idea that the best way to do that was to build a good road." That "good road" would replace the well-established Seep Ridge Road through Middle Canyon over the Book Cliffs and down Hay Canyon into Grand County. This would satisfy the initial purpose for the special service transportation districts to support more energy development. The Grand County Roads Special Service District teamed up with the newly organized Uintah Special Service District to steer the proposed highway through the planning phase.[13]

On their end, the Uintah County district pushed quickly on the highway construction, using a six-million-dollar loan from the Community Impact Board that would be repaid using mineral-lease funds.[14] But from the beginning, the highway scheme seemed a shady business deal. The company that received the first contract to build the initial section of the road through the Ute Indian reservation, Creamer and Noble Engineering, had lobbied for the state to pass legislation returning mineral-lease money directly to counties. David Knutson admitted to Jim Stiles in 1989 that county officials did not even consider giving the contract to another construction company.

"Basically we told [Steve Creamer] that if he could find the money for Grand County to do this project, he could do the engineering on it. It was more of a gentleman's agreement." Knutson's comments later became public, and Steve Creamer, in an interview by KTVX News in Salt Lake City, "shakily denied any wrong-doing," according to Stiles.[15]

That was not the only commercial interest to benefit from the new road. Highway proponents did not hide the fact that the road would principally serve the oil and gas industry, justified on the basis that mineral-lease funds would pay for it. The highway would also facilitate increased tourism and revenue in eastern Utah, they defended. But access to energy resources in southern Uintah County and the greater Book Cliffs area was clearly the end game. The Grand County transportation district's 1989 "Application for Transportation and Utility Systems and Facilities on Federal Lands" indicated that the highway's "primary purpose" would be "to provide improved access into the tar sand, oil shale, natural gas and oil deposits located on public lands in that area."[16] Commissioner Max Adams had noted the need to access "some of the richest oil deposits in the world."[17] Tom Wardell, manager of the Uintah Special Service District, bluntly admitted, "We are trying to give something back to the [gas and oil] companies by providing them with a better road system."

Proponents of the highway took for granted they had the community's full support to push forward on the project. Even the Ute Indian Tribe, expressing support for a road running from "Ouray to East Cisco," granted a twenty-five-year right-of-way for construction across a portion of the reservation.[18] The major challenge seemed to be construction costs; the Utah Department of Transportation had estimated a price tag upwards of forty million dollars. Along most of the Uintah County side, the new highway would traverse an existing alignment, but straightening and widening it would require major engineering feats. Particularly in Grand County, some parts of the proposed road would have to be built over an entirely new alignment. None of the current alignments through the Book Cliffs would be easily negotiated by construction crews facing isolated and otherwise inadequate working conditions. For some county road advocates, the route that would be the easiest to build—through East Canyon—would also be nonsensical, since it would drop motorists close to the Utah-Colorado line and would save motorists a mere thirty-seven miles of driving distance.[19]

By October 1990, the Uintah Special Service District had already spent more than a million dollars on the highway. Continued highway construction was invariably dependent on funding and coordination between the two counties as well as the Environmental Impact Statement (EIS) then being prepared to determine the highway's environmental impact.[20]

Wilderness advocates touted the greater Book Cliffs region as one of the largest and last-remaining protected "roadless" areas in Utah. During the initial wilderness inventory initiated in 1979, the BLM had earmarked practically the entire region for consideration. When the BLM eventually settled on proposed Wilderness Study Areas, Unit 100 and Unit 068 were within the Book and Roan Cliffs. Unit 100 even overlapped the original existing route that was the template for the proposed highway. The BLM eventually whittled the units down to more modest-size areas hugging the western and southern boundary of the Uintah and Ouray Indian Reservation.[21] Yet the longstanding "Citizens' Wilderness Proposal for Bureau of Land Management Lands in Utah," endorsed by the Southern Utah Wilderness Alliance and other environmental groups, identified large sections of intact wilderness lands in what the proposal called the Book Cliffs–Desolation Canyon region.[22]

Conservationists sharply criticized oil and gas development as the most serious threat to the environmental integrity of the Book Cliffs region. Earlier, in December 1981, the Utah Wilderness Association filed suit in the federal district court against the BLM to cease "significant road construction" within wilderness inventory units in the Book Cliffs. The plaintiffs alleged that the permits for road construction in wilderness units had been issued without proper attention to environmental laws.[23] Although the BLM had highlighted potential impacts of road construction and petroleum development in the Book Cliffs region in its 1982 Grand Resource Area Resource Management Plan (RMP) and EIS, environmentalists found federal protection to be lacking.[24] Before a congressional audience, Sierra Club representative Debbie Sease pointed specifically to how the Book Cliffs RMP left the "widest range of action" because it "does not set goals and priorities for these various resources." According to Sease, the RMP avoided designation of "critical" areas and provided inadequate protection of land and resources. "What seems to be missing is the will of the agency to enforce and implement the spirit and the letter of the law," Sease said, speaking of the 1976 Federal Land Policy and Management Act.[25]

In truth, there was no clear management directive for the Book Cliffs region. Although the BLM ostensibly attempted to satisfy multiple interests, each group had its own designs for the land. The region was a blank sheet, but questions remained. Would Congress designate large sections as wilderness, or would it largely remain open to petroleum development? Might oil and gas development be curtailed to minimize impact? Would there be special land-use designations to protect large-game wildlife for hunting interests? How would private landownership remain compatible, if at all, with public land use? Competing interests jockeyed the BLM to allocate land to their favored use, marshaling their strongest arguments and portraying other uses as largely incompatible.

One vision that increasingly drew attention was the Book Cliffs as wildlife preserve. In 1970 an elk herd was successfully reintroduced into the region, and other rewilding efforts have concentrated on bison, which had once occupied the area. (The Spanish missionary Francisco Silvestre Veléz de Escalante in 1776 recorded a buffalo-herd sighting north of the cliffs near present-day Jensen, Utah.) The Ute tribe introduced a small herd of bison on the Hill Creek Extension of the Uintah and Ouray Indian Reservation in 1986. Since then, bison have begun to repopulate the Book Cliffs.[26]

When the Uintah and Grand County districts teamed up to push for a Book Cliffs highway, Fish and Wildlife Service officials protested the "increases in traffic and hunting" that would follow. On one hand, the road promised to provide better access to hunters who valued the region as a premier hunting ground, and in turn, more game wardens would be required. Conversely, sportsmen expressed alarm that the road might adversely affect wildlife and lobbied that "pristine areas [ought] to be maintained for protection and management of trophy hunting." The Fish and Wildlife Service believed there were "large trac[t]s of land that could be closed to road traffic in order to preserve pristine conditions." Yet county commissioners staunchly resisted mention of closing land for private hunting or any other preservation purpose, instead pinning their hopes on economic development through oil and gas extraction. In 1987, Uintah County commissioners balked at pressure to close

Seep Ridge Road to create a "private game reserve," which they felt would set a dangerous precedent. It is unclear what was meant by a "private" reserve, but at any rate hunting interests had lobbied to protect the region's elk and other game.[27] Members of the transportation district supported the commission's position and "reiterated their commitment to an improvement through this area of Oil leases," although they did acknowledge the need to balance "oil development, tourism, hunters, and adversaries" through "cooperation and communication between parties."[28]

Hunting and conservation interests were dually satisfied with the creation of the Book Cliffs Conservation Initiative in 1990. A year earlier, purportedly while sitting around a campfire somewhere on the Book Cliffs, personnel from the BLM and the Utah Division of Wildlife Resources concocted a plan to buy up privately owned ranches, phase out or limit grazing, and populate and reintroduce some game species into the area. In time, state and federal agencies joined forces with the Rocky Mountain Elk Foundation, the Nature Conservancy, and a handful of longtime ranchers and private landowners willing to sell their property for this purpose. Within a few years, the conservation area encompassed approximately twenty thousand acres of public lands. Grazing leases were retired on more than six hundred thousand acres of state and federal lands to encourage more wildlife. As reported in the Grand County Roads Special Service District meeting, "Originally [the conservation area] had boundaries nearly identical to the tar sands deposits in the Book Cliffs" but had then "expanded to the Indian lands on the West and to the Colorado line on the east down to the WSA on the South."[29]

The initiative garnered support not only among environmentalists and sportsmen but also among locals—at least early on—in part because it did not aim to cut off oil and gas access and development entirely and because hunting areas would provide significant economic benefits to local communities. Grazing would also be permitted to a lesser degree. When the Utah state legislature appropriated two million dollars to the Division of Wildlife Resources to purchase the 7,515-acre S & H Book Cliffs Ranch, it used carefully crafted language acknowledging "major reserves of gas, oil, coal, and other mineral resources" and the continued desire to develop them. In particular, the bill prioritized energy development over conservation on state-trust lands. The state was also careful to not support extended federal ownership or control; through land swaps, it ensured that the conservation initiative would not result in a net gain of federal lands.[30]

If the conservation area did not seriously threaten oil and gas development in the Book Cliffs region, wilderness designation did, and vice versa. The proposed highway would ostensibly impact the region's wilderness characteristics and wildlife resources, bisecting the Winter Ridge WSA and passing immediately adjacent to the Flume Canyon WSA. In a record of decision, the BLM allowed sections of the proposed route in the WSAs to be surveyed for environmental effects. In September 1991, the Utah Chapter of the Sierra Club and the Utah Wildlife Leadership Coalition appealed a BLM decision, debating that it violated section 603 of FLPMA, directing the BLM to manage WSAs "in a manner so as not to impair the suitability of such areas for preservation as a wilderness." They also asserted that the BLM should have conducted a full-scale environmental inventory to determine impacts of the proposed highway on endangered species like peregrine falcons, bald eagles, and other wildlife and plants.[31]

Wilderness advocates were further alarmed when in 1991, a full year before the release of the BLM's draft EIS, Utah congressman Bill Orton confidently declared that "there will be a road through [the Book Cliffs] area." Orton threatened to introduce legislation to "delist" the Winter Ridge WSA if the EIS concluded that the proposed Book Cliffs highway through it would "do the least damage to the environment, cost the least amount of money, be the easiest and safest to maintain, and so on."[32] With this option on the table, highway opponents anxiously awaited the EIS release.

In Grand County, the roads district circulated a pamphlet entitled *Book Cliffs Highway: The Pathway of Progress.* The cover image displayed a rod-straight road slicing through an unnecessarily enormous swath of the Book Cliffs with comical precision. The second page stated in bold, "The Book Cliffs Highway will be the only paved road through a multiple-use region about as large as the states of Connecticut and Rhode Island combined."[33] Along with facilitating mineral revenues to the county, the highway would provide a public north-south access serving hunters, hikers, and mountain bikers. Motorists would enjoy a smooth drive through cragged country and intermittent scenic stops that showcased the character of the place. Indeed, the pamphlet underscored the vision of the basin's first community builders who dreamed of roads, towns, dams, and prosperity.

The need for a Book Cliffs highway reflected that founding vision, deeply rooted in the Turnerian narrative of American history and magnified through a particular lens of progress. Glenn Anderson, arguing for the proposed highway, penned in a letter to the editor, "The Lord made the earth for everyone and admonished Adam to subdue it and produce for the good of man." Believing the road-building task to be divinely ordained, he stridently advocated it and dismissed "this non-sense" of the road affecting wildlife. Anderson and other highway proponents merely assumed that economic growth would benefit the county and trickle down to locals, that roads would enable the aged and disabled to access the region's magnificent landscape, that roads benignly impact wildlife populations and could not possibly ruin a place as expansive as the Book Cliffs. These were plausible arguments that appealed to deeply entrenched notions of progress and the ideal of advancing a prosperous society.[34]

But not all locals—and certainly not the highway's opponents—bought into this line of thinking. Gary Martin, a recent transplant to the Uinta Basin, spoke of the virtues of living in a place where "it's quiet, the air is clean and my wife and children are safe on the streets." He, too, could appeal to the traditional, conservative impulse of the community in opposing the road and questioning the notion of growth for growth's sake. "Go back east and look at what people like you and the county commissioners have done, or simply go visit Springdale or Moab, here in Utah," he said. "The world is a crowded place and sitting here in the Uintah Basin you don't get a fee[l] for it. If you have any sense you will do your best to keep people out of here for as long as you can. There is only so much free space and when it is gone there will be no more."[35]

Critics questioned not just "growth for growth's sake" but also the prudence of spending millions on a road project that would better support communities in other ways. Will Durrant of the Uintah Mountain Club recommended the money go to education or repairing crumbling infrastructure. Many decried millions being spent to build a new road—and potentially millions more to maintain it until the state took it over, if ever—primarily to benefit one industry. "What could this community do with a fraction of the money it will take to pave this White Elephant across the unpaved Book Cliffs?" queried Durrant. "For a fraction of the $80 million, could we have a fully-staffed and accredited four-year college in our town? Sure we could. Could we have a permanent endowment fund for the library? A perpetual scholarship fund for deserving high school seniors? You bet we could."[36]

Martin and Durrant were a few of the voices that by 1992 were publicly questioning the proposed highway and its implications. In scoping workshops to acquire public input prior to the EIS draft, the Utah Trail Machine Association inquired about ORV recreation in the region. The Utah Hunters Federation had no concern other than detrimental effects on hunting opportunities, the Ute tribal chairman opposed an alternative route that would cross partway through the Hill Creek Extension of the reservation, and the Utah Division of Wildlife held that "a high quality, all season highway can only detract from the Cisco Desert and Book Cliffs attractiveness as remote wildlands."[37]

These legitimate concerns nonetheless, members of the county transportation districts forged ahead, confident that the BLM would provide the green light with the EIS release. In Grand County, one resident speculated that "perhaps by the first of the year work on the project may begin."[38] Conceivably based on that overarching optimism, the district threw more money at the project in the hopes of generating public support. They mulled over producing a film to showcase the project in a positive light or setting up a booth at the county fair. These activities would be funded by the district; the county allocated at least fifteen thousand dollars for the promotional film. Although some criticized these expenditures as wasteful and that the district was overstepping its authority, in a closed-door meeting the district reaffirmed the original motion to allocate funds, with only Ollie Knutson in dissent.[39]

Meanwhile, public officials queued up along either side of the proposed highway. In June 1992, the Vernal Area Chamber of Commerce Board of Directors voted its support. Roosevelt mayor Leonard Ferguson backed it, in part because it would enable locals to travel more quickly to Moab. Not long after, the Moab City Council, the mayor of Vernal, and the Duchesne City Council came out publicly opposing the highway. Even some oil and gas companies operating in the Book Cliffs region like Beartooth Oil & Gas and

Northstar Gas withdrew support, instead advocating a general improvement to the region's dirt roads.[40]

The BLM at last released the draft EIS in September 1992. It recommended a compromise, concluding the existing alignment could be paved without significant widening or grading. The proposed highway from Ouray to I-70 would generally follow the Seep Ridge Road to Pine Spring Canyon and there extend into Main Canyon and Pretty Valley Ridge. It would then continue on a dirt road along the ridge, connect to an existing route through Hay Canyon and East Canyon, and extend south to I-70 near Cisco. In total, the highway would shorten the driving distance between Vernal and Crescent Junction by a paltry thirty-eight miles.[41]

The EIS also sought to evaluate the possible presence of unknown wildlife species. Based on a "historic sighting" of a Mexican spotted owl near P. R. Springs in 1958, the Fish and Wildlife Service recommended the BLM survey suitable owl habitats that might potentially be disturbed by road construction. The BLM had apparently identified owls—possibly spotted, a federally listed threatened species—but members of the Grand County Roads Special Service District expressed skepticism, noting that "no such reports [have been] given to the sponsors of the survey." Jerry McNeil of Moab maintained that BLM personnel played a tape recorder with the sound of a spotted owl but spotted no actual owls in the Book Cliffs.[42]

Defenders of the highway urged the BLM to proceed in other ways, as planned, with the project. At a public meeting, Jay Mealey of Crown Energy extolled the road's benefits for tar-sand development. The proposed road would "dramatically improve access/economic viability for developing tar sands in Uintah Basin and PR Springs." Crown Energy representatives anticipated the benefits of tar-sand development at "five million barrels of oil, thousands of jobs, and millions in tax revenue."[43]

The BLM received about seven hundred letters, mostly from critics. Chief arguments centered on threats to the region's biological diversity and the road's impact on a remarkable landscape. William R. Russell, an attorney in Salt Lake City, wrote, "Such a highway would put huge numbers of wildlife at risk, befoul a rather pristine area, and change the character of these remote Cliffs *forever*!"[44] George Nickas of the UWA believed the highway "threatens to blow apart one of the greatest opportunities we will ever have to restore, on one small part of our planet, the wildlife heritage that once existed in North America." He worried that "it will take much more than the initial steps contemplated in the Book Cliffs Conservation Initiative, but it's a good beginning. Conversely, the Book Cliffs Highway is probably the greatest step backward imaginable."[45] A slew of oppositional voices in fact came from local residents and officials, particularly in Grand County, and to a lesser degree in Uintah County, where a new demographic challenged traditional convention.[46]

From 1970 to 1995, the interior West grew faster than the rest of the country, and folks making a home in communities like Moab and Vernal little resembled the traditional populations characterized by the Old West.[47] They were river runners, mountain bikers, backcountry enthusiasts, artists, writers, and winter birds, and they came for the scenery, wide-open spaces, clean air, climate, and recreational opportunities. The cultural, political, and environmental impact of this new, emergent demographic was unmistakable, and, to some, unsettling. Yet to some, the benefits of a diverse, vibrant population far outweighed the attendant challenges. "Moab's good and creative people are experimenting, working hard to craft a sensible relationship between our species and a jagged, erratic, redrock stretch of land that not long ago we scorned but that we now know is sacred," noted attorney Charles Wilkinson.[48]

It was this shifting mind-set among the emergent demographic in rural Utah that would decisively put an end to the proposed highway project on Grand County's side. They not only killed the proposal, but also modified the county political system to ensure that a similar proposal would never crop up again. In the 1992 local elections, fed up with the political in-dealings of the commission, Grand County residents soundly voted for a complete rehaul, replacing the commission-style government with a council system, in large part due to the former's spearheading of the Book Cliffs highway proposal. Within a few months of the election, the entire highway proposal had collapsed. The new Grand County Council passed a resolution that revoked the authority of the county transportation district and terminated the Book Cliffs Highway memorandum of understanding (MOU) between the BLM and the Grand County Roads and Uintah Special Service Districts. They also withdrew the county's right-of-way application to the Book Cliffs highway alignment. With the MOU no longer in force, the BLM halted work on the

EIS. Newly appointed Grand County Council chairman Charles Peterson justified the move: "The benefits of the Highway would not justify its costs; geophysical evidence shows that the proposed route is not a suitable place for constructing or maintaining a highway, nor would the highway provide useful access to Grand County's oil, gas, and mineral reserves; and, finally, public sentiment in the County is strongly in favor of putting the County's limited resources to work on other priorities."[49]

Grand County's withdrawal left Uintah County in a tricky position. The right-of-way application jointly filed by the two counties was now defunct, and Uintah County was left to start over and go at it alone.[50] County officials have never officially surrendered the idea. In Uintah County the proposal to pave Seep Ridge Road never met with the same resistance that it did in Grand County.

To Jimmie Walker, the former Grand County commissioner, the defeat was devastating. He publicly criticized environmentalists and federal personnel for "sabotaging" the highway project and took a swipe at the Book Cliffs Conservation Initiative, which he referred to as a "real boondoggle." Walker later disparaged oil interests who "never learned how to fight" and those who abandoned him when he needed their support the most. "It put me in a position of how Custer felt," he lamented. "They made a big enough deal over the Book Cliffs thing, how it was going to do all this damage, and how it was costly, and whatever other excuse." To the end, he upheld his position that thirty-seven or thirty-eight miles saved meant a lot to tourists and the long-haul trucker and that the highway would have provided the county net benefits.[51]

For all the good Walker claimed the project would do for Grand County residents, he could not possibly perceive why it attracted such intense opposition. Critics not only feared the highway would impact adjacent WSAs and wildlife populations. They also lamented the highway's impact on the feeling of wildness in the Book Cliffs. There was a sense of loss from the growing realization that large roadless places on earth were becoming fewer, with resulting effects irreversible. These lost places would never be reclaimed, environmentalists affirmed, with growing populations ever crowding into shrinking land areas.

Individuals responded to increasing population pressures, justifying the need to develop or preserve resources, depending on their perspective. Environmental activists, considering the larger Book Cliffs region to be a bastion of wildness, argued that it warranted protection precisely because of increasing pressure for resources, just as others thought the region's vast mineral resources ought to be developed for humans' betterment.

The notion of the highway slicing through a roadless and pristine wilderness belied the reality of development in the Uinta Basin–Book Cliffs region. The area contains an extensive network of oil and gas roads and pumping wells, as well as future possibilities for mineral-lease development. Some liked to reference the massive energy potential of the Uinta Basin and other petroleum-rich regions in the West, although it is still not always technologically possible or economically efficient to tap these resources. Supporters of the Book Cliffs highway, however, regarded the presence of these minerals as justification for the road. "What really galled me about this whole damn thing, we kept talking to our governor and our people from the state level, and they wouldn't have done anything about biting off this damn wilderness being put right on top of that damn thing," complained Ray Tibbetts of Moab. "I mean, here's the breadbasket of Utah and Uintah County, with all these minerals and reserves of energy, you can't believe, and they weren't worried about it being locked up forever." He then referred to recent success in developing these resources, particularly natural gas. "There's more natural gas being passed along the Book Cliffs than you can shake a fist at."[52]

Yet Tibbetts's blanket statements are misleading: it is hardly a uniform landscape, and resources have not been locked up, albeit the northern portion of the Uintah County region was much more intensively developed than areas in Grand County. In a letter to BLM district manager Daryl Trotter, John Wilson describes driving the length of the proposed highway alignment "to see what the route and the area in question was like." In a four-wheel-drive vehicle, Wilson crossed the Green River and for twenty-five miles "saw a lot of oil truck activity." Continuing, he encountered "a beautiful, pristine, and deserted area."[53] To many familiar with the area, the region to be carved by the proposed highway could not be characterized by generalizations. Contrasting the heavily developed gas lands in southern Uintah County to the less developed portions of the Book Cliffs and East Tavaputs Plateau—classifying the region as either "energy rich" or "pristine wildlands"—captures only a fraction of the land's character. Classification is a narrative device that does not reflect real land-use designations.

Furthermore, assessing whether the region is an energy field or a wilderness is, in part, a matter of perspective. The stereotype of the Book Cliffs as "wild" lingers because on the surface it appears to be a barren, inhospitable place. Some may view it as devoid of qualities worth preserving in pristine form—an expansive wasteland exhibiting little by way of scenic wonder and beauty or richness in ecological diversity. Yet arguments along this line enabled the development oriented to advance their own self-interest while appearing benign. If the land is worthless, if it is relatively barren, unseemly, and unforgiving, why not turn it over to the oil and gas interests? Why not put it to its highest use, which to them was clearly energy development?

To many, the natural order of nature suggested its own use. From an economic or utilitarian perspective, the high, inaccessible mountain peaks may best be allocated for wilderness, the lower wooded slopes for timber production, the grassland valleys and canyons for grazing, and mineral-rich areas to mining and energy development. The idea of a best and highest use implies that each area of land offers a variety of values and that each area of land should be allocated to that use which maximizes present net value. Nature establishes the order, dictating where people settle, work, and move about the land. Sometimes this was a matter of limitations imposed by a lack of technology or resources—it is not possible to build cities or graze cattle or construct roads just anywhere—but here it especially seemed to confirm the natural order of things. The debate over the Book Cliffs highway reflects these dominant perceptions. Because the region contained what some believed to be nearly unlimited economic potential and because it did not conform to idealized expectations of beauty, developers easily justified their actions. By contrast, by the late twentieth century, some had become awakened to the region's own qualities that made it worthy of defense against roads and energy development. Many today recognize within that landscape beauty, life, vitality, wonder, and spirituality that likely escaped the imagination of early visitors. This way of seeing the land—quite different from the perspective that merely notes utilitarian purpose—enabled one visitor to the Book Cliffs to wonder "why anyone would pave a highway across this somewhat barren but unique ecosystem?"[54]

By contrast, early explorers and even settlers expected little from what they considered a barren landscape. In the nineteenth and early twentieth centuries, the Book Cliffs, Uinta Basin, and other arid areas were places to shun. Even the millenarian-minded William H. Smart, a Mormon leader who spearheaded settlement in the basin in the early twentieth century, late in life was disappointed to realize, according to his biographer, that his initial dream of a growing, flourishing Mormon settlement in the Uinta Basin could not be realized.[55] Yet it is a curious thing of history how perceptions change. Smart would likely be astonished at how much wealth is extracted from a place he so tirelessly attempted to develop. The basin still supports ranching and marginally productive irrigation farmland, but the region's most lucrative industry is petroleum extraction. According to a 2007 report of the Utah Governor's Office, crude oil production in the Uinta Basin (comprising Uintah and Duchesne Counties) reached 11.4 million barrels and natural gas production reached 226 billion cubic feet in 2006. The oil and gas industry directly and indirectly accounted for nearly half of all employment and 38.7 percent of all property taxes paid in the basin. Uintah and Duchesne Counties also collected a combined $30.3 million in federal mineral royalties. The region has economically benefited in recent years from a spike in the value of crude oil and natural gas.[56]

Other landscapes have similarly been reconsidered. Once valued only by ranchers and farmers, the groundwater in central Nevada and western Utah is now believed to be a valuable source for southern Nevada's insatiable growth. Indeed, the perceptions of abundance paradoxically derive from the reality of scarcity. Only after Las Vegas overused its water rights to the Colorado River and its tributaries did it begin to notice the "abundant" groundwater reserves in central Nevada. The same might be said of energy development in eastern Utah: the added urgency to tap into energy resources rose in large part from the national debate over the scarcity and rising prices of domestic energy supplies.

The parallel between water and energy resources may be further extended. In both cases, the development dreams defy economic or technological possibility. Even if Pat Mulroy of the Southern Nevada Water Authority was able to successfully claim water rights for southern Nevada, the challenge and cost of piping it to Las Vegas would be enormous, though likely not prohibitive.

Yet, not surprisingly, this groundwater supply is finite. In the case of energy development, the resource is there in abundance, but the ability to extract it in economically and environmentally viable ways remains elusive. The technology simply does not yet exist to extract oil from shale. Perhaps the main point is that both resources—groundwater and petroleum—are nonrenewable and can easily be depleted. Managing for wildlife, recreation, and healthy watersheds is an activity that does not entail extraction to depletion, unless done improperly, whereas extracting fossil petroleum and fossil water is a short-term project that must ultimately be replaced with something more sustainable. Advocating for responsible development of renewable resources is acknowledging the limitations and long-term needs of the land. By contrast, nonrenewable resource development is very often shortsighted in the long-term health of the environment as well as the living things that make it home.

As we have seen, the debate surrounding the proposed Book Cliffs highway largely hinged on the dual expectations of the land as barren and unproductive versus the land as full and valuable. Constituents on both sides "discovered" the bounties of the land, and they variously used these to advance their positions. The West contains countless other places that have attracted or will attract attention for the values that people see in them. The perpetual challenge in the modern West is the same challenge that confronted advocates and opponents of the proposed Book Cliffs highway.

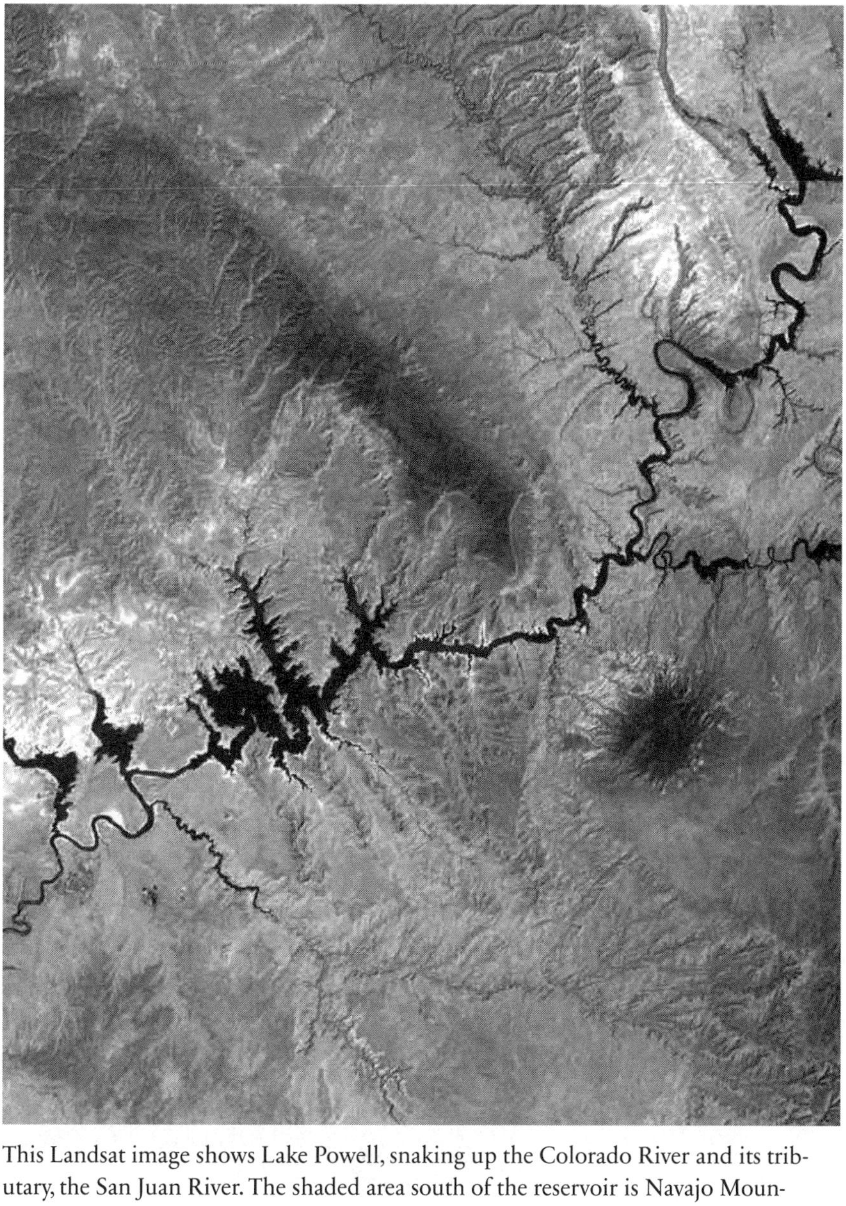

This Landsat image shows Lake Powell, snaking up the Colorado River and its tributary, the San Juan River. The shaded area south of the reservoir is Navajo Mountain; the large shaded area northwest of the reservoir is the Kaiparowits Plateau. The Escalante River, a Colorado River tributary, parallels the Kaiparowits to the northeast. *Courtesy the Landsat Project digital archives, part of a joint endeavor of the US Geological Survey and NASA.*

Reenactment of the Hole-in-the-Rock expedition, 1971. This view is looking northwest with the cleft in the Hole-in-the-Rock in the background. *Photo by Robert Clayton. Used by permission, Utah State Historical Society, all rights reserved.*

Looking westward toward the Kaiparowits Plateau. This photo was taken after Kluckhohn and his party had scaled the walls of Glen Canyon, emerging through Hole-in-the-Rock. James Hanks wrote his sister, "I suppose that you can get some idea of [the land] from the pictures, but the colors which you do not see, make the country far more beautiful" (Hanks to Mrs. Arthur Mailer, July 3, 1928, James J. Hanks Collection, Cline Library, Northern Arizona University). *Courtesy Northern Arizona University, Cline Library, James J. Hanks Collection.*

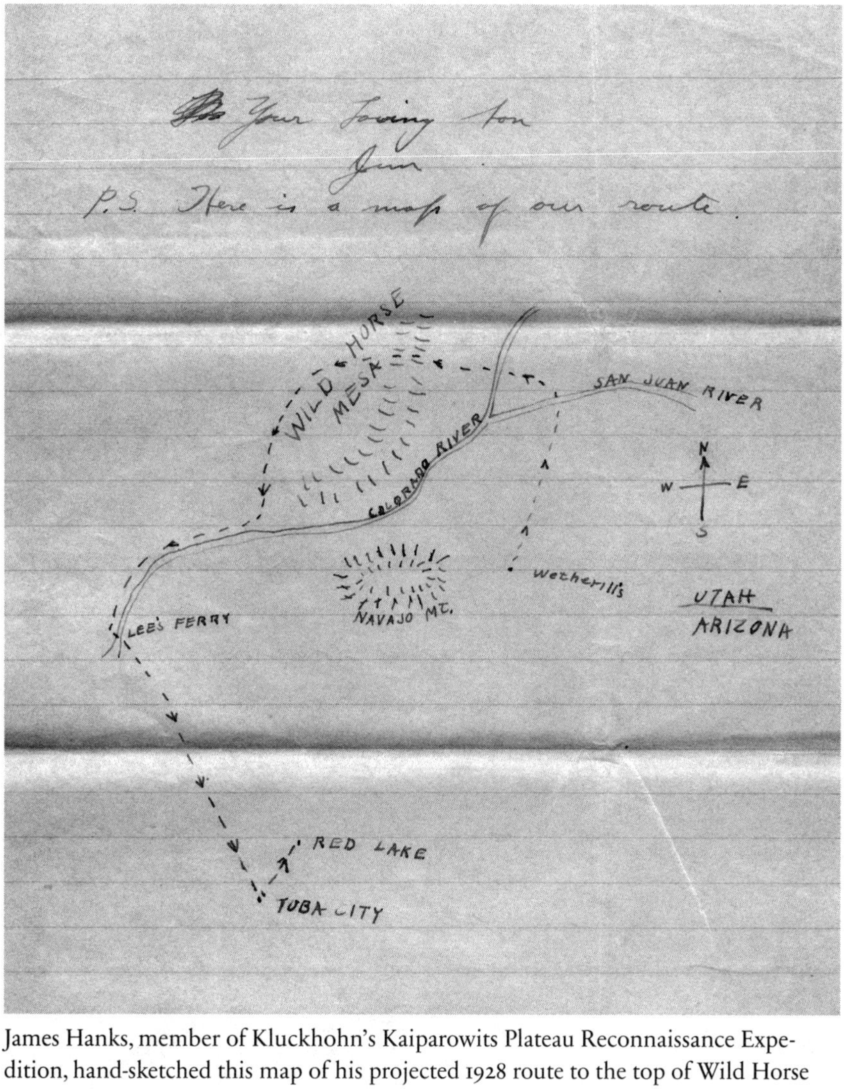

James Hanks, member of Kluckhohn's Kaiparowits Plateau Reconnaissance Expedition, hand-sketched this map of his projected 1928 route to the top of Wild Horse Mesa. *Courtesy Northern Arizona University, Cline Library, James Hanks Collection.*

The celebration at the dedication of Navajo Bridge, at Marble Canyon near Lee's Ferry, 1929. Until completion of the bridge, Kluckhohn wrote in *Beyond the Rainbow*, "The rockribbed, unapproachable chasm of the Colorado, for a thousand miles unbridged, was an almost invincible barrier." *From the A. L. Inglesby Collection. Used by permission, Utah State Historical Society, all rights reserved.*

Automobile being pulled out of a river, possibly the Green River, 1921. *Used by permission, Utah State Historical Society, all rights reserved.*

Parade of the Elephants in Arches National Monument, southeast Utah, 1945. Edward Abbey, who spent two seasons as a rancher in Arches, wrote in his journal on April 8, 1957: "DICTUM: NO AUTOMOBILES IN NATIONAL PARKS. . . . God Bless America. Let's Save Some of It." *Used by permission, Utah State Historical Society, all rights reserved.*

Calvin Black, circa 1976.
Courtesy Merri Shumway.

Ferry crossing at Hite, Utah, September 18, 1946, the day after the dedication of State Highway 95. Art Chaffin operated this ferry on the Colorado River from 1946 to 1964. *Used by permission, Utah State Historical Society, all rights reserved.*

The new steel arched bridge over the Colorado River, with the location of the old Hite's ferry in the background, June 3, 1966. The other bridges dedicated were the Dirty Devil River Bridge, about a half mile from this bridge, and the White Canyon Bridge, several miles to the south. *Bureau of Reclamation photo by Mel Davis. Used by permission, Utah State Historical Society, all rights reserved.*

Old State Road 95, in its harrowing descent of Comb Ridge, early 1950s. *Used by permission, Utah State Archives, all rights reserved.*

Construction of Utah Highway 95 through the formidable Comb Ridge. *Used by permission, Utah State Archives, all rights reserved.*

On July 4, 1980, Grand County commissioners organized a protest to "upgrade" a road at the boundary of a Wilderness Study Area. *Used by permission, Utah State Historical Society, all rights reserved.*

A bulldozer returned to Mill Creek Canyon on July 7, 1980, after Grand County commissioners learned that the bulldozer did not make it into the Wilderness Study Area the first time. *Used by permission, Utah State Historical Society, all rights reserved.*

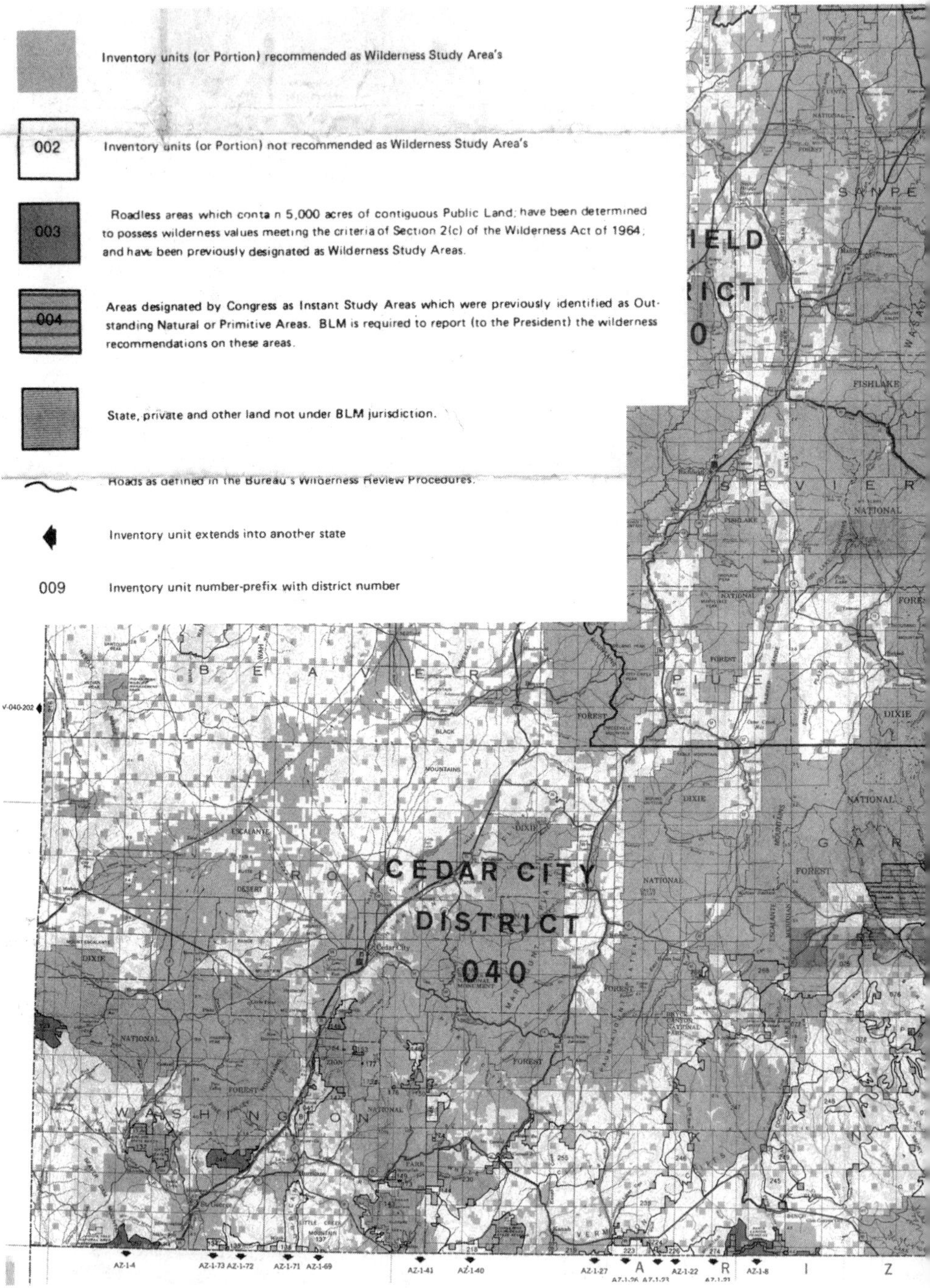

Department of the Interior, Bureau of Land Management, "Utah BLM Intensive Wilderness Inventory, Wilderness Study Areas," November 1980. In this map Negro Bill Canyon had been eliminated from wilderness consideration. BLM officials later reinstated it as a WSA.

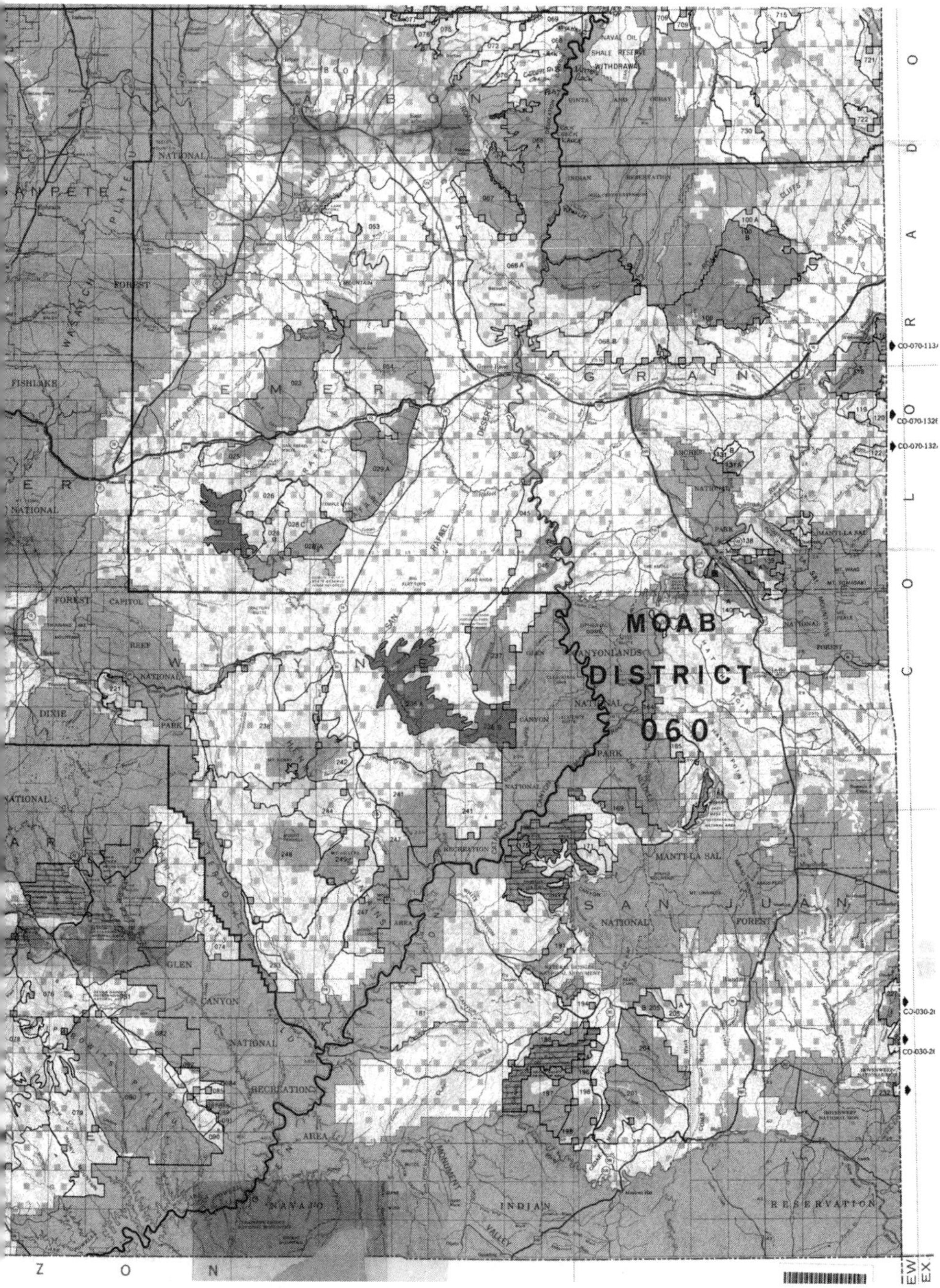
MOAB
DISTRICT
060
CARBON
EMERY
GRAND
WAYNE
SAN JUAN
SANPETE
COLORADO
NAVAJO
INDIAN
RESERVATION
MANTI-LA SAL
NATIONAL
FOREST
CAPITOL
REEF
GLEN
CANYON
NATIONAL
RECREATION
AREA
FISHLAKE
DIXIE
ARCHES
CANYONLANDS
CO-070-132
Z O N

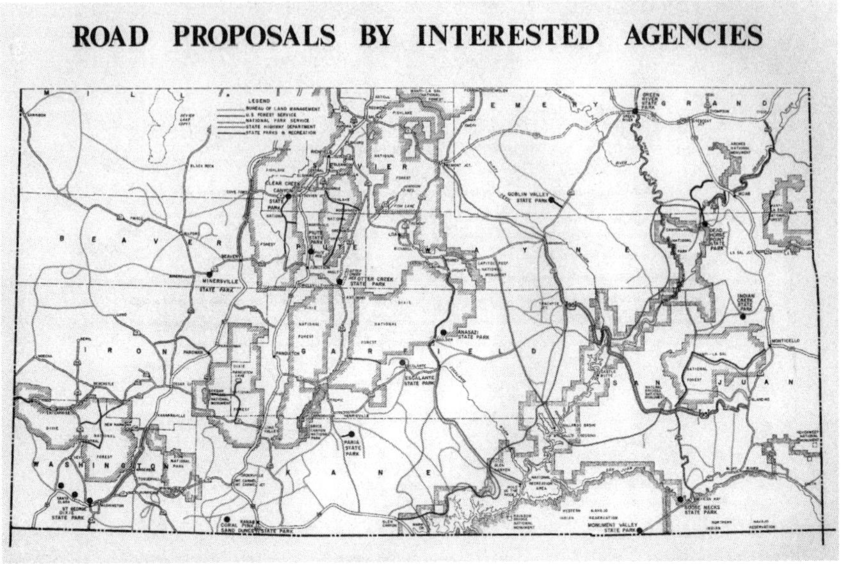

This map, circa 1965, shows the extensive web of roads multiple government agencies were proposing for the Golden Circle region. *Used by permission, Utah State Archives, all rights reserved.*

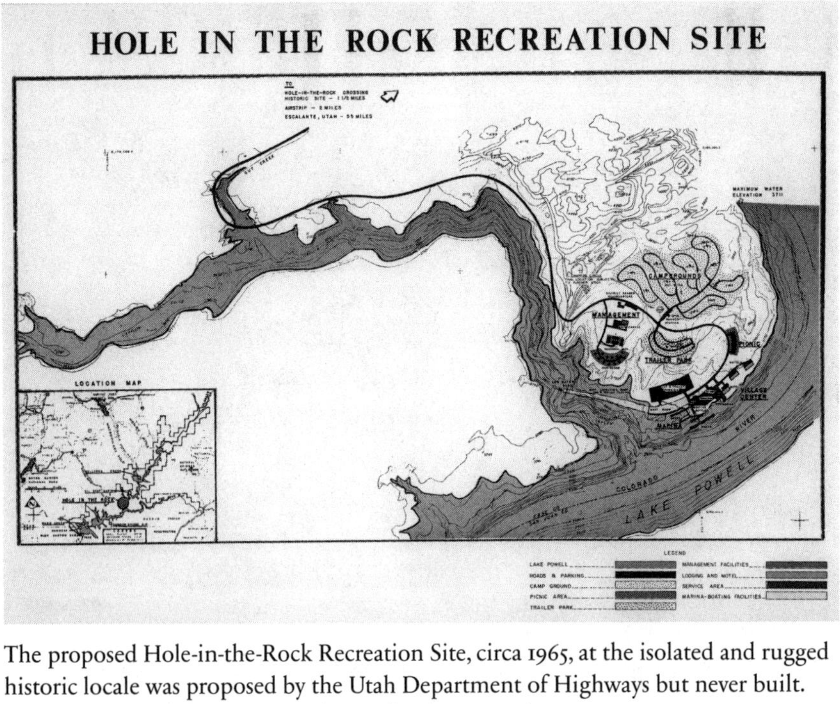

The proposed Hole-in-the-Rock Recreation Site, circa 1965, at the isolated and rugged historic locale was proposed by the Utah Department of Highways but never built. *Used by permission, Utah State Archives, all rights reserved.*

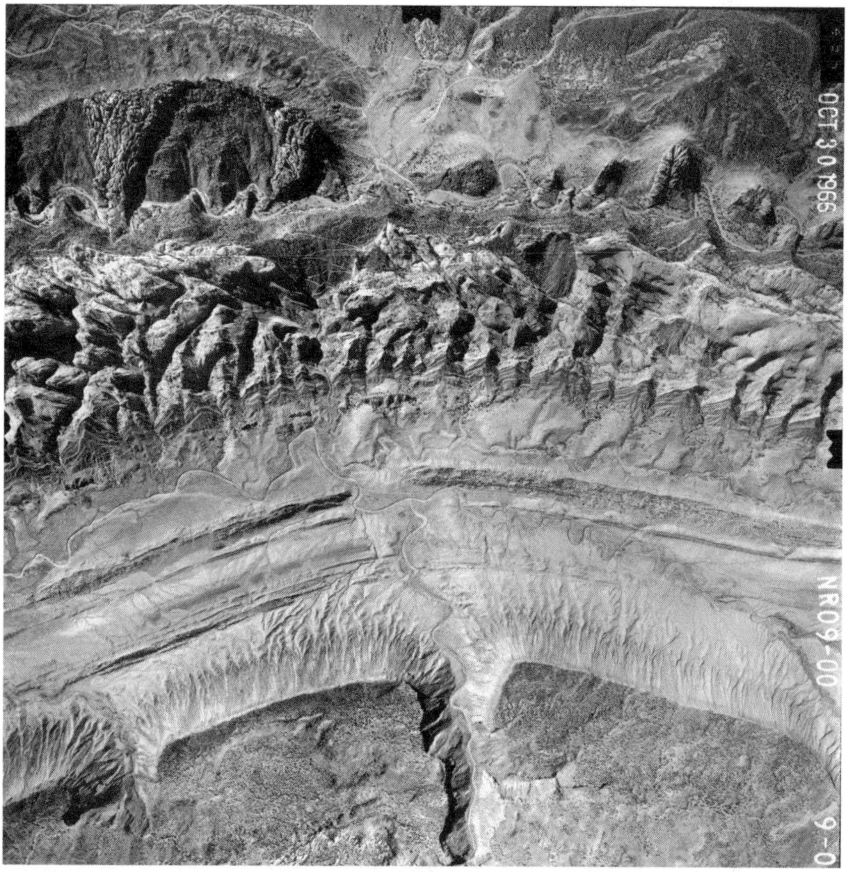

An aerial view of the Burr Trail with its hairpin switchbacks through the Waterpocket Fold, October 1966. *Used by permission, Utah State Archives, all rights reserved.*

Drill pads in the Uinta Basin, south of Vernal. *Copyright Lin Alder.*

A structure at the abandoned town site of Pahreah, Grand Staircase–Escalante National Monument. *Photo by the author.*

The wide channel of the Paria River, just north of Pahreah. The Paria, running the length of the Grand Staircase–Escalante, was once a travel corridor for Mormon pioneers and is now claimed by Kane County as an R.S. 2477 road. *Photo by the author.*

Moab Jeep Safari, April 14, 1979. *Used by permission, Utah State Archives, all rights reserved.*

An archaeological site in the Arch Canyon proposed wilderness. *Copyright by Liz Thomas/SUWA.*

Illegal ORV ride up Arch Canyon, with peaceful protesters. *Copyright by Liz Thomas/ SUWA.*

Off-road-vehicle tracks at Factory Butte in Wayne County east of Capitol Reef National Park. *Copyright by Ray Bloxham/SUWA.*

six

Heritage on the Grand Staircase–Escalante

The Paria River captures the drainage from the Paunsaugunt Plateau before meandering south and southeasterly through the Vermilion and White Cliffs and ultimately joining the Colorado River near Lee's Ferry. About halfway between the headwaters and confluence, where the Paria carves through the Cockscomb—a distinctive geologic formation resembling a rooster's comb—nineteenth-century Mormon settlers colonized the town of Pahreah. The Paria River was the lifeblood of the community, as channel waters were diverted for irrigation to the flat, sage-scattered valley. As many as forty-seven families lived there in the late 1870s. Like so many other hardscrabble communities in the pioneer West, its years of prosperity were short-lived. Perennial flooding was the primary culprit, often destroying a season's harvest and at times even homes and buildings. Today few human remnants remain of this fly-by-night place: a cemetery plot, two fallen buildings, an old sluice used to mine gold. In 1963 a movie set for the film *Sergeants Three* was erected at the site, and a handful of westerns were shot here. Now even those structures no longer stand.[1]

The fragile, low-flow Paria River channel is now, fascinatingly, one of thousands of "roads" claimed by southern Utah counties. Kane County officials point to it as the main transportation corridor for early Mormon settlers, connecting the towns of Pahreah and Adairville to northern settlements. In the pioneer era, the river afforded easier movement than overland travel across the mesas, crags, and canyons of southern Utah's deserts. But since the abrupt designation of the Grand Staircase–Escalante in 1996—a 1.8-million-acre national monument encompassing the Grand Staircase and Vermilion Cliffs, the imposing Kaiparowits Plateau, and the canyons of the Escalante River—pioneer-era roadways have been thrust to center stage. Locals cherish them. To them, these passageways not only provide access to backcountry but also embody their heritage here. A national monument, they fear, severely restricts access and erases human markings from the landscape. By invoking county R.S. 2477 rights to roads within the monument's borders, they have fought back. Kane County officials pushed for roads to be recognized in the monument's management plan and, since 2003, asserted control by removing or replacing road signs. The dispute between Kane County and the BLM—each exerting jurisdiction over monument roads—has yet to resolve, and because each road must go through its own legal process of recognition, these contentions may extend indefinitely.

When we probe into the historical and cultural meaning of roads, they emerge as symbols of a broader disquiet over rural communities' rights in the modern American West. There is just a hint of paradox that in their attempt to preserve tradition and culture, many locals oppose a land-use designation with celebration of heritage as its design. President Bill Clinton recognized the place's rich human history, and he intended for that to serve as one purpose of the monument. But many opposed to the designation yearn not to memorialize the place's history but to retain a sense of culture and tradition that they believe is best exemplified through autonomy to live, work, and move about the land as they please. Roads are more than mere props employed to assert control; they are objects of considerable social and political significance that represent a way of life and livelihood. The staunch position of Kane County officials and citizens is, in fact, a deep-rooted umbrage over being marginalized in the changing political climate of the modern West. They view the monument as another design of the federal government and environmental groups to force them off their land for the sake of preserving wild, untrammeled landscapes.[2]

Almon Thompson, John Wesley Powell's brother-in-law and the first person to survey and map the region that would become Grand Staircase–Escalante, discovered a cache of coal embedded in the Kaiparowits at Fifty-Mile Mountain. That was in 1875, four years before the Hole-in-the-Rock expedition. In 1931 Herbert E. Gregory and Raymond C. Moore projected in *The Kaiparowits Region* that enough coal could be had for a major commercial development. Then with construction of Glen Canyon Dam, major energy companies rushed to acquire leases or prospecting permits for coal mining.[3] But plans for large-scale development did not materialize until the 1960s, when a proposal was put forth to construct a massive three-thousand-megawatt power plant on Fourmile Bench, deep in the heart of the Kaiparowits. Four underground mines would supply the plant with coal, and a network of roads, power lines, and pipelines would fuel the operation. A new town would even spring up on East Clark Bench to house workers and their families, similar to Page, Arizona, the Bureau of Reclamation town near Glen Canyon Dam.

For a time, it seemed as though the power plant would be built. California and Arizona utilities promoted, and Utah officials and citizens overwhelmingly supported, a project anticipated to cost $3.5 billion and employ between eight to ten thousand people. But national environmental groups pushed back, warning that the plant and attendant development would irreconcilably alter the character of the wild landscape. This opposition, coupled with other economic obstacles, doomed the proposal, and the sponsors pulled out in 1976.[4] That is why when William Least Heat-Moon drove through Kane and Garfield Counties in 1979, he called the region "the largest unexploited coalfield in the country. A land certain one day to be fought over."[5]

Heat-Moon was right: gas, oil, and coal dreams—and schemes—persist. During the BLM wilderness inventories of the late 1970s and early 1980s, Kane County officials protested proposals to designate county lands as wilderness, given "the manifest and manifold imprints of man and the vast reservoirs of mineral resources scattered throughout the proposed Wilderness Study Areas of Kane County." (The Kaiparowits Plateau reportedly contains 11.375 billion tons of recoverable coal, according to the Utah Geological Survey.)[6] Officials urged the BLM to allow the Gulf Mineral Resource Company and Exxon Mineral Company to scout for uranium deposits on Fifty-Mile Mountain and Fifty-Mile Bench.[7]

When a Dutch mining company, Andalex Resources, Inc., received leases from the BLM to extract 2.5 million tons of coal per year on the Kaiparowits Plateau near Smoky Hollow in the late 1980s, the prospects of energy development again brightened. By Andalex estimates, the proposed mine would provide hundreds of jobs and $10 million a year in state and federal taxes. Proponents of the mine also pointed to the relatively benign surface disturbance of the mine. The Western States Coalition commended the "40 acre coal mine that could supply the State of Utah with enough energy for a thousand years."[8]

The Southern Utah Wilderness Alliance filed an objection to Andalex's application. The Smoky Hollow Mine proposal, SUWA maintained, would penetrate the heart of the Kaiparowits, located adjacent to two Wilderness Study Areas: Wahweap and Burning Hills. The surface disturbances from the mine would indeed be minimal, as proponents promised, but the underground mines would generate impacts of their own: namely, subsidence potentially harmful to wildlife and archaeological resources. Perhaps most damning, mining operations would require movement and construction across the landscape on a grand scale. Twenty-two miles of paved roads and power lines would be necessary to access the mine. SUWA estimated that large industrial trucks would leave the mine on average every five and a half minutes for forty years, creating unsafe driving conditions and huge taxpayer expenses to build and maintain the roads.[9] Indeed, the prospect of publicly financed roads on the Kaiparowits enabling trucks to move coal from the mine to rail spurs near Cedar City, Utah, or Moapa, Nevada—more than two hundred miles away—concerned not only environmentalists but also the local communities surely to be impacted by the operations.[10]

These serious objections notwithstanding, the Andalex coal mine on the Kaiparowits seemed destined to be realized. In early 1996, Kane County officials, eager to advance the project, offered to construct a public road to the Smoky Hollow area. Their proposal would ostensibly supply safe and convenient access to county public lands and school-trust lands; enable federal lands resource development; provide access for recreation, hunting, wildlife management, grazing, and mining; improve transportation from Kane County to Escalante; and create a scenic byway. The commissioners voiced their "full and total support of responsible development of all the natural resources in the Smoky Mountain area." They advocated using public funding to build public access roads, promising a large economic return to the county and state.[11]

The question of whether to open Utah's canyon-country lands to large-scale industrial development like the Andalex mine proposal dates back to at least the 1930s, when President Franklin D. Roosevelt's secretary of the interior, Harold Ickes, campaigned to create a gigantic monument encompassing nearly four and a half million acres and spanning from present-day Canyonlands National Park to the Utah-Arizona border. The proposed Escalante National Monument came up empty-handed. Many locals had opposed it. Ranchers had worried that expanded Park Service authority would push out cattle and sheep in favor of tourists. Some, such as Dodge Freeman, disputed the designation on grounds that it would attract hordes of tourists, and thus cheapen the wilderness experience that could be had. "To me," he penned, "the charm of the wilderness along the Colorado rests far more in its inaccessibility and freedom from trodden paths than in its admitted wonderful beauty. I often asked myself last summer whether I would get the same sense of pleasure and enjoyment I got riding through that country on horseback if I were to go through by motor bus or auto with a lot of rubber-neck tourists ogling around and making inane remarks—I trust you can satisfy yourself as to the answer that came to me!"[12]

Congress ultimately designated within that original park proposal other national monuments, parks, and recreation areas—Capitol Reef National Monument in 1937, Canyonlands National Park in 1964, and Glen Canyon National Recreation Area in 1972—but the rest of the region remained undesignated BLM land. Would these areas remain a part of the BLM estate, and thus open to mining, grazing, and other land uses, or might the government impose another designation that would close off certain land uses? This remained a viable concern well into the 1990s.

The Escalante Canyons Study Act of 1991, H.R. 4015, directed the Interior Department secretary to conduct a study to determine the suitability of a national park designation for the Escalante Canyon region. In 1992, another bill, H.R. 5415, proposed establishing the Canyons of the Escalante National

Conservation Area, recommending mixed land-use designations at the secretary's discretion. Some areas would permit grazing, others would become wilderness, and still others—like Fifty-Mile Mountain—would be released from wilderness consideration.[13]

Two years later, in 1994, Utah governor Michael Leavitt organized a task force to consider yet another proposal called "Canyons of the Escalante, A National Ecoregion."[14] It was novel in its attempt to bring competing interests together to cocreate a plan for the region, and some headway was made among traditional land users and environmentalists. In the end, though, the task force came to nothing. In a workshop in Boulder, Utah, locals overwhelmingly objected any form of government involvement. Some in the environmental community worried because the proposal emphasized economy over ecosystem management. "If this proposal is to succeed it must transcend the idea that the wild and natural lands are not as important as the multiple-use or enterprise lands," wrote Dick Carter of the Utah Wilderness Association to Brad Barber, deputy director of the Governor's Office of Planning and Budget. To Carter, the proposal was "driven by production of revenue rather than preservation of the Escalante ecosystems," an observation essentially echoed by Thomas C. Jensen of the Grand Canyon Trust and Terri Martin of the National Parks and Conservation Association.[15]

By 1996, wilderness advocates eager for a mantle of federal protection and movement to end the state's wilderness stalemate were seeking to "nationalize" the debate over preservation and development on the plateau. Some advocated making the Kaiparowits region the poster child for the Utah Wilderness Coalition's 5.7-million-acre wilderness proposal on BLM lands; others recommended pushing for national monument status—a designation that unexpectedly came to fruition.[16]

In the summer of 1996, the Clinton administration by its own initiative quietly forged ahead on a plan to designate a large national monument at Utah's southernmost border. The broad executive authority to do so came from the Antiquities Act of 1906. Clinton and his team had no obligation to consult local and state interests not likely to endorse the designation. So they didn't, though they did work with a number of Utah residents and environmentalists in drafting the proposal. Just a few hours before the administration announced the monument on September 18, 1996, Secretary of the Interior Bruce Babbitt asked William B. Smart, Utah's representative on the Grand Canyon Trust board of directors, what would make the monument designation more palatable for Utahns. Smart recommended that the administration promise to trade Utah school lands in the monument for federal lands of equal or greater value and to expedite trades of other school lands throughout the state for more accessible federal land. That promise was included at the last minute in the president's proclamation—a promise the federal government subsequently fulfilled.[17]

The last time a president had wielded the Antiquities Act was in 1978 when Jimmy Carter created fifteen new national monuments in Alaska. President Bill Clinton, strapped with a reelection campaign, must have surmised that creating the monument would be a politically popular move—possibly bringing Arizona into the Democratic column—although it would further alienate Utah (which was solidly in the Republican camp anyway). But Clinton also presumed the move to safeguard a region deserving of protection.[18] In his speech announcing the new monument he explained: "This high, rugged, and remote region, where bold plateaus and multi-hued cliffs run for distances that defy human perspective, was the last place in the continental United States to be mapped. Even today, this unspoiled natural area remains a frontier, a quality that greatly enhances the monument's value for scientific study. The monument has a long and dignified human history: it is a place where one can see how nature shapes human endeavors in the American West, where distance and aridity have been pitted against our dreams and courage."[19] In sweeping literary language reminiscent of the Wilderness Act of 1964, Clinton spoke movingly about the region's frontier qualities as well as its human past. Far from portraying nature and culture in tension, the president spoke of a natural world that perfected human endeavors on the land and of a history every bit worthy of its environment. He evoked the romantic notion of the settler and rancher braving a new frontier, and through awed and reverenced speech for the place and its history, he no doubt intended to pay praise to contemporary residents.

Residents of the towns like Kanab surrounding the monument's edges loudly protested the designation. For most Kanab residents and those in the tiny communities ringing the monument's outer edges, the image of Clinton and Vice President Al Gore standing at the Grand Canyon's rim in Arizona—not at the monument's actual site in Utah—lent a maddening appearance of outsiders imposing outside interests. "This whole thing burns me up," former Kane County commissioner Vance Esplin avowed. "Clinton didn't even have enough guts to come here. He stayed 70 miles away." In an editorial, resident Gerald W. Berry went a step further with an unsubstantiated claim that Clinton's proclamation was in the presence of "hundreds of people who neither live in the state, nor have vested interests here."[20] Despite Clinton's lack of direct ties to southern Utah (in his address, Clinton could only reflect on a memorable trip to the Grand Canyon, where he "found a place on a rock" and "was all alone" to contemplate the majestic scene before him), there were many Utahns who heartily welcomed the monument. The explosive rhetoric of some southern Utahns merely reflected a flawed perception that prowilderness interests came only from outside the state.

The sense was not of a designation deserving of the land or of their history and culture. The history was theirs, they felt, and although Clinton's memorializing would celebrate the human past, it would no doubt stymie their future. The monument allowed some traditional uses like existing grazing operations to continue, while prohibiting other uses on 1.8 million acres of southern Utah public lands. Some locals believed it was one thing to celebrate the hardy pioneers who explored and settled the region, but it was quite another to shut out their descendants from pursuing an economic livelihood on the land. The *Southern Utah News* editorialized that "tourists may someday drive through our towns and tell their kids, 'look honey, that's where a lot of hardy people used to be able to live.'"[21]

It did not help that the announcement came at the heels of the Kaibab Forest Products mill closure in Fredonia, Arizona, just seven miles south of Kanab, costing some two hundred jobs. Locals surmised that the closure resulted from a lawsuit filed by outside environmental groups that challenged logging impacts on the Mexican spotted owl and northern goshawk. In editorials locals referred to themselves as an endangered species trying to eke out a living in a "hostile" environment. In their anger and desperation, many targeted environmentalists as a convenient villain, even if some problems perhaps derived more from nebulous economic forces of modernization and globalization than from SUWA's legal arm. "There are groups that don't live here and yet tell us how to govern the people," growled Kane County commissioner Joe C. Judd. "There are groups drawing the line in the sand."[22]

Within a week of Clinton's announcement, commissioners held a "Loss of Rights" rally where they released into the air black balloons of protest. At a press conference after the rally, county commissioner Judd and Kanab city councillor Roger Holland spoke about a meeting with the Utah and Arizona congressional delegates. There they had learned the full extent of the monument's designation: previous to the September 14 announcement in the *Washington Post,* not even Utah's congressional delegates had known of the impending designation, let alone how large it would be. They reported that the previous week's rally attracted the Capitol's attention, and the rally that day "brought a lot of impact" in terms of media coverage. Showcasing to the world the harmful local impacts would, they hoped, stir up sympathy and public indignation.[23]

By October the commissioners had conceived another protest by reenacting what in southern Utah had become a grand tradition: calling out bulldozers to put blade to dirt on their own county roads within the monument's boundaries. Protest of the monument designation primarily prompted the action. So did a bill titled America's Red Rock Wilderness Act then before Congress patterned after the Utah Wilderness Coalition's Utah's BLM wilderness proposal. On the eighteenth, the BLM filed suit against the county (and Garfield and San Juan Counties, also involved in illegal road maintenance).[24] The Utah Chapter of the Sierra Club and SUWA, suspecting the protesters were "taking bulldozers and scrapers and widening old two track jeep roads" to deliberately hijack the area's wilderness characteristics, asked to intervene in the suit "to prevent the federal government from caving in or otherwise compromising on any key issues."[25] Volunteers fanned out into the backcountry to document and map roads claimed by the counties. A Sierra Club group witnessed firsthand the bulldozer damage in Right-Hand Collett Canyon on the Kaiparowits Plateau. They reported that at one point, the dozer cut a "completely new route through a wash," while another grader had to back up after taking a wrong turn and running up against a gully. "Obviously, the vehicle tracks the grader was following were so faint he couldn't tell where the so-called road was," surmised Susan Sweigert of the Wasatch Mountain Club.[26]

At the time of the designation, more than six thousand R.S. 2477 claims were then in contention in Utah, by far the largest count in the western United States. The status of these claims was still pending. Secretary of the Interior Donald Hodel's R.S. 2477 policy during the height of the Burr Trail conflict in 1988 had asserted that the Interior Department could "administratively recognize" certain R.S. 2477 claims. Later, in a 1993 report to Congress, the Interior Department stated the administrative acknowledgments of R.S. 2477 claims under the Hodel policy "are recognitions of 'claims' and are useful only for limited purposes" and "are not intended to be binding, or a final agency action." The report asserted that a final determination of the validity of an R.S. 2477 claim would be made in the courts. The following year, however, the Interior Department introduced a proposal that would require a process resulting in "binding determinations of [the] existence and validity" of R.S. 2477 claims.

But Congress soundly rejected this proposal or any attempt to make a final determination on R.S. 2477 claims without express congressional authorization. Indeed, the Clinton administration further alienated R.S. 2477 proponents when in 1997 Secretary of the Interior Bruce Babbitt revoked the Hodel policy, although the department would continue to "give its views" on asserted R.S. 2477 claims in cases where there was a "demonstrated, compelling, and immediate need."[27] This policy only forestalled any immediate resolution between locals who claimed R.S. 2477 rights and others who insisted that advocates of R.S. 2477 rights would need to "prove" their claims.

Nearly everyone took it for granted that the monument would be turned over to the National Park Service, the traditional caretaker of national parks and monuments. These designated locales are always afforded some kind of protection, but the number of facilities designed to accommodate and encourage tourism and what development is permitted within their boundaries vary widely. Since the NPS's origins, debates over what it means to keep national parks "unimpaired" have persisted between those who wish to fully outfit parks for mass tourism and those who advocate minimal development. The prospect of the NPS transforming the Grand Staircase–Escalante into a recreational mecca concerned some. "Which is worse—a coal mine on the Kaiparowits Plateau, or visitor center, large over-crowded campgrounds, RV dumps, millions of visitors, ranger housing, etc., etc. at Calf Creek Falls?" Ron Hamblin of Monroe, Utah, wondered. "I started fighting coal mining on the Kaiparowits in the 1970's, but I would rather see that than what the park service will do to the Escalante River."[28]

In a surprise move, the Interior Department announced the BLM would assume jurisdiction, a pragmatic but also conciliatory move for the local anti-monument crowd more accustomed to that agency's management style.[29] To environmentalists, this presented both a challenge and an opportunity. On one hand, some worried that the BLM would be captive to industry and development interests, just as it had been prior to the designation. During the Andalex mine debate, for instance, opponents of the proposed mine accused BLM employees responsible for the EIS process of "publicly display[ing] consistent bias against citizens perceived as 'environmentalists.'"[30] They likely foremost referred to Mike Noel, a native Utahn and BLM employee with a master's degree in plant biology. Noel had refused to comply with the environmentalists' Freedom of Information Act request to view traffic information on the Andalex mine road, and he later quit his federal job with the BLM shortly after designation of the national monument.[31]

On the other hand, the BLM would be more likely than the NPS to manage the monument as more of a scientific laboratory and ecological preserve than a mass tourist destination. Charles Wilkinson, who served as special counsel to the Interior Department and helped draft the proclamation, noted that the original intent was to make Grand Staircase–Escalante a "wilderness monument." The proclamation declared the purpose was to preserve an "unspoiled natural area," which suggested to him that even the BLM would minimize roads and development. Although historically the BLM had been wedded to extractive land uses, the Clinton administration purportedly considered the new management move as also a way to redefine the BLM's mission.[32]

Conservationists took the stance that the monument's principal value lay in its wilderness characteristics. They expected the BLM to act the part of the good environmental steward, and they vigorously challenged the notion that the BLM was just a safe haven for motorized vehicles and industrial development. SUWA vowed to "work vigilantly to stop" lawmakers from appropriating funds to build roads and visitor centers. Roger Holland found this environmentalist position to be duplicitous, recalling the words of Ken Rait of SUWA that local people "ought to learn which side their bread is buttered on, [that] tourism is their salvation." Wilderness enthusiasts now sought to minimize tourism where they had previously trumpeted it as the future of southern Utah's economy.[33]

Further, environmentalists hoped to snuff out vestiges of mining in the monument, including the highly controversial proposed Andalex mine. On this matter, Clinton had been very clear: "We can't have mines everywhere, and we shouldn't have mines which threaten our national treasures.... I hope that Andalex, a foreign company, will...work with us to find a way to pursue its mining operations elsewhere." Although Clinton did not immediately put the coal proposal to rest, the monument clearly presented severe challenges to the mining operation—particularly in securing environmental clearance to push roads and power lines to the mine site over monument lands. Any mining must now be compatible with purposes that Clinton had hinted at but had yet to define clearly.[34] By early 1997, though, the Andalex prospect ended when the Dutch-based company withdrew its application to mine coal on the Kaiparowits.[35]

With a coal mine now out of the picture, some Kanab residents began to advance tourism as the monument's primary use with the call to act the part of good hosts. While some believed their rage would evoke sympathy, not distaste, from visitors, others insisted they move forward and accept the new reality rather than fight, gripe, and bicker, no matter how frustrating the situation. Just after the monument's designation, Porter Arbogast, a Kanab businessman and member of the local Chamber of Commerce, conveyed concern over "portraying ourselves negatively, for the world to see." He affirmed that "as hard as it is to accept this new national monument, it is futile to resist in principle." Arbogast urged a reasonable course of advantageously using their position to seize control of how the monument would be managed instead of burning Robert Redford in effigy. County commissioners similarly conceded that the monument was there to stay, but they insisted the best way to fight it was to earn concessions from the BLM through either funding for county planning or legal avenues.[36]

Thus, while many locals and politicians spoke out strongly against the monument, they nevertheless hoped to significantly influence how it would be managed. Governor Michael Leavitt told Kane County locals that he felt "strongly about co-operation and helping to plan the National Monument," perhaps because it might serve their advantage.[37] The governor's position, however, raised the ire of some hard-liners; Melvin K. Dalton of Monticello, Utah, wrote Leavitt that had he been in his place, "the ink would not have been dry on the Escalante National Monument proclamation before I would have had a bulldozer building a road to each one of the state sections in the monument."[38]

For all their rhetoric, county officials resigned themselves to the monument's reality, hopeful to at least have a say in shaping its management plan. Shortly after the designation, the Kane County Commission passed a resolution declaring insistence upon "tourist centers and paved roads."[39] Local politicians supposed they had every reason to believe the monument would serve as a tourist park; county commissioner Judd assumed Interior secretary Bruce Babbitt and President Clinton intended for a park with roads to provide access to the visitors who would surely come. Judd even imagined that the monument might be made to "serve us"—meaning, of course, to help bolster the region with a strong economic base.[40] Further, while county officials recognized that Clinton had specifically excluded coal mining from the Kaiparowits, they presumed other economic ventures might be viable. Some hoped to strike a balance between preservation and development, as Porter Arbogast noted on January 14, 1997, to have "industry and ecology working together to maximize profit and minimize impacts" and to "make sure trail developments don't impact ranchers or ecology."[41]

Jerry Meredith, the new Grand Staircase–Escalante National Monument director, told a gathering at the Kanab-Fredonia United Church in December 1996 that he understood the challenge of trying to please so many different constituents. "Cows are way easier to manage than people," he joked. He assured the crowd that Bruce Babbitt wanted "a multiple-use monument," and he encouraged citizens and county government to offer input for the monument's management plan.[42] In a public meeting on June 12, 1997, the

Kane County Commission also urged locals to provide feedback for the management plan, for they must have genuinely supposed they would have a say in it. "This is an opportunity to determine the out come of the Monument if we are smart enough to use it," the commissioners told the local crowd.[43]

In November 1998, county officials signed an agreement with the BLM that would essentially settle the question of roads and access within the monument's boundaries. The November 4 agreement would dissolve county R.S. 2477 rights to two roads within the monument—Skutumpah and Smoky Mountain Roads—and the Moquith Mountain Road outside it. In exchange, other monument roads would remain open; even those that the BLM planned to close to the public would still be accessible to ranchers and other land users with existing rights.[44]

Some county residents lambasted the commission's handling of the monument's roads. In a February 1999 meeting of the Kane County Commission, Jesse Frost, president of People for the USA, a recently organized pro–states' rights grassroots group, argued that the November 4 agreement had illegally "relinquished R.S.2477 rights in the monument," and the following week he raised the issue again, remonstrating curtailment of county rights. Mike Noel, vice president of People for the USA, similarly protested. "This agreement does give up rights," he said. "Most roads are R.S.2477 in Kane County. State statute to close public roads requires a public hearing and even the BLM cannot close a road without public comment. We do not need to give up our roads, heritage and culture."[45] Judd responded, insisting he hoped to avoid a lawsuit, to which rancher Calvin Johnson further urged the commission from signing the agreement.

Responding to the accusation of trading its birthright, the commissioners maintained they simply signed the agreement to keep the county out of court and that fighting a costly legal battle might drag out for months, possibly years, with no guarantee of a desired outcome. Judd had learned enough from their Garfield County neighbors about the expensive, dragged-out Burr Trail suit. He also agreed with the county's position on wilderness proposals within their borders. Nevertheless, the commission would refrain from a final decision until the public had also weighed in on the issue.[46]

The local public response was swift and decisive. At a public meeting in June 1999, Mark Habbeshaw of the Canyon 4x4 Club stated, "90 percent of southern Utah roads qualify for R.S.2477 status and are vested property rights with constitutional rights of protection." Lamar LeVevor from Garfield County advocated "unlimited access" to the monument's roads. Bob Ott from Garfield County endorsed maintaining major roads in the monument—Skutumpah, Kodachrome, and Cottonwood—and urged the paving of at least one road "all the way through the monument." Karl Shakespear of the local cattlemen's association also spoke out against road closure.[47] According to People for the USA, not one citizen of Kane County who had been polled wanted the county to sign the road agreement. "These people feel it would be a grave mistake to sign away our granted rights," J. H. Frost and Brent Mackelprang wrote to the county commission. "These rights were granted by congress and are protected by the constitution, they should not be given up or traded for a privilege that can be revoked by the BLM."[48]

The county commission came under increasing pressure to back out of the road agreement and to mount an aggressive campaign for county road rights. At another public meeting in July 1999, Terril Honey of the road committee likely spoke for all present when he acknowledged "the effects this road closure will have on the people of Kane County." He spoke of the environmental "extremists" who wanted "zero access." "If we turn the roads over to the government we are turning the power over to the extremists," he said. Mike Habbeshaw then requested that the commission make a policy for R.S. 2477 roads and commit not to sign the agreement.[49]

Two weeks later, commissioners convened another public meeting, attended by about six hundred people, at the local high school. The speakers there were particularly resolute, even belligerent. Mike Noel, the former BLM staffer, told the crowd that "BLM authorization is not required for work on roads" and urged the county to contest the lawsuit "with all the might that you have." Another resident claimed that in conversations with Utah's congressional delegation, "they are all appalled that the County is signing this agreement." The commissioners closed the meeting by bowing to the public's wishes to pass a motion essentially informing the BLM that the county would assert its R.S. 2477 rights.[50] The next month, the commission officially motioned to "abandon the signing of the Road Agreement" and to "continue to work on a way to identify Kane County Road rights within the Monument."[51]

That August 1999 decision to renege on the road-closure agreement would prove pivotal. Although the BLM administratively determined to proceed with its management plan and close some county-claimed R.S. 2477 roads in the monument (while still leaving open nearly one thousand miles of roads to motorized vehicles), Kane County has officially resisted the closures in the courts *and* on the ground. The proaccess group People for the USA was one group to push the county to fight in court. Even after the group disbanded in 2000 due to lack of funds, some have continued to openly contest their assumed R.S. 2477 rights.

The county's assertion of rights to the dirt routes and roads within the monument received a major boost in 2003 when the Interior Department under the Bush administration entered into a memorandum of understanding with the State of Utah that established a process for the department to evaluate certain R.S. 2477 rights-of-way on BLM state land. The MOU permitted the state or any county to use the disclaimer process for "eligible roads." Governor Leavitt defended the MOU by affirming that it was high time to resolve a thirty-year dispute through "an open administrative process" instead of by "a closed process decided by the courts."[52]

The new regulations and the MOU had plenty of critics, nonetheless, who argued that leaving the matter of R.S. 2477 claims open to administrative decision would, in the words of SUWA attorney Heidi McIntosh, "disqualify vast, spectacular scenic territory from congressional protection as wilderness or other protective status." Indeed, McIntosh insisted that the MOU offered loopholes that would allow R.S. 2477 rights to be recognized without establishing the legal claim that the route was a "highway" and had been "constructed."[53] A group of conservation-minded members of Congress also weighed in, concerned that the regulations might be "contrary to law" and "devoid of any standards or criteria to be applied in assessing the validity of asserted claims." Colorado representative Mark Udall and eighty-six other members of Congress urged the secretary to suspend the disclaimer regulations: "Whether intentional or not, issuance of the Department's new disclaimer regulations has prompted an accelerating wave of road-building expectations in many States." Perhaps nowhere more so than in Utah.[54]

In 2003, buoyed by the softened R.S. 2477 policy, Kane County commissioners made their most daring move yet: they unilaterally removed thirty-one BLM road-closure signs on limited-access monument roads in defiance of the monument's transportation plan. Mark Habbeshaw, newly elected to the commission, instructed that the signs be delivered to BLM headquarters in Kanab with a note defending their actions. The department initiated a criminal investigation of Kane County officials involved in the sign removal, but no legal action was ever taken. Two years later, in the spring of 2005, the drama escalated when officials undermined federal authority by placing their own signs on county-claimed routes within the monument. These signs, in some cases placed alongside BLM markers that limited or closed routes, invited ORV use. This time the Wilderness Society and SUWA interceded by initiating legal action against the county under the Supremacy Clause of the Constitution. The Tenth Circuit Court agreed with the suit and in 2008 required the county to remove the signs and to use only permitted roads within the monument. Kane County appealed, but the court upheld the monument's transportation plan, which closed hundreds of roads to motor vehicles. The BLM announced that it would start to enforce road closures within the monument.[55]

Kane County officials sprang into action. "The Paria Canyon road would be the first public highway actually closed in Kane County by federal action but it would not be the last," county commissioner Mark Habbeshaw wrote his constituents on May 3, 2009. "The Paria Canyon road must become the issue that brings the people together to oppose and protest federal actions threatening what little sovereignty we have left as a rural people."[56] To that end, county officials staged a "protest ride" with all-terrain vehicles (ATVs), dirt bikes, jeeps, and a few trucks up the Paria River along a route recently closed by the BLM to ORV traffic. A group of counterprotesters quietly sat by as the three-hundred-plus motorists revved passed. The scene was civil, but both sides knew what was at stake. A portion of the claimed route cut through the Paria-Hackberry Wilderness Study Area, a route that if recognized would disqualify much of it as wilderness. Those participating in the protests defended it as an established road, traveled for more than a hundred years. And closing it to motorized travel threatened other historic routes and the status of R.S. 2477 claims throughout the West.[57]

In Utah many more county roads are contested than in any other state.[58] The status of the majority of these claims remains unresolved, the old Paria route included. Given the enormously divergent perspectives on what constitutes a road and who owns it, road claims seem destined to limp sluggishly in courts indefinitely, despite FLPMA's original intent for swift resolution of R.S. 2477 claims within a few years of the act. And rather than settle the claims all at once, the process will almost surely proceed road by road, plausibly spawning ceaseless litigation and courtroom theatrics.

There is some evidence that a new era of understanding and coexistence is stirring in rural communities like Kanab. Monument supporters predicted in the 1990s that even hard-line locals would in time welcome the monument as their own. That may now be true for some. In fact, the overwhelming demographic majority of pioneer-stock Mormons in Kanab has slowly eroded. As Joshua Zaffos observes in the *High Country News,* Kanab is now home to a world-premier animal sanctuary and a growing community of wilderness lovers and progressives. Although newcomers sometimes still sense a tension of unwelcome from old-timers, recent move-ins seem to have a moderating presence. Zaffos comments that "a kind of détente appears to be emerging" in "Utah's bitter cultural wars."[59]

Antifederal sentiment cannot be easily eradicated, though. It is interwoven with deep resentment over the perceived erosion of culture, heritage, and tradition in the rural West. The federal government and its alleged environmental allies make an easy target. In Kanab and elsewhere in the West, the story line often goes that for generations ancestors lived and worked on the land, often just scraping by but always making do on the endowments of nature and their own fortitude. In recent decades, residents now feel that their fierce independence has been unfairly tempered by an overbearing, even dictatorial federal government focused on imposing strict environmental regulations and land-use restrictions. And the matter is not merely economical. It is also about what some regard as attrition of local culture and heritage. "New West, Old West, that's what this is about," said Kane County commissioner

Habbeshaw. To him it is honorable to resist New West changes to preserve—for a short time, at least—what remains of the Old West. "Are we going to eventually lose the Old West, the traditions and the culture, [and] shift towards a New West and urban life? You bet we are. But why rush to it?"[60]

Thus, the road—the object celebrated as a means of progress—has become a metaphor and sword for tradition and heritage. Roads become artifacts, reminders of the past. Far from being merely a catapult to growth and change, as many generations once understood them to be, roads are now also symbols of an eroded local culture and tradition. The irony, of course, is that leaders of Kanab had for years supported industrial development that would have irrefutably transformed their towns and landscapes—on the Grand Staircase, on the Kaiparowits, in the Escalante region. Indeed, locals may not entirely understand the factors influencing cultural changes in their communities. "Nearly everywhere traditional economies are in decline, creating hardship, dislocation and no small amount of desperation," notes Bill Hedden of the Grand Canyon Trust, "and neither [environmentalists] nor Bill Clinton did it to us."[61]

From one perspective, the creation of Grand Staircase–Escalante was an attempt to push southern Utah and northern Arizona communities into a post–Old West era. The monument designation encouraged the collection of scientific, economic, and policy-related information that would consider biota within the monument and the changing nature of nearby communities. It was designed to regard rural people and their communities as a part of the monument "ecosystem"—to sustain and protect human and natural ecosystems side by side. Even conservationists eager to welcome the Grand Staircase–Escalante to southern Utah's constellation of parks acknowledged the need in the management plan for a mechanism to satiate all these needs—economic, environmental, and cultural. The foremost goal would be to meet these communities' needs without their becoming "overdeveloped, commercialized gateways," in the words of two environmentalists. In formulating a policy to protect the environment as well as the human presence on the land, the Wilderness Society suggested considering the impacts of humans—of hunting on wildlife, cattle on cryptobiotic soil, water management on floods, roads on vegetation—and their role in the broader ecosystem.[62]

Yet in advancing the monument as an acceptable middle ground where humans, animals, and wildness exist harmoniously, the Wilderness Society and other conservation groups either dismissed or underestimated the major cultural forces that contributed to its opposition. Many assumed that when locals learned of the material gains to be had from the monument, they would happily embrace it. This assumption is too easy and implies a naked material self-interest. The issue is as much cultural as economic. The road itself does not matter as much as the freedom that it represents. Locals had become accustomed to moving about the landscape as they pleased. Many attributed the freedom of the road with family, home, and community. Roads enabled fathers and grandfathers to take their children camping or hunting. Roads bridged generational gaps. Without motorized access, "our parents (in their 80s) and our kids (as young as two) have made these trips and wouldn't have been able to see this great country close-up any other way," penned Bruce Bolander of Irving, California. He urged the BLM to keep routes in the monument open.[63]

Locals convinced that the monument designation was an abuse of presidential power would also avow that the closure of roads degraded local heritage and culture. Mormons in southern Utah cherish how their ancestors settled in the outposts of the West to flee perceived federal oppression. Utah representative Thomas V. Hatch and Garfield County commissioner D. Maloy Dodds referred to Brigham Young as "a visionary leader" who directed the settlement of southern Utah, "where [Mormons] could make their own decisions and practice a lifestyle sacred and peculiar to them." The monument was a perceived continuation of government tyranny stemming back to the nineteenth century when Congress waged a war against the Mormon practice of plural marriage and the church's iron grip on politics in the Territory of Utah. To Hatch and Dodds, President Clinton "wiped out economic freedom from southern Utah" and permanently altered the "home" that had been a shelter for Mormons for nearly 150 years.[64]

To some, management of the monument had also obscured this human heritage. The official monument map distributed to tourists by the BLM details only a handful of roads open to travel and omits the rest, giving a flawed impression that movement within the monument is orderly. By design perhaps it is, but there is an extensive underworld of roads and trails (often no more than rut marks) that have yet to be reclaimed to grass and brush. What are we to believe about these? Are we to think anything at all about them, to consider their original purpose or future utility? The BLM and the environmental community claim these roads no longer serve a useful purpose either as artifacts or for practical design and that the land's highest use is to revert back to nature. Many locals, in contrast, insist that obscuring these roads on official monument maps puts visitors in danger of losing their way or taking a wrong turn. What appears comprehensible, even friendly, on the maps may be chaotic, disorganized, and dangerous. The roads themselves, like the land they traverse, are random, uneven, rough.

The specter of roads still casts a shadow over the nation's largest national monument. Some, like the route along the Paria River, are "phantom" roads; others are more visible. All are imprinted on the hearts and minds of many residents. Whether closed by the BLM or open to motorized travel, their presence is enduring. Discovering a straight path to resolution is dubious; these are winding, haphazard, and bewitching roads over a twisted landscape.

seven

Off-Roading in Arch Canyon

Arch Canyon, a side canyon of Comb Wash in San Juan County, Utah, is considered by locals and visitors alike as a rare gem. Near the mouth is Arch Canyon Ruin, a major Ancestral Puebloan site. For those who made this dwelling home between seven hundred and one thousand years ago, it afforded close proximity to the slow-flowing, perennial stream and fertile soils of the canyon bottom. Farther along the canyon lies more evidence of ancient habitation. Indeed, around every turn is a new and delightful site, some near the base, others situated higher up on the canyon walls. Farther up still loom the stately natural sandstone formations of Cathedral Arch, Angel Arch, and Keystone Arch. All these sites are easily accessible just off Utah Highway 95. It should be no surprise, then, that this enchanting place draws large numbers of visitors.

Although the chronicle of Arch Canyon echoes earlier conflicts, this one turns the others on their heads. Off-road vehicles have added a whole new dimension and problem to the road debate. Instead of merely following a road or trail to a desired destination, ORV drivers blaze their own trails, often with no apparent purpose. ORVs are technologically adapted to the rough landscape, and they ideologically suit those who believe the landscape ought to be traversed as one pleases. For these reasons, they are wildly popular among some, ardently derided by others. Federal and state land managers are obliged to maneuver around these constituencies, determining where to allow ORV access and where and how to restrict it. Arch Canyon is at the center of this controversy. This story is worth telling because it highlights the evolution of a relatively recent controversy in the canyon country as a pervasive presence, presenting threats to the land's integrity, challenges to land managers, and flash points of contention.

Arch Canyon is dually managed by the BLM in the lower canyon and by the Forest Service in the upper canyon and the area north all the way to the Abajo Mountains. Their specific challenge is to manage a place with a long history of use, one that is coveted by many interests who similarly value the canyon but advocate different ways of managing it. The BLM has played an active but inconsistent role in directing vehicle access in Arch Canyon, at times proposing limited access and other times recommending full vehicle access to the canyon. In 1973, in its South San Juan Management Framework Plan, the BLM determined to close the canyon to ORVs to protect resources.[1] Despite its implementation, the decision seems to have been weakly enforced—although one witness claimed that from at least 1972 to 1976, a fence at the mouth of the canyon blocked vehicle access.[2]

Whatever the barriers to entry into Arch Canyon, off-road motorists four-wheeled up the canyon increasingly by the late 1970s. A 1978 BLM report noted that the canyon was "receiving increased ORV traffic approximately five miles from the mouth of the canyon," which was contributing to the erosion of the hillside below Arch Canyon Ruin. BLM employee Fred Blackburn recommended closing Arch Canyon to vehicles indefinitely.[3] But the damage sustained was more than on the hillside; in 1979 BLM rangers noted "extensive ORV tracks" for six miles up the canyon and "pot holes dug either earlier this year or last year near [the] mouth of Arch Canyon in a large ruin area."[4] According to William R. Haase of the Utah Chapter of the Sierra Club, damage from ORV use was extensive in Arch Canyon compared to adjacent Mule Canyon, which in its upper reaches remained "absolutely pristine and contains no evidence of modern man."[5]

The illegal practice of disturbing ancient Indian sites like those in Arch Canyon was then becoming widespread in southeastern Utah. In 1979 and

1980, BLM's Kane Gulch Ranger Station documented dozens of incidents of "heavy vandalism" and "fresh diggings" in the San Juan area. The official incident report observed the vandalism "to be very Blatant, and becoming more numerous especially in locations close to Blanding." At one location, BLM personnel followed motorcycle tracks veering off beyond the dead end of a narrow road to a small dwelling site that had been vandalized for its treasures. "Of significance here is that motorcycles may be being used to comb wide areas of land for archeological sites," the employee wrote. "This abuse of ORVs may be of consideration in the ORV planning and designations of areas where site densities are high."[6]

These incidences suggest the problems that ORV use presents to land managers. By definition, ORVs veer off the designated road, using their small frames and specifically tailored gears to maneuver over and around rugged terrain. In fact, no road construction equipment is necessary; these vehicles simply push the road farther on—beyond to places even new to road builders. ORVs literally extend the road. And their tracks are not light, especially on fragile desert soils. These impacts were beginning to be understood; in 1977 the National Science Foundation and the Geological Society of America produced *Impacts and Management of Off Road Vehicles*, a report that detailed the heavy-use impacts of motorized backcountry travel.[7]

Edward Abbey produced a most searing critique of ORV use on the public lands in a 1976 letter to the editors of *Esquire*. ORVs were "a goddamned plague," he penned, and a lazy way of experiencing nature. Here is what he wrote of the people who use them:

> The fat pink soft slobs who go roaring over the landscape in these oversized over-priced over-advertised mechanical mastodons are people too lazy to walk, too ignorant to saddle a horse, too cheap and clumsy to paddle a canoe. Like cattle or sheep, they travel in herds, scared to death of going anywhere alone, and they leave their sign and spoor all over the back country: Coors beercans, Styrofoam cups, plastic spoons, balls of Kleenex, wads of toilet paper, spent cartridge shells, crushed gopher snakes, smashed sagebrush, broken trees, dead chipmunks, wounded deer, eroded trails, bullet-riddled petroglyphs, spray-paint signatures, vandalized Indian ruins, fouled-up waterholes, polluted springs, and

> smouldering campfires piled with incombustible tinfoil, filtertips, broken bottles. Etc.

Abbey castigated federal land managers for "doing far too little" to "stop this motorized invasion of what little wild country still remains in America."[8]

If Abbey unfairly characterized ORV users, he hinted rightly at the enormous challenge they present to land agencies charged with protecting public land resources. Roads are tidy; they can be followed and tracked, connecting point to point. ORV tracks, conversely, wind around, over, and through, weaving across the land in erratic marks like a pattern on a crazy quilt. These kinds of "roads" are not the products of careful planning. They are the imprint of impulse, of humans' drive to seek out a new place beyond the next ridge or around the next canyon bend. This is not to say that ORVers do not or cannot follow existing routes, but it would seem that the impulse to discover and even conquer is not easily repressed. As one of the BLM staffers noted in May 1980 regarding a patrol of Alkali Ridge in San Juan County, "A great number of new roads that have been developed in the area...made it difficult to see if there was any new archaeological vandalism in the area."[9]

Some environmentalists opined that new motorized tracks in Arch Canyon and elsewhere in the county had been created with sinister motives. Brian Beard of the Utah Chapter of the Sierra Club alleged that San Juan County officials had instructed people to "dig in ruins" and "drive four wheel vehicles to establish roads" in an effort to damage the wilderness characteristics of these areas so they could not be set aside for protection. He and other environmentalists petitioned the BLM district manager in Moab to close Arch Canyon, pursuant to Executive Order 11989 that directed land managers to "immediately close such areas or trails to the type of off road vehicle causing such effects."[10]

The BLM response in no way complied with Beard's request to close the canyon to vehicles. BLM personnel reported that "the road follows the drainage bottom the entire length of the canyon" and that "travel through the canyon appears to be extremely light." In fact, ORV traces were so minimal, the agency said, that vegetation had begun to grow back along the roadbed due to little use in the spring and summer of 1979. The district manager refused to budge—the canyon would remain open to ORV use. "Perhaps, BLM plans to turn Arch Canyon in to a[n] ORV play ground prejudice their eyes into seeing only 'slight damage,'" speculated a member of the Utah Chapter of the Sierra Club.[11]

To get a sense of just what an ORV playground might look like, visit the annual Jeep Safari in Moab or one of Jeep Jamboree USA's events held throughout the country. Every year since 1967, thousands of ORV enthusiasts converge in Moab, Utah, to drive their vehicles along designated routes in the redrock backcountry. The Jeep Jamboree USA, sponsored by Jeep-Chrysler to "access the inaccessible," holds events in out-of-the-way places, with a good number in southern Utah. And in 1989, Jeep-Chrysler held its first annual jamboree in Arch Canyon.

The advertised event did not go unnoticed by environmentalists disquieted about the impact of ORV use in the canyon. Prior to the jamboree, the Southern Utah Wilderness Alliance called the BLM office and requested a copy of the environmental assessment for this large gathering. The event, the BLM responded, would be "categorically excluded" from environmental review. After being pressured to complete the assessment, the BLM produced an EA and released it on March 28, 1989, three days before the scheduled event. SUWA then requested a stay of the event to force the BLM to hold the outing "in a non-riparian area," which the BLM refused to do. Thus, one hundred jeeps congregated as planned for the first annual Arch Canyon Jeep Jamboree.[12]

SUWA refused to let the matter rest and appealed the decision. The US Department of Interior Board of Land Appeals determined on October 12, 1989, that the BLM had improperly permitted the jamboree. The IBLA also ruled that the BLM had not properly validated county R.S. 2477 rights-of-way claims. Based on this decision, Scott Groene of SUWA concluded that the BLM was responsible for actively correcting ORV misuse in the canyon, and he echoed Brian Beard's recommendation ten years earlier to close the canyon to motorized vehicles and enforce the closure. "The BLM has created this problem and now must take steps to solve it," Groene wrote.[13]

Although the BLM field office deemed it had authority to validate county-asserted R. S. 2477 claims, the IBLA decision clearly directed the BLM of its obligation "to define and determine" the county right-of-way before permitting its use on the basis of county assertion. Even after this decision, however, the BLM continued to operate as though the county had a legal right-of-way to Arch Canyon road when, in fact, this claim had yet to be decided.[14]

To cover its bases, pursuant to the IBLA ruling and in anticipation of another Arch Canyon Jeep Jamboree the following year, the county filed materials with the BLM for consideration of R.S. 2477 status. Once again, SUWA contested the adequacy of the county's application and otherwise demanded that the BLM take action to close the canyon to ORV use and deny Jeep Jamboree a 1990 permit. The BLM district manager, Kenneth Rhea, responded that under Interior Department secretary Donald Hodel's policy, the BLM had full authority to make a "factual" determination as to whether Arch Canyon road satisfies the following provisions: the land is public land, construction occurred, and the road is considered a public road.[15] Meanwhile, locals mailed letters with the hopes of convincing the BLM that the road met these criteria. Calvin Black, then battling cancer, even wrote in, saying that he had used the road for multiple purposes several times a year since 1959. "I have personally used a shovel and picked and rolled rocks out of the way through the years and have removed trees occasionally as they have fallen across the road," he maintained.[16] All the same, environmentalists claimed a victory when Jeep Jamboree announced it would cancel the event at Arch Canyon and move it to a less sensitive area.

Not to be outdone, a roughly organized group of twenty-five jeepers congregated at Arch Canyon on the same weekend the jamboree was scheduled. Drivers were intent on riding up the canyon in direct violation of the BLM's dictate to close it while awaiting a final R.S. 2477 determination. The man to observe and report the offending motorists was none other than SUWA attorney Michael Heyrend, who had anticipated a quiet weekend of backpacking in Arch Canyon. No sooner had he started up the canyon by foot when he heard the roar of motors. Rushing back to the canyon's mouth, Heyrend witnessed the vehicles in a row, revving up for entry. "It looked like Patton's army," he recalled. Heyrend confronted the motorists: "This is closed to off-road vehicles.... Legally you guys can't go up." After learning that none of the jeepers had permits for entry, he further insisted. "Watch us" was the reply, as they proceeded past him. "The people who were going up the canyon were very hostile to me—their facial expressions, they muttered, that kind of thing.... I felt like a civil rights worker in 1962 in Selma, Alabama." Heyrend did manage to jot down some of the license plate numbers as they drove by. When he returned to his car several days later, he found a T-shirt with an obscene drawing of a man in hiking boots. The accompanying note read: "With Our Compliments. We could have used your tactics & Screwed your Vehicle Up."[17]

Later, BLM's Ken Rhea would defend the ORVers as "just a bunch of people who apparently go together...up the canyon." Since it was not a commercial outing, Rhea supposed that no charges would be made.[18] Incensed, BLM district manager Gene Nodine spoke out. "Here we've been doing our utmost to cooperate, and [get] everybody to be a partner in the whole thing. Then we find out that this particular incident has taken place." He threatened that the purported perpetrators could face legal consequences, although evidently no charges were ever filed.[19]

In 1990 BLM manager Edward Scherick signed an administrative decision acknowledging San Juan County's R.S. 2477 rights to the Arch Canyon road. After SUWA appealed the decision, the IBLA determined to suspend the status until the Department of the Interior developed its own R.S. 2477 policy. Like nearly all dirt roads in southern Utah with R. S. 2477 claims, however, an official decision on the Arch Canyon route has yet to be made.[20]

The question of road jurisdiction would resume in 2004 when the BLM rejected a multiyear permit for Jeep Jamborees in Arch Canyon. But Lynn Stevens, San Juan County commissioner and state coordinator of the Public Lands Policy Coordinating Office, defied the BLM by leading a jamboree up the canyon anyway. When the BLM then reversed course and granted the permit, environmentalists promptly appealed. The permit wound its way through a maze of legal procedures and in the end was remanded back to the BLM.[21]

In 2006 the BLM issued a five-year permit to hold Easter Jeep Safari events in Grand and San Juan Counties. Arch Canyon would now be opened up to the Jeep Safari sponsored by the Red Rock 4-Wheelers of Moab, Utah. "It really makes a mockery of the BLM's statements that they're trying to take care of the land and make things better when they go and open the

Jeep Safari to new routes," Dan Kent of Red Rock Forests, an environmental group, vented. "Arch Canyon is a unique and valuable place biologically, and for them to go and dump a big event like this into such a pristine area is just a sham. It's beyond the pale." BLM Monticello Field Office manager Sandra Meyers insisted, though, that the BLM had carefully reviewed the proposal, evaluated all the trails in the San Juan County for consideration, and ultimately determined that Arch Canyon would be a suitable site. "We studied it very hard and we feel we made the right decision," she stated. "We care very much, but we are a multiple use agency."[22]

Meyers's implication that multiple use essentially demands that motorized use of America's public lands sit side by side with wilderness use strikes at the heart of these debates. In the public's eye, multiple use suggests human commercial or motorized uses, the type of use often involving work: timber cutting, mining, livestock grazing, and so forth. By contrast, the public generally equates wilderness as a single or "dominant" use, when in fact wilderness is not only one of many uses but multiple use. It protects watersheds, ecosystems, and wildlife, and it provides recreational, scenic, and spiritual values. It seems that the BLM often operates on and the public discourse revolves around the assumption that closing off certain places from off-road use violates the principle of multiple use.

In October SUWA attorney Liz Thomas appealed to the BLM once again to close what she called the Arch Canyon "ORV 'route'" after it sustained damage from high floods. Thomas pointed out that at least in the lower portion of the canyon that she had observed, the floodwaters had "essentially obliterated" the trail. She even argued that the ORV ruts made the flood worse than it would have been, pointing to the "deep trenches, gullies and ledges that resulted as flood water was channeled down these linear tracks." Without the aid of a clearly defined route, she posited, ORV users attempting to maneuver up the canyon posed a threat to the environment as well as to themselves. Because the contemporary San Juan Management Resource Plan for Arch Canyon limited motorized vehicles "to designated routes," and because the BLM had yet to officially designate a route in the canyon, Thomas urged the Monticello Field Office to close the route to vehicular traffic.[23]

In response, the BLM sent personnel to inspect the road in Arch Canyon to determine what needed to be done. Meyers concluded that the flood event did not warrant an emergency closure. Instead, she posted closure signs and barriers where some vehicles had "detoured" to maneuver around the deep incisions created by the flood along portions of the road. The BLM field office manager also allowed local volunteers to reconstruct the original route. On November 18 and 25, 2006, members of San Juan Public Entry and Access Rights (known as SPEAR) and other locals repaired road damage from the storm using shovels, picks, and other tools to remove debris and rock from the road's bed. BLM personnel joined in the work, posting more signs and barriers where ORV users had veered from the main road.[24]

Rejecting the BLM response as utterly unacceptable, SUWA sought a ban on motorized recreation in Arch Canyon and in December filed its four-hundred-page "Petition to Preserve Arch Canyon's Natural and Cultural Heritage." Mustering support from tribal leaders and local business owners, conservationists showed how ORV use in the canyon threatened both cultural resources that were significant to the Navajo and Hopi tribes and the integrity of the natural ecosystem. Given the threat of new routes to the canyon's riparian bottom and the potential damage to more ancient artifacts, environmentalists again implored the BLM to close the canyon to motorized use. "There are thousands of miles of ORV routes in southern Utah located in less sensitive areas where ORV use may be appropriate," asserted Liz Thomas of SUWA. "But some special places should be protected."[25]

In 2007 the BLM denied SUWA's petition, provoking a stern reaction from SUWA's Scott Groene.[26] In February 2010, however, the BLM agreed to reconsider the petition by assessing the effects of motorized vehicle use in Arch Canyon. In the petition's official review, the BLM determined to keep the route open, although it acknowledged that "a large increase in ORV use beyond the current levels in the Canyon could pose future risks" to the canyon's resources. The BLM agreed to outline steps that could be taken to minimize potential damage from ORV use.[27]

The story of Arch Canyon reveals both the challenges and the promises of land management in the plateau region today. At first glance, the Arch Canyon conflict reads like others explored in this study: two opposing sides at loggerheads and largely unwilling to bend. Even the options seem diametrically opposed—either close or open the canyon to motorized use. Furthermore,

ORV use in particular exacerbates the conflicts. ORV users tend to line up on one side of the cultural spectrum and demand the right to access; driving an ORV to experience nature in out-of-the-way places is a symbol of freedom and Americanism. On the other side, critics maintain that ORV use is a lazy and environmentally destructive way to enjoy nature, and that indeed true freedom and Americanism are experiencing nature without being confined to a machine. These are two philosophical positions regarding how to experience wild places, and both make their way into debates over public land access and use.

Yet the proliferation of ORV use on public lands also suggests a new road-related management problem. ORV use is a blending of the so-called Old West and the New West. It is a form of mass recreation that complements nicely the tourist economy of the New West, but it is also a pursuit enjoyed by traditional land users who have long valued mobility in a broken country. Vehicles allow them to traverse the untraversable, to view the country how they want to, unfettered by the confines of a road. It is the modern version of the horse. Contrary to Edward Abbey's prediction in 1976 that "the coming and inevitable day of gasoline rationing...will retire all these goddamned ORVs and 'escape machines' to the junkyards where they belong," the ORVs have not only grown up with the New West, playing an integral role in its transformation, but steadily increased in popularity.[28]

Because ORV use is a blending of the Old West and New West, the sides of the debate between permitting or restricting ORVs on public lands are not so clearly defined. Development-minded southern Utahns have widely embraced ORVs as recreational, but so too, historically, did many conservationists. The ORV allowed access into the celebrated outback of the canyon country. SUWA may have contested Jeep Safari events held on public lands, but, at least according to Ken Davey in the *Canyon Country Zephyr,* many local environmentalists in Moab welcomed the events as well. "The Safari has always stressed the importance of responsible land use, and by publicizing the beauty of the region, it tends to promote preservation of undeveloped canyons," Davey writes. Besides, the events pump tourist dollars into a twenty-first-century regional economy that relies heavily on tourism.[29]

Edward Abbey himself is a bit of a contradiction, because he railed against the very form of transportation that he often used to penetrate the backcountry. In Abbey's writings, he describes rocky adventures on what could hardly be called a road into some of the roughest and most isolated pockets of the canyon country. Clearly, he preferred the experience of jeeping the rocky backcountry trail to driving the slick-paved highway. Moving quickly over the landscape was not as important as feeling and seeing and braving it as one would by jeep over a rugged backcountry trail. That very line of reasoning drove him and others to contest construction of the new paved road in Arches National Monument (now Arches National Park), the Trans-Escalante Highway, Utah Highway 95, the Burr Trail, the Book Cliffs highway, and other road projects. Yet Abbey also posited that use of even primitive trails by off-road motorists ought to be limited. In response to a 1974 National Park Service proposal to designate wilderness in Canyonlands National Park, he suggested additional steps to close roads that he himself had once used for exhilarating backcountry experiences. Abbey justified his proposal on the basis "that the preservation of wildlife...takes priority over motorized recreation, that most of the canyon country remains wide open to jeep and trailbike exploration, and that if wilderness is to be preserved at all, it must be preserved in our national parks and in areas extensive enough to be meaningful."[30]

Some critics like Abbey may ever insist that areas off-limits to ORV use are never enough, but many if not most constituents may be pleased with how public lands are managed. It may not always be a matter of either-or. At Arch Canyon, the BLM field office manager decided to allow ORV use but to take future steps to limit it if they determined it posed a threat to resources. Moreover, the BLM has attempted to keep ORV use to specific trails—to open the main road up the canyon to ORV travel but to close off the branch trails that had developed over time. It is a management scheme that works well enough, at least for the time being.

In other words, the BLM does not and need not operate within a black-and-white paradigm. Federal land managers daily make decisions that cater to a wide-ranging constituency, which is reflected in the BLM's waffling management decisions. Several times land managers have changed course by variously restricting access and then opening it back up. This behavior has led environmentalists to charge the BLM with not doing its job to protect the land from destructive uses. ORV users could be just as frustrated by the BLM's inconsistency. Few people are entirely satisfied by the BLM's management of Arch Canyon. Whereas some conservationists recognized the BLM's efforts to protect the canyon's invaluable natural and archaeological treasures from motorized use by placing designated route signs and barriers, Veronica Egan, a member of Great Old Broads for Wilderness, recognized that "the agency has neither the personnel nor the funds, and the public often lacks the self restraint," to prevent damage from occurring.[31]

Yet even if the BLM did have the personnel and funding, it would likely be impossible for the agency to please everyone anyhow. For one thing, places like Arch Canyon—previously out of the way and used only by a handful of locals—are now being discovered and "loved to death." "A few years ago, no one had heard of Arch Canyon," said Robert Turri of the San Juan Resource District of the BLM in 1990. "Now we get several calls a day from people asking what's there and how to get to it."[32] Land managers often do not have adequate resources to manage the public lands properly. Beyond that, determining the right way to manage the lands is a matter of contention. To expect land managers to please all user groups is disingenuous. As we have seen in previous chapters, managing the public lands (in other words, negotiating controversy) is a highly localized and subjective affair, contingent upon a number of variables, including personalities, culture, and circumstances.

Even many of the highly politicized and contentious New West land-use conflicts are being handled by land managers and personnel on the local level. It may be true that some refuse to compromise or to find solutions in the best interest of all groups, but there are many others willing to negotiate. In some cases, the decision made is to open a road to ORV use, in others to close it. In still others, federal land managers negotiate a range of issues, from the issuance of grazing permits to management of a newly designated national monument. These hard decisions, navigated daily by land managers alongside varying interests, are often made with little fanfare or appreciation, but they are essential to the management of our public lands.

eight

Making a Desert Landscape

When people look upon the canyon country of southern Utah and northern Arizona, they overwhelmingly see nature—a great wilderness expanse. They see the magnificent vistas, the redrock spires, the wide-open spaces. What they observe might delight, terrify, intrigue. They may also take note how the place has been altered and transformed by people. They can't miss the towns, roads, reservoirs, cows, and other human creations. But what people see is not merely a matter of what physical objects litter the land. Landscape is more deeply revealing than that. As British geographer H. C. Darby observed, landscape is "Art as well as Nature," or, in other words, physical space as well as mental space—how we think about land and act on it.[1]

The landscape of the canyon country has been continually and continues to be created and re-created according to the ideas and values that people bring to it. Both the form of the landscape and the ideas behind it developed slowly, organically, as preconceived expectations, worldviews, and experiences collided in a great palimpsest. For nineteenth-century Mormons who founded communities in southeastern Utah, the deserts and canyons were a stage where their religious aspirations would play out—driven by the impulse to domesticate and conquer the land and shape it to their perception of what land was supposed to be. Others who have called the plateau country home or who identify strongly with the region embraced or rejected that impulse to varying degrees. All groups confronted a material reality that tested, shaped, and reshaped them. They all attempted to impose their own vision on the land with limited success. Material modifications on the landscape reflect these contending values and their alternating triumphs.

The canyon country will yet be transformed according to the perceptions humans bring to it. The challenge today is for the various groups with a stake in its future to come together to create a landscape that aims to satisfy all. Finding common ground will not be easy and may ultimately fall short, but the long-term process of envisioning and acting on the land should nevertheless move forward. The process will require contemplating how to blend the built and natural environments. Addressing the role of roads is central. Despite their polarizing influence as symbols of both desired progress and lamented exploitation, roads have yet held the promise of integrating the human and natural landscapes into a cogent whole. We can start this collaborative process by examining the history and meaning of roads in American culture.

To begin imagining the role of roads on the landscape, start by contrasting them to rivers. Rivers are in constant motion. Their flow transforms landscapes in gradual and at times rapid increments, taking millions of years to trickle and ebb through a rock canyon or altering, leveling earth in a matter of minutes with a rush of floodwater. The energy produced by rivers is immense, to say nothing of the energy required to channel and contain them. Roads also require energy to construct and maintain and serve a similar function to rivers in transporting humans and their cargoes, but the similarities seemingly stop there: roads are static, inorganic, and unnatural; while they can be moved and create change when built and rebuilt, they indicate permanence and sheer resistance to change.

Just as water strikes the best possible compromise between shortest distance and negotiable terrain, so, too, can roads. Particularly in the past, the land's natural contours dictated how and where people moved and lived on the land. Not unlike early irrigation canals built in gullies and soil depressions, early roads were built with an appreciation for the land's terrain. And to some degree, this remains true. Nature predominantly dictates how people and machines move across the land, for roads are built to rise and fall and turn with the landscape. "When you walk out here," Craig Childs writes of the canyon country, "you walk the places where water has gone—the canyons, the low places, and the pour-offs—because travel is too difficult against the grain of gullies or up in the rough rock outcrops."[2]

But nature can always be improved upon. "The 'proper' channel for a river is not necessarily the one it has carved for itself," John Seelye observes in *Beautiful Machine.* "By means of canals and locks it can be guided by men along a straight and level line, thereby improving upon natural design."[3] The reclamation movement in the West existed largely to "free" rivers from their natural course and steer them into channels to serve human needs. Technology could also do for roads what it did for rivers: enable engineers to carve roads up, over, and through some of the roughest terrain on the planet. It may be that this overt intention toward the landscape—the impulse to improve upon nature and subdue it for human purposes—has largely contributed to the image of roads as a dominant force.

The road has long played the role of vanguard in mediating between wild and civilized places. In sixteenth-century Europe, roads ventured into primeval forests and wildlands previously unknown, even feared. They introduced people to new and bewildering wildlands. "Sixteenth century Europeans saw the road not as good or evil but as enticingly mysterious," writes John Stilgoe. It offered the "joys of wandering..., in wandering itself, for the roads that passed from landschaft into wilderness promised excitement and fortune." The road was celebrated, too, by villagers, because it meant an infusion of wealth and goods. But it was at the same time viewed cautiously, for the road also brought in new and different people and ideas reflecting the chaos of the wild and not the stability of the village.[4]

In early America, roads tended to be rougher and more local in design than their European counterparts owned and maintained by centralized authority. Public officials recognized roads as means and symbols of progress and civilization. Thomas Jefferson argued in 1808 that surplus federal revenue ought to be used for public road and canal projects. "Shall [the revenue] lie unproductive in the public vaults," he queried, "[o]r shall it not be appropriated to the improvement of roads, canals, rivers, education and other foundations of prosperity and union?"[5] Not until the 1840s did the United States undertake a comprehensive system of "internal improvements," and long-distance travel gradually became viable, leading Horace Bushnell in his 1846 pamphlet *The Day of Roads* to proclaim his as "an age of Roads."[6]

Indeed, at that time, few did, or could, contest the moral authority of roads as facilitators of prosperity and stability. Roads served a basic human need—to move from one place to another—but they also facilitated nearly every other human endeavor. Nineteenth-century travel accounts referred to the developments along the road as an index to progress. Politicians, businessmen, poets, writers, and artists all applauded these built features and their contribution to American society. In "Song of the Open Road," Walt Whitman used the road as a symbol of freedom, a metaphor depicting one's journey:

> *Afoot and lighthearted I take to the open road,*
> *Healthy, free, the world before me,*
> *The long brown path before me leading wherever I choose.*"[7]

The metaphor of the open road remains common, but the road is not necessarily a monolith of virtue, particularly on wildlands. Consider the direct physical impacts. Ecologists speak of the ecological fragmentation that occurs when roads partition wildlife and plant communities. Unpaved rural roads present erosion hazards; water glides over the compressed and impervious roadbed, corroding the adjacent soil. But erosion and pollution impacts are even more severe from paved roads. Automobile leaks, salts, and chemicals contaminate land and water. There is the adverse effects on vegetation—seeds, plants, trees—and animals. One estimate places the cumulative damage of roads to public lands in the western United States at about one hundred thousand square miles, an area approximately the size of Arizona.[8]

Next consider the tremendous collateral damage of roads. Yes, roads facilitate growth, industry, and recreation. But herein lies the problem: in the midst of facilitation, roads threaten the viability and integrity of untouched wild places. Early conservationists recognized this. Historian Paul Sutter has persuasively argued that the modern wilderness movement emerged from concerns about automobiles and the environmental impacts of outdoor recreation. The road opens and facilitates, but it also defiles. The founding members of the Wilderness Society—Aldo Leopold, Robert Sterling Yard, Benton

MacKaye, and Bob Marshall—intentionally created a definition and hence a perception of wilderness as roadless.[9]

These are two ways of perceiving roads—as symbols of progress and of exploitation. A third, ambivalent, position underscores a middle way: the road as desired yet lamented. While people value access, they bemoan the effects of modernization on the landscape. Leo Marx called their ideal the pastoral dream, the middle landscape wherein people hoped to enjoy just the right mix of nature and artifice, wildness and technology. Marx argued that the struggle to reconcile the idea of a pastoral landscape and the reality of an urbanized, industrial landscape has long been a part of the American imagination.[10]

In the nineteenth and early twentieth centuries, road builders posited that such a middle landscape was possible. An engineer of a mid-nineteenth-century railroad that would hug the western shore of the Hudson River responded to critics who feared the new rail might destroy the artistic landscape. "To a very great extent the construction of the Road will improve the appearance of the shore," he noted. "Rough points will be smoothed off, the irregular indentations of the bays [will] be hidden and regularity and symmetry imparted to the outline of the shore...adding to the interest, grandeur and beauty of the whole."[11] Later, twentieth-century architects designed American parkways (landscaped highways, often intended for recreational driving) to blend seamlessly into the natural and built landscapes. These roadways reflected the democratization of the automobile and also the modernist impulse to create roads that served motorists. The intent was to merge engineering and nature harmoniously so as not to dominate local tradition or despoil the landscape. As Timothy Davis writes, "Parkways helped to mediate the tension between progress and nostalgia."[12]

Created in the wake of World War II, the interstate highway system would overwhelm nostalgia, boasting functionality, efficiency, and modernity. A new standard of design prized for its utilitarian value, the interstate moved masses to their destinations in the shortest distance possible. This is not to say that highways eliminated in the postwar era the graceful landscape curves and striking vistas of parkways. William Least Heat-Moon's best-selling book, *Blue Highways,* documents his thirteen-thousand-mile road trip in 1978 along back roads to locations largely untouched by the modern interstate.[13] Yet these places had become increasingly difficult to find. Parkways satisfied America's demand for an integration of landscape aesthetics, traditional values, and modernity, but increasingly the need to accommodate higher speeds and heavier traffic overwhelmed the desire to showcase historical sites or local culture. Over time, engineers would streamline road building by forgoing scenic or recreational features.

Whereas some roadways in the United States were designed with an aesthetic intent in that they blended into the landscape and gave motorists pretty views, roads constructed in the canyon country tended toward a utilitarian design. Debates in the postwar period zeroed in on their competing values. Creating roads to serve the extractive industry promised to give birth to a vibrant tourist economy showcasing the region's scenic wonders. Advocates were quick to declare that roads would bring tourists and commerce into their communities. But questions lingered over how to walk the fine line between upgrading roads to encourage tourism without making communities flybys for high-speed motorists. At any rate, few rural folks presumed tourism would be a panacea to the region's economic woes.

Increasingly, more people began to recognize and regret the road's role in the loss of wild landscapes. A growing chorus advocated preserving wild areas because they represented the last remnants of primeval America and ought not to be opened to extractive, commercial, or tourist industries. For some, roads on public lands took on a foreboding nature since they facilitated clear-cut logging, industrial mining, and off-road vehicle recreation. Environmentalists became ever more skeptical that the middle landscape could be preserved. At the same time, wilderness proponents began asserting that roads did not belong on many wild landscapes at all. The threat of roads has been a major impetus to wilderness preservation, and it continues to drive environmental debates to this day.

The idea of wilderness derived from apprehension over the mechanized world, and wilderness founders in the 1930s organized a new conservation group that aimed to protect places "from the mechanical sights and sounds and smells." The notion was born that some places ought to remain untouched by humans' industrious, tinkering hands. Roads above all threatened the wilderness experience—more than resource commodity use, more than desire for recreational pursuits, more than biological diversity or endangered species.[14] Aldo Leopold, who practically and philosophically outlined the principles behind wilderness in his 1949 posthumous *The Sand County Almanac*, railed against roads of any kind. "Recreational development is a job not of building roads into lovely country," he penned, "but of building receptivity into the still unlovely human mind."[15]

For advocates of southern Utah wilderness, progress has advanced at an agonizingly slow pace. In the original 1964 wilderness bill, no wilderness areas in Utah were allocated. By 1980 Congress had designated as wilderness only about 30,000 acres of forestland all in the Lone Peak area. In 1984—"the Year of the Wilderness"—Utah's congressional delegation, led by Senator Jake Garn, shepherded a wilderness bill through Congress that set aside nearly 750,000 acres in the state's national forests along the Wasatch Front and in the Uinta Mountains.[16] Designated BLM wilderness lands are much fewer. In 1984 Congress also set aside the Beaver Dam Mountains and the Paria Canyon–Vermilion Cliffs for a total of 26,630 acres. The Cedar Mountain Wilderness Area due west of Salt Lake City was designated in 2006, and the Omnibus Public Lands Management Act of 2009 appropriated 129,000 acres of BLM wilderness in fourteen areas. Except for 23,000 acres in the Paria Canyon–Vermilion Cliffs and 5,000 acres in the Black Ridge Canyons, none are in southeastern Utah.[17]

In the American imagination, forests have more immediately recognizable wilderness qualities than deserts, so it is understandable that most designated wilderness in Utah is mountainous. Wilderness imagery evokes the fecund, verdant, vegetation-rich places. High mountain peaks and forested areas evoke a sublimity that people have come to expect of wilderness. The intent of the Utah wilderness bill in 1984 was to protect water at its source by keeping forests free from logging and grazing. Development advocates supported the bill because it would "release" from statutory protection forested land for potential economic use.

No such arrangement has been made on the deserts managed by the BLM. For generations, lands were either considered not worthy of wilderness protection or areas that had thoroughly been worked and thus disqualified for wilderness status. But the perception of these areas as wastelands is no longer true: they are variously coveted for their natural resources *and* for their wilderness qualities. Dick Carter of the Utah Wilderness Association, the architect of the 1984 wilderness bill, worried even conservationists were slow to recognize the threat of losing these lands to development and recreation interests. "These are the last great remains of wilderness in the United States and they have been discovered and coveted, if you will," he told an audience in 1985. "And they will be lost unless we look truthfully at BLM lands and quit hiding them in our collective romanticism."[18]

In 1995 two disparate Utah BLM wilderness bills came before Congress, one representing SUWA and the environmental community and the other toted by politicians and residents generally opposed to wilderness. The Utah Public Lands Management Act of 1995 (H.R. 1745) proposed designation of 1.8 million acres, later increased to 2.1 million under the Senate version of the bill (S. 884)—more than 1 million acres less than what some rural county commissioners said was acceptable but about 3.6 million acres less than the Utah Wilderness Coalition's long-standing BLM wilderness proposal of 5.7 million acres. The Utah Public Lands Management Act of 1995 made provisions for hard-release language, recognition of R.S. 2477 rights, vehicle use, and dam building within wilderness areas. America's Red Rock Wilderness Act of 1995, introduced by Representative Maurice Hinchey (D-NY) and celebrated by wilderness activists, incorporated the Utah Wilderness Coalition's 5.7-million-acre statewide wilderness proposal. Although the same bill, or variations of it, has been introduced several times in the House and Senate, it has failed to come up for a vote each time.[19]

Both sides have little incentive to compromise, according to Mark Walsh of the Utah Association of Counties. The environmental community would get less acreage than is now being managed as WSAs as though they were wilderness. To those opposed to wilderness, the amount of wilderness already designated in the state is more than they originally wanted anyway. At this point, a wilderness bill would result in less or more wilderness than either group wants.[20]

Roads are not only a key threat to wilderness, but also the prop that opponents use to contest wilderness designation. Roads and wilderness are conjoined. They have a shared history and follow a similar trajectory. The same legislation—FLPMA—that initiated BLM wilderness inventories also canceled R.S. 2477, except for existing rights. For nearly four decades, both have remained a long way from being resolved. It is nearly inconceivable to settle one without the other. Utah representative James Hansen has said that tying the fate of R.S. 2477 road claims "to Utah Wilderness or any wilderness ... is a worn out scare tactic and does not hold water." Although he is right that environmentalists sometimes use roads as a scare tactic, the connection between R.S. 2477 claims and wilderness in Utah is clear: the future of wilderness will not be decided until we have some resolution to thousands of road claims.[21]

Not just in Utah but elsewhere in the West, roads and road building impede wilderness designation. One of the most significant environmental initiatives of our time was designed to keep new roads out of remaining unprotected forestlands. On national forests, roads total, by one account, more than 440,000 miles.[22] The Forest Service's Roadless Area Conservation Rule (known as the Roadless Rule), published in 2001 in the closing days of the Clinton administration, protected 58 million roadless forested acres from new roads. The Roadless Rule has its own messy history: in 2005 the Bush administration rescinded it, but a district court in 2006 and a federal appeals court in 2011 upheld it. But in southern Utah, the prospect of resolution is even dimmer than nationally on the Roadless Rule question. There the central issue is R.S. 2477—a very different roads issue. Whereas the Roadless Rule aims to curtail new road building on forested lands, R.S. 2477 applies to validating and improving existing roads on what was in 1866 public land "not reserved for public uses." This is a messy process of acknowledging prior use and negotiating competing, often conflicting, contemporary uses to determine whether a route becomes a recognized "public highway."

In the absence of legislative and judicial resolution to R.S. 2477 claims, wilderness critics and proponents use roads as leverage. Roads assume a primal importance. Critics fear the onerous process, for the longer wilderness issues remain unresolved, the more possibility that many of the contested roads will be reclaimed by nature, even disappear from the landscape. "This is one of the rubs we're in right now," Walsh worries. "We're identifying lands that may not now meet the [wilderness] criteria, but if it's managed in a certain fashion for a while it very well may.... I think that's the intent with respect to roads."[23] One reason county officials call out dozers for road work is to keep the road's imprint fresh for fear that disappearance would qualify the area for wilderness. On the other hand, wilderness proponents fear the passage of each new year without official protections as a whittling away of wilderness areas.

In fact, as we saw in Negro Bill Canyon, road marks do not automatically disqualify an area from wilderness consideration. Long ago Congress rejected the erroneous notion that only "pristine" lands would be eligible for wilderness designation. Thus, debating whether road scars or an old cabin or mine tailings exist in areas considered for wilderness designation in fact masks the central issue: determining which of the remaining roadless areas on public lands will be left in a wild and natural state and which ones will be available for development. Some argue for the unsuitability of wilderness wherever there is any visible human imprint on the land, insisting that humans and wilderness are incompatible. On the spectrum's other end, wilderness proponents sometimes embrace the historic human presence as compatible with preservation.

This runs contrary to historian William Cronon's argument in his article "The Trouble with Wilderness; or, Getting Back to the Wrong Nature" that the idea of wilderness promotes and enforces a human-nature dualism. By treating nature and culture as separate categories, he claims, the modern wilderness movement creates "a dualistic vision in which the human is entirely outside the natural" and does not reflect the right way to live in the world.[24] Cronon's argument is valid: at least in perception, wilderness and civilization are two polar ends. But this duality is enforced more by folks opposed to wilderness who insist on defining it as out-of-the-way places largely untouched by and inaccessible to humans than by wilderness proponents. This is not to say that environmentalists do not see worth in defining distinct geographic boundaries and characteristics. Breaking down the demarcation between "untrammeled" wilderness and human landscapes leaves room for developers to further justify their activities on the land, contributing to what environmental activist Doug Scott calls "nibbl[ing] away at wild places in an insatiable, creeping process fatal to wilderness."[25] Still, conservationists have not advanced the position that wilderness reflects a wide divide between nature and culture.[26]

Yet roads are important not because they defile the land or because their presence detracts from the wilderness experience, although they can do both. Rather, they have come to betoken something much larger than themselves:

their absence suggests wilderness, and their presence suggests human history and culture. Wrongly or rightly, roads suggest a stark choice between wildness and civilization.

Every road now in contention has a history. Each represents continuity between generations. That is how descendants of the pioneers who built and used them see it. Garfield County commissioner Louise Liston, speaking before Congress about the Burr Trail, remarked that "150 years ago our ancestors in Utah sacrificed and struggled to open up that land by using these very roads and now we are having a sacrifice and struggle to keep those lands open to those who want to close them."[27] To her, the struggle of her forebears and the struggle of her generation could not be separated. And the struggle to which she refers stems directly back to her Mormon ancestry.

The roots of that struggle merit some final contemplation. When in July 1831 founding Mormon prophet Joseph Smith first arrived in Jackson County, Missouri—what he declared the center place of Zion—he surveyed the area and wondered, "When will the wilderness blossom as the rose; when will Zion be built up in her glory[?]"[28] His was the view that Christ upon his triumphal return to earth would flatten out the mountains "into a gently rolling countryside" ideal for agriculture.[29] To Smith and many of his contemporaries, the built landscape was prized over unused, unimproved land. Smith envisioned not only a place where people could live, but a *well-ordered* place, as reflected by the plat for the City of Zion that he and his counselors produced in 1833. This idealized view—the quintessential pastoral landscape—possessed a redemptive quality that fitted squarely with the nineteenth-century biblical view of land ordained by Providence for "the use of man."

Later, when Smith's successor, Brigham Young, directed the Mormon migration and settlement of the Great Basin and the Intermountain West, Mormons brought with them religious beliefs about land and their role on it. In the late nineteenth century, Mormons entered the canyon country with idealized views of the land, originating in the well-watered East and refined by the religious assurances of a promised people. Their views of land and community are well represented by their handiwork. They may have looked forward longingly to the millennial day when the high places would be made low and the crooked places straight, but they did not have to wait. Their work, as revealed through their roads, was to realize that dream. It was a spiritual and temporal endeavor, and it gave meaning and vitality to the act of settlement and survival in that arid desert country. Mormons may have looked upon the canyon country and seen a cursed wilderness, but they fully believed they could impose their will on it. Beginning in the late nineteenth century, they set about settling it, planting its fields, attempting to control its rivers, and putting down roads that would endure. Many descendants of original settlers still live today in the canyon country and do their part to carry on that work of redemption.[30]

Contemporary residents of southeastern Utah often view their history as a tale of progress, not much different from the way Frederick Jackson Turner described settlement of the West. Enterprising humans ventured first into the wilderness, clearing and cultivating the land. Trails became wagon routes that became well-traveled roads. Roads stood as the vanguard of "a continually advancing frontier line," in other words "the meeting point between savagery and civilization," and the act of moving about the land extended the frontier westward. Humans who encountered the wilderness were at first at its mercy, until they slowly transformed it. As the wilderness receded and the "lines of civilization" advanced, settlement moved into a more advanced stage. From animal trail to well-traveled highway, the road evolved in tandem with society.[31]

Approaching the task of settlement with communal energy and religious cohesion, Mormons planted communities where other groups had failed. Of all the virtues of the agrarian myth, self-sufficiency and independence are among the closely guarded and highly valued in Mormon society. Living off the fruits and riches of the land is a powerful notion. Mormons were farmers, industrious and generally successful at plying their trade. They established the first modern irrigation system in the West and created a self-sustaining inland empire in the mountains that lasted nearly through the nineteenth century. Even today, that region is part of the Mormon cultural zone, dotted as it is by Mormon towns, many still reliant on agriculture and other traditional land-use activities.[32]

In the Mormon cosmos, the earth is in a fallen state, and man as steward is destined to redeem it. The notion of a steward is usually understood as gardener, one who improves upon the land. "There is a great work for the Saints to do," Brigham Young told his people in 1860. "Progress, and improve upon, and make beautiful everything around you. Cultivate the earth and cultivate your minds. Build cities, adorn your habitations, make gardens, orchards, and vineyards, and render the earth so pleasant that when you look upon your labours you may do so with pleasure, and that angels may delight to come and visit your beautiful locations."[33] The idea was not so much about living in harmony with nature as it was bringing nature harmoniously into the human-defined ideals of a celestial place. Stewardship was more an act of creation than preservation.

But the deserts of southeastern Utah were not easily manipulated. Here was land that did not conform to worldviews. Religious ideas about land and experiences in the desert country made the Hole-in-the-Rock pioneers and their descendants develop an adversarial relationship to the land. Early Mormons did not linger for a time in the canyon country and marvel at it. They planted crops, built homes and communities, and grazed their cattle there. They sought to create a society in the wilderness, work that continues even as new generations have come to admire the beauties of the redrock and cherish the wide-open spaces. In all the rhetoric of longtime residents, the land is something to admire and behold, but it is still to be improved upon. If it appears current residents are changing their tune, it is likely because they are at long last enjoying the fruits of their labors. The land is no longer feared or avoided—not because its essential nature has changed or because perceptions have evolved, but precisely because it has been worked and reworked over the generations to conform to imposed ideals.

Now residents of small rural towns in southeastern Utah marvel at the ingenuity and grit of their forebears, not without a hint of romanticism. Robert Redd of La Sal, Utah, hopes that historic spots are there for future generations: "There's a strong feeling of kinship with things like the Hole-in-the-Rock. These are features of the landscape that have been the curse and the blessing to us settlers. They have endeared themselves to us, and we're still connected going back a hundred years.... It'll be nice if it isn't just a memory and it's not just pictures of the stuff, but if you can actually go back and feel some of those same feelings and connect with nature in a personal way like the old timers did."[34] To local Joe Finn Lyman, discovering an "old pioneer trail" is "the most euphoric feeling, especially if I think I'm the only one who knows where it is." The history of roads and trails intrigues him. "My cousin and I found an old crossing below the highway," he continued. "We thought, 'What's it doing here? Why did they build it?' All of a sudden, these old trails became alive.... We get our life from these histories, our forebearers, and their sacrifices. When you go out and find these old trails, it brings it all together in a really meaningful way."[35]

Many contemporary residents value the freedom to move about the landscape just as their pioneer ancestors did before them. The historic sites, the wide-open vistas, the rough trails, the prehistoric sites make San Juan County one of the finest places to experience the West—what Andrew Gulliford of Durango, Colorado, calls "one big outdoor museum."[36] Oliver Harris, a longtime resident of Blanding, mused about hiking the backcountry around Blanding. With his large family, he would explore places with little foot traffic, encountering ruins with corncobs scattered about, cliff dwellings high above the canyon floor, and cliff art in Arch Canyon that to him resembled the Holy Trinity.[37] Whether encountering it on an ATV or by foot, scrambling up a rock-faced ledge or relaxing from the front seat of a car, the canyon country holds the promise of exploration and discovery in open spaces. Few San Juan County residents want a mediated landscape, one that is controlled and patrolled by a watchful eye. They generally cherish the freedom to experience the land on their own terms, not with road signs directing traffic, maps indicating the location of historic sites, or roadside displays detailing the lay of the land. Not in San Juan County. This is where the enthusiast strikes out into the backcountry, the hiker sets out to uncover the ancient past, and the ATVer cruises a faded trail to see what lies around the next bend.

Locals in general do not much worry about the impact of their roving activities on the land. Oliver Harris pointed to places that bear the human imprint. "There's a place down in Recapture [Canyon] where you can see that a Cat [tractor] went across the solid rock and left cleat marks all the way, but they're almost gone. In another hundred years, they'll be gone. There's too much hysteria about man's footprint on the land." Marks by four-wheelers, he opined, are not permanent, although he admitted he resents finding motorized tracks in places he "hiked hard and climbed high" to reach. But above all, Harris valued access, a word imprinted on his license plate.[38]

Longtime residents often begrudge outside interests dictating one's activities on the land. Complaints against government interference go way back.

Joseph Smith formed his secretive Council of Fifty to seek out a place for the Mormons to settle outside of the United States, and Brigham Young realized that objective in the Great Basin in 1847. Following the Treaty of Guadalupe Hidalgo, Young found his people back on US soil. Subsequent years of theocratic-democratic wrangling in Utah territory over control and autonomy have left distaste for federal oversight. Even as Mormons abandoned the original lightning rod of dispute—polygamy—and incorporated into the mainstream in the late nineteenth and early twentieth centuries, in one area the federal presence remained strong: ownership and, increasingly, regulation of the public lands. In southeastern Utah where ranchers generally had free rein to graze livestock on public lands, the feds carved districts now managed by the BLM. Their homeland is now (and has been for generations) a patchwork of federal designations: the forested high country is managed by the Forest Service, the celebrated landmarks including the whole of Lake Powell and vicinity by the NPS, and the remaining public lands—most of it arid desert—by the BLM. That leaves a relatively small percentage of state and privately owned land to those who may feel entitled to control the whole of it.

When San Juan County locals like Gary Shumway talk about "the freedom to get on a four-wheeler and drive through the country with it being just as quiet and calm and peaceful," they reference notions with deep resonance in the Mormon tradition.[39] Many with Mormon heritage see the land not just as a physical form to be used but also as a spiritual form to be worshipped. This may be because in the Mormon tradition, the spiritual and the material realms are one: roads as physical markers of an earlier generation's sacrifice. We, too, can almost sense the trials associated with traversing or building a road across this rough-hewn land, because we can feel the discomfort when we step out of our vehicles and walk sections of it. The roads, the land, the markings are all reminders that we are material beings, limited in space, thoroughly grounded to the soil beneath our feet.

The Mormon presence in the canyon country is sometimes obscured. In the American imagination, the redrock desert of Everett Ruess and Edward Abbey is largely an unpeopled place. One can travel on paved and dirt roads for miles, with no sign of human habitation in sight. Tracing the Hole-in-the-Rock trail, writer Phyllis Rose wanted "to see what the settlers saw, and, in a general way, I did, for the landscape remains as it was then, a site of mind-numbing immensity and sameness, with geological features that continue unchanged for 50 or 100 miles at a time."[40] The visitor will note that the entrance to Arches National Park lies a few miles from a city of about five thousand, but Moab is auxiliary to the actual character of the place. These perceptions are products, in part, of official Utah campaigns beginning in the 1940s to brand the canyon country as a place apart, outside Mormon country.[41] The bare sandstone and windswept plateau only faintly resembles the places where Mormons congregated, particularly the valleys at the base of the Wasatch Mountains. To the visitor, the small communities at the edges of the canyon country are little noticed and serve primarily as stations to fuel up. Aside from the chapel house at the center of each town, the tourist would not necessarily know these are Mormon towns—settled, tended, and worked for generations by hardy pioneers.

This is a perception of the canyon country that suits environmental advocacy groups intent on branding the region as a mostly unpeopled wilderness deserving of protection. Ward J. Roylance, a longtime writer and photographer, referred to the country in 1986 as an "enchanted wilderness," "one of the largest relatively undeveloped parts of the 48 contiguous states," a veritable landscape of natural wonders, scenery, and spectacle.[42] Conversely, the argument is also made that parts of the region are altered—even defiled—by local communities courting industrial interests and by increased populations and recreational use. Both notions—of a last remaining unprotected wilderness and of a defiled landscape—play to environmental groups' oft-cited claim: that time is of the essence to save unprotected lands before the relentless march of commercialization and industry destroys it forever.

True, the region's land appears to the naked eye much as pioneers encountered it more than a hundred years before. Certainly, the canyon country has not changed on an ecological scale as, say, the Great Plains, which saw the disappearance within a single century of native tallgrasses and bison, or as Navajo country directly south of the San Juan River, which endured degradation of the rangeland from overgrazing sheep and horses.[43] This is not to say that if examined closely within this vast country, one would not find instances of abuse and degradation. Mines, power plants, and water projects have enduring environmental consequences, and grazing has altered the land as much as anything else. Cattle grazing in places like Butler and Comb Wash contributed to the growth of invasive species such as the Russian thistle (tumbleweed). The damages are not just to the natural landscape; many ancient Ancestral Pueblo sites have been vandalized and picked clean by raiders.[44]

The proprietary mentality inherited from Mormon tenets is responsible, in part, for some acts of environmental degradation in the canyon country. But the Mormon communal system and land ethic can be looked to as a blueprint in determining how to move forward. Wallace Stegner once extolled the practicality of the old Mormon village in the desert. The settlers lived communally, working as a group to live in an arid environment. They had what he called the Mormon "dream of Millennium, not of quick fortune."[45] Some Mormons advocate a return to this ethos—one that recognizes the virtues not just of community but of living in true relation to nature, an ethic of the Hole-in-the-Rock pioneers that not only attempted to conquer nature but to work in a dialectical relationship to it.[46] Mormon pioneers may have wanted to conquer and tame the land, but they also understood its tremendous power and limitations—in the best of the Mormon tradition—as good stewards. True, Mormon scripture variously speaks of the earth as "full" and ordained for the use of man, but it also commands stewardship of the earth and its animals, plants, and resources. Scripture evokes both entitlement and reverence, and both are at work here.

If we look only to a few of the more fanatical Mormon folks, we might be tempted to surmise that the logical extension of the Mormon land ethic would be unfettered ORV access, mining, and livestock grazing. But some Mormons may inspire wise use of resources more in the tradition of San Juan County rancher Charles Redd, son of Lemuel Hardison Redd Jr., one of the original Hole-in-the-Rock pioneers. Well ahead of his time, Charles Redd and his herders often went about the public domain where they grazed livestock and replanted eroded spots with clover or crested wheatgrass. He worked closely with BLM and Forest Service personnel to improve range conditions. In response to Redd's directive to hold the cattle in the low country to protect the grass in the higher elevations, cattle foreman Chet Smith remarked, "I thought we were in the cow business to raise cows, but Charlie just wants to raise grass." Redd's was a commitment to traditional agrarian land-use practices and a care for the land. As a man with deep cultural roots in southeastern Utah, Charles Redd believed land ought to be cared for to last for generations, not for immediate profit. And this impulse was a religious one in which he found spiritual expression.[47]

It is *this* land ethic that can yet be reclaimed in a canyon country threatened by overgrazing, strip and coal mining, and what Abbey called "industrial tourism." We need to reclaim a cultural vision with a fierce devotion to protecting the character and spirit of the land. More people are discovering the public lands and recreating on it, but they are not necessarily coming to know it better than earlier generations. Andrew Gulliford of Durango talks of the hordes who come for "hard exercise" to places like Moab. "It's not a pioneer ethos. It's not about respecting the landscape. It's pretty self-serving, and it bothers me."[48] By the same token, locals sometimes fail to recognize that mining and industrial development erode not just the land they hold dear but also the culture and traditions that make the region unique. Conservationists could do better to articulate a vision that recognizes the culture, identity, and needs of rural people instead of treating these as collateral damage in the quest to preserve nature. Boulder resident Loch Wade points this out in an article in Jim Stiles's *Canyon Country Zephyr.* "This will mean that in some cases, humans will have to come first," he notes. "But if this pragmatism is based on a willingness to strike a balance that moves towards overall sustainability, then there is a chance for rapprochement between the greens and working people."[49]

It may yet be possible for conservation groups to steer southern Utahns against a proposed water pipeline from Lake Powell to St. George on the grounds that it would not only draw on a precious resource in short supply but likely welcome unwanted population growth. It may yet be possible for environmentalists and southern Utah residents to align together against defacing development projects on the grounds of harming the region's tourist industry.[50] Wilderness advocates *must* begin to legitimize the deeply held cultural connection that many locals have with the land. When southern Utahns as a whole equate the health of the land with the health of their communities and the revitalization of local culture and heritage, then they may begin to see wilderness advocates as allies instead of ideological enemies. Then they may truly be in a position to reclaim their heritage.

The redrock landscape of southeastern Utah has long been and will continue to be imagined and re-created. Throughout time humans have worked and reworked the land, attempting to shape it to suit their needs and expectations. This vision has butted heads with another human impulse—to keep nature as it is. This is an ongoing process of thinking about, working and living on, and reshaping the places we know and cherish. Landscape evokes the image of garden or yard, but making a landscape is a process of altering as well as conceptually imagining the land; it is both "comprehensive and cultural."[51]

As for the network of existing dirt trails and roads, Mormon pioneer descendants may yet be able to concur that enough now crisscross our public lands, with many accessible under federal management plans. More dirt roads are not needed, and in fact many existing roads—particularly those that no longer serve an economic function—ought to be permanently reclaimed by the land. Residents may yet recognize that permanent land-use designations ought not to be held hostage to future predictions. Wilderness may be the most divisive of all designations, but it is essential to any land-use scheme on the Colorado Plateau. In a country—a world—that is increasingly developed one acre at a time, we need these wilderness areas to keep us rooted. The plateau region is one of the few places where large tracts of wildlands yet exist.

Yet neither should we insist on a roadless landscape. The Colorado Plateau is a mix of nature *and* culture. In our modern society, it is impractical to maintain an entire region that is pristine and unpeopled. As we have seen, even wilderness areas contain traces of human markings—and this should be welcomed as we continue to deem what land-use designations are best suited. The road has its place on the landscape. The question now is which existing roads should be closed and which areas protected as wilderness from future road construction or mechanized transportation. Roads needed for fire suppression, public lands management, intercommunity travel, and a handful of other purposes may be maintained. Old uranium mining roads wandering and crisscrossing the desert—perhaps not.

The model that both sides might embrace would represent neither full-bore development nor a New West inhabited by hordes of recreationists nor a landscape devoid of the human imprint or habitation. We are in the West an eclectic mix, and we ought to create a landscape to match the culture, just as we need a society to match the scenery. Landscapes are a blending of culture, history, and nature. This layering is important. We should not fashion a landscape of stark difference: wilderness here and civilization there. We ought to protect the wilderness characteristics of the whole region while maintaining the built environment in harmony, as much as possible, with its natural surroundings. This might mean restraining suburban growth in small towns like Kanab or Moab, or scaling back or eliminating coal production. It will certainly mean finding strategies to minimize impacts on a sensitive desert environment. We can yet work for a middle way.

Somewhat ironically, the Burr Trail story suggests a possible course. Many in the environmental community once fretted that a paved Burr Trail would invite despoliation of the surrounding environment, but these fears have largely turned out to be unsubstantiated. Use of the road has certainly increased in the past two decades, but the immediate environment remains largely undamaged, and some real wilderness still exists on either side. There is evidence that the traffic, in fact, has deterred vandalism. The land's WSA status limits what is permissible on the dirt roads leading off the Burr Trail. So far the BLM has not caved in to lobbyists who would open the area to motorized vehicles. The BLM's management of the Burr Trail and surrounding environment is similar to how the NPS manages the national parks: they restrict movement and keep development principally to the roads while ensuring that the more inaccessible backcountry remains as primitive as possible.

Any land-use plan must acknowledge—and perhaps reflect—the values and traditions of the residents who make it home. Consider Hole-in-the-Rock, the road running south from Escalante to the rim of Glen Canyon and beyond into the San Juan country. Here is a road of deep cultural meaning to locals. It is a central artifact of their history and celebration of pioneer ingenuity and hard-rock perseverance. No land-use scheme would be acceptable without acknowledging its significance and permanence on the landscape. But how might we celebrate this road: by paving it, as Garfield County engineer Brian Bremner wants to do? Paving would certainly enable easy access to the notch where in 1879 Mormons and their horses and wagons made the perilous descent down the canyon's rim. But it would completely obliterate the *experience* of the Mormon trek. The rough-hewn road, still available to those adventurous enough to brave it, is the heritage. Neither paving it nor erasing it from the landscape would do.

As we conceptualize the landscape of the New West, we will be wise to contemplate the role of the road. Roads reveal a great deal about how people have built and rebuilt, adjusted and adopted, and transformed the land. They reveal how generations approached and judged the land. Roads and their absence provide a starting point for how to maintain a working landscape while protecting the character of the land that westerners cherish most. The road is not merely a symbol of progress or exploitation; it is an essential feature on the middle landscape. Roads—those intermediaries between nature and civilization—may yet help us fashion the balance we need.

Still, conflict will persist in America's most iconic and celebrated desert landscape. The competing worldviews represented by the treks of Hole-in-the-Rock pioneers and Kluckhohn—and played out by Abbey and Black—remain soundly in place. If the history of the Colorado Plateau reveals anything, it is that contesting worldviews endure. In southeastern Utah, the notion of supreme local control and sovereignty over the land derives from religiously learned and culturally inherited ideas. They do not easily evaporate. Decades of each side responding headstrong to the other have only added layers of grievance that, like sediment, have agglomerated over the years. In this history, I have attempted to peel back some of these layers, revealing, at least to a small degree, the bare rock of human perception and impulse.

No one group can claim a privileged right to the land. But proroad advocates and wilderness activists alike can legitimately claim a connection to it and its history, each free to fashion the region into their own sacred space. It is precisely this raw connection to the land that helps to explain the sense of loss for both. Environmentalists lament a single acre no longer assignable as wilderness. Grant Johnson expressed "melancholy or worse at seeing 30 years of change in the canyon country."[52] Likewise, development advocates—many with deep affection for and cultural ties to the canyon country—express similar sentiment. For them, each primitive road, each canyon or wash, each mesa top is precious and in danger of being "closed off" by environmentalists or federal land agencies. Sometimes both groups feel similarly thwarted, as when the BLM issued a five-year permit to the Red Rock 4-Wheelers, and neither was happy with it. Ber Knight of the 4-Wheelers expressed disappointment over permit modifications: "It's a game of attrition, really. Every year we lose a little more."[53]

Not surprisingly, both sides blame losses on the other. Because each may feel powerless and melancholic over changes to the landscape and trepidation over a future of increasing competition among resources, they may view themselves as victims of the other's avarice. During the past fifty years, the region has undergone a tumultuous transition from Old West to New West, escalating the power struggle. The old resource economy has been expiring while a new one is tentatively taking its place. This, coupled with a growing concern over environment and wilderness protection, has created a perfect storm. As various sides have butted heads over how to make sense of these changes, conflict has operated as the dominant paradigm.

In some cases, players displayed obstinacy beyond their own material self-interests. Commissioners bulldozed roads in symbolic protest, built roads, and prolonged lawsuits just to make a point. In the Book Cliffs, some insisted on a paved highway at an impractical, exorbitant cost through exceptionally rough terrain. In Kane County, locals claimed roads as their entitled birthright, even if the roads no longer served a useful purpose—indeed, the road's sole purpose became to show that it once had a purpose. Roads transcended their physical utility. And these environmental battles escalated, becoming more than attempts to save the land from plundering or to prevent one dirt road from being paved. They are conflicts over which vision will win out—a battle for the heart and soul of western culture.

The problem becomes that over time, these hard-line ideological positions both categorize and caricature, deepening the divisions. The story for many longtime locals morphs into claims that environmentalists are outside interests intent on "locking up" resources, when in fact many are native to the region. Environmentalists similarly misrepresent locals as simple-minded denizens concerned only with making a buck. As divisions persist and intensify, new story lines emerge that emphasize not collaboration but despair. Mormon pioneer descendants may think less of the promise of entering a new landscape—theirs by birthright through the sweat of their ancestors and theirs to domesticate as they choose—than of their frustration inhabiting a place they perceive as dominated by undue regulations. For environmentalists, the narrative is less about the discovery of a new landmark just around the canyon's bend than a landscape mucked up by cows, bulldozers, and humans.

The Abbeys and the Blacks can make the world seem black-and-white. They are easily caricatured. But in the modern West, we face shades of gray, and we confront the reality that the good guys are not always good, and the bad guys not always bad. This has always been so, but the canyon-country conflicts in the 1970s to the present seem to have identifiable foes. Edward Abbey and Calvin Black provided the ideological and philosophical underpinnings to the debates. They were social critics who articulated a particular worldview, generating interest, passion, and righteous anger. As outspoken advocates of their positions, they framed the contours of the debate, and as symbols of an ideology, they are still meaningful to people invested in the future of the West.

Although some may mourn the blurring of these categories, the black-and-white of Abbey and Black is in the narratives we tell about them. They are a narrative device. We may hold them up as timeless symbols of contradictory ways to understand progress, but they were in real life—as all of us are—complex products of culture and environment. We may reflect on these narratives that continue to play out in southeastern Utah, but we might also forge our own way—tethered as we are to our own culture, heritage, and preconceived notions of the land. There are alternative voices in the West today more attuned to specific circumstances and needs in the region that fall somewhere in the middle of the ideological spectrum.

In other words, ideologues may have their place in the West, but they do not represent the whole continuum, nor do they ultimately make the decisions, nor should we use them as role models for how to address the challenge of balanced, sustainable, responsible land management on the Colorado Plateau. Perhaps what we need now is to blur the distinction between good and bad, since those categories may have exacerbated the conflicts in the first place. The land ethic and respect for all living creatures—humans included—that is needed for the health of the land and rural communities can be achieved only when we do away with categories altogether.

Epilogue

The Old Spanish Trail predates any of the R.S. 2477 roads in Utah now in dispute. Twelve hundred miles long, the pack route linked Santa Fe, New Mexico, with San Gabriel, California, creating an important trade corridor between the far-flung outposts of the Spanish and, later, Mexican frontiers. The canyon-country portion forms an upward arc through what is now central Utah and adeptly circumvents the Colorado and San Juan River canyons.

The main route chiefly headed northwest through southwestern Colorado, entered Utah near present-day Monticello, then extended into Spanish Valley and across the Colorado River. From there it continued northwest and crossed the Green River before angling southwest down Castle Valley near the San Rafael Swell. Especially at first, the route was not clearly constructed or defined. Those traversing the path followed it in portions but abandoned it in others. It was a route dictated by nature. The trail's crossing of the Colorado River (near Moab) and the Green River (at Green River Junction) occurs at breaks in the canyon walls where the water was placid enough to cross.[1]

For two decades, thousands of Mexican traders passed through this country along the Old Spanish Trail, scuttling goods and trades—Indian women and children as slaves from Utah included—between New Mexico and California. By the late 1820s, Mexican traders had perfected a route, tracing portions of Indian trails and even following sections of Dominguez and Escalante's trail.

What resulted was a well-traversed trade route, born of an economic need—a road if not for its smoothly constructed tracks, the function it served.

Although long since abandoned for its original purpose, the trail is still visible in places where modern infrastructure has not yet obliterated its ruts. Not surprisingly, some modern transportation routes parallel the old trail's course, and in places have been overlaid on top of it. Here is a case of the organic evolution of a road from pack trail to high-speed highway.

But the old trail's durability is beginning to fade, and a race is now being run to survey and inventory what portions of it can still be traced before all vestiges are gone forever—either to the restless march of development or the gradual erosion of nature. This could happen within a generation or two if preservation efforts are not done quickly, according to archaeologists under contract with the BLM.[2] The aim is to reclaim the trail and preserve it for future generations. But this is a complex task. The trail was not indelibly imprinted on the land in the first place and never followed a clearly defined path. Nearly two hundred years have passed since the trail was in use, and the landscape has morphed over the generations. The BLM is now strapped with the task of determining the best method of preserving the Old Spanish Trail as well as teasing out its broader cultural and historical meaning for the present.

Consider other premodern roads, like those of the ancient Chacoans in the Southwest, parts of which are also still visible. These roads ostensibly connected points aligned on a meridian. Archaeologists at first supposed the roads fanned out from Chaco in New Mexico and connected to outlying communities in the Southwest. Although some scholars believe this was true of short roads, in other cases roads project out for a few kilometers and then abruptly end. These roads appeared to merely point the way to a traveler's destination but were not built the entire distance. A seeming exception is the Great North Road—which nearly links Chaco and Aztec—which was built over a long distance. Commencing at Pueblo Alto in Chaco Canyon, the road runs due north and then curves at Kutz Canyon. Beyond here the road has never been found, but some archaeologists are convinced that at one time, it extended north to Twin Angels Pueblo, northwest to Salmon, and due north, connecting to Aztec.[3]

The Chacoans knew how to lay roads in a straight line over long distances and, more remarkably, possessed the engineering capacity to construct them.

Their roads provide the shortest but—curiously—not necessarily the easiest routes to various destinations. When centuries later the Navajo built roads in the Four Corners area, for the most part they did not retrace the Chaco routes—perhaps due to this detail. Stephen Lekson asks why the Chacoans would construct wide roads over rough terrain when a simple footpath over easier terrain would likely suffice. Were the roads built with a purpose beyond utilitarian value? Undoubtedly, they were used to move goods and people, but they further appear as expressions of cultural and technological power, perhaps even cosmic value. The Great North Road indeed seemed to have "connected an old place with a new place, an *emerging* place." Aside from, or in lieu of, its usual function, the road represented a monument to an earlier age and time, what John Stein and Andrew Fowler call "time bridges, symbolic umbilicals that linked one age to another."[4]

Although the Old Spanish Trail apparently served a more utilitarian purpose than the Chacoan roads, it, too, is a time bridge of sorts. Every road is. Roads as much as any other material object reveal epochal layering. Modern roads typically have antecedents; cow trails become wagon ruts that develop into well-traveled roads and then highways. Theirs is an enduring presence on the landscape, and as such they are symbols of efficiency, technological prowess, conquest, and cultural values. That is to say, roads carry meaning beyond their utilitarian function as objects that intimately disclose the human relationship to not only land and nature but also other people.

The Old Spanish Trail is being remembered and preserved in large part because it is national, even international, in scope. In the nineteenth century, it connected the vast northern domain of Spain and, later, Mexico. What remains today navigates portions of the entire length of six states. More than any other road discussed in this book, its reach extends far beyond the Colorado Plateau. It is part of the national historic trails system, a federal program designed to protect the remains of overland trails significant to our national history.

But the act of preserving and even commemorating the Old Spanish Trail raises some intriguing questions as we consider the future of roads in dispute in the canyon country. Who determines which roads are important to preserve? How do we decide at what point to celebrate a trail or return it to its "natural" state? Put another way, what separates the line between celebrated trail and degrading highway?

In the controversies over R.S. 2477 claims and road development in the canyon country, the arguments cycle back to road definitions. This is clearly a matter of considerable debate. Many southern Utahns are inclined to call any two-track route a "road," even if it no longer serves its original purpose. The environmental community contends many routes should not be recognized and in fact should be reclaimed to the land. Federal criteria for R.S. 2477 rights-of-way are that a road must have been constructed by some means beyond the mere passage of vehicles and been in continuous use (in Utah, for ten years) prior to 1976.

Under these technical criteria, the Old Spanish Trail would not qualify at all. It was not constructed or maintained as a road. It was a track for mules, horses, and pedestrians, not wagons or wheeled vehicles like the Hole-in-the-Rock road, ephemeral prospector tracks, and some of the other local routes now claimed under R.S. 2477. And its disappearing trace suggests that it is not a permanent feature of the landscape.

In some ways, though, the Old Spanish Trail fits the definition of road better than others currently claimed under R.S. 2477. The trail had a specific purpose to convey people, goods, and commerce, and it connected two disparate points on a map. It was a transportation route. Traders did not move through the canyon country for a particular affection for redrock scenery or its potential for economic enterprise. The old trail is a physical expression—arguably the only one—of an age prior to the late nineteenth century when the canyons of the Colorado were something to avoid, a mere spot on the map that did not conform to idealized views. But traders used the trail because it afforded them passage from one place to another and benefited them economically. In that sense, it served the purpose of a road more than countless now claimed.

Preserving and commemorating the Old Spanish Trail today beg the question of whether other nineteenth-century roads ought to be similarly celebrated and restored. The answer, of course, depends on whom you ask. It might rely on the road's local, regional, or national significance or how it was used and what role it continues to serve. It would surely depend on how the road would be preserved and whether it would impinge on the wild and primitive qualities of the landscape.

The central point here is that no one is entirely consistent in their analysis of roads. Certainly, some who would advocate creating a roadless landscape and eliminating all traces of roads within proposed wilderness areas would welcome the preservation of the Old Spanish Trail. Road designations are often arbitrary. A road is a road or not depending on whose interests it serves. For some, the value of a road is its utility to move people and goods across the landscape or as an assurance of future economic development and productivity. Some base value on ease of transportation, commercial opportunity, or an ideology hinging on free and universal access or local sovereignty and tradition. The central question is not so much whether a road is a road or not as much as what benefit that road is to society at large: indeed, whether the value of the road in offering transportation, cultural renewal, and so forth outweighs its impact on the natural landscape and on human opportunities associated with wilderness.

At the beginning of the twentieth century, another old trail—the Oregon Trail—had begun to fade. In a delightful tract derived from his lecture on the advance of civilization, George Washington Martin lamented the passing of "landmarks" along the trail even as he celebrated the advance of civilization. "The twentieth century pilgrim finds a change fallen over all the scene of the old route," he noted of the Oregon Trail. Only the ruins of a few trading posts along the course remained, yet he instructed "the inquirer" to read into the natural landmarks and remaining human traces for "the stories and the history of the trails and the roads which have united and developed an empire so diversified into our one matchless country."[5]

Modern observers may or may not celebrate with Martin the creation of a continental empire, but the point that stories may be read on the landscape is well taken. Just as each generation rewrites its history, landscapes are being reimagined and re-created to suit the times. The roads chronicled in this book will be similarly reexamined, for we will continually reconsider the features we wish to preserve or ignore or perhaps even erase from the landscape. Their ultimate fate is a matter of contemplation and debate. How and where we place our roads, which ones we preserve, and which places we keep off-limits to vehicles that create roads should not be taken lightly.

Certainly, in the canyon country, it is no small matter. The road is an artifact that extends in time as well as in space. The act of commemorating, remembering, erasing, or restoring roads on the landscape is an intimate act, for each road imprinted on the landscape is a reflection of the culture and people who created and used it.

Acknowledgments

The origins of this book go back to my childhood experiences in the canyon country, and I owe a great deal to my parents who introduced me to it. Sadly, my dad, Randy Rogers, has since passed away, but my memory of the man is as solid as redrock. Kristen Rogers-Iversen remains by my side through life and all things history related, and her bright mind and support improved this manuscript greatly. I also owe a great deal to my grandparents William B. and Donna T. Smart, both writers and historians and longtime admirers and wanderers of the canyon country. Through personal association and the printed word, Bill Smart brought the land and history of that region to life for me.

Isaac and Lincoln, my two boys, grew up with this project, and they are now old enough to know something of what it means. Only my wonderful partner, Holly Rogers, can fully appreciate the road this book has taken, and she above all deserves my appreciation. She has edited and commented on my work many times over, but her greatest contribution has been her steady guiding hand and unflappable support.

To those I met and consulted fortunate to call the canyon country home, thank you for allowing me to interview you and for directing me to out-of-the-way places and records. Cal Black's widow, Carolyn, and his daughter, Merri Shumway, turned over to me historical materials in their possession. Grant Johnson offered his perspective on the Burr Trail fight. Maxine Deeter in the BLM Monticello field office and Bill Stevens in the BLM Moab office graciously opened their records to me, as did the staff of various county offices in southern and eastern Utah. I appreciate the staff and archivists at the Utah State Historical Society, Utah State Archives and Records Service, Special Collections and Archives at the University of Utah, Special Collections and Archives at Utah State University, Special Collections at the University of Arizona, Denver Public Library, and Huntington Library in Pasadena, California, for permitting me to consult their records.

I could not have traveled any of these trails without financial assistance, and I thank those institutions that provided it: the Charles Redd Center for Western Studies at Brigham Young University, Arizona State University (the Office of the Vice President for Research and Economic Affairs, the Graduate Research Support Program, and the Graduate College at Arizona State University), Arizona State University's Department of History, and the Mountain West Center for Regional Studies at Utah State University. My two employers during the period I drafted the manuscript—the US Bureau of Reclamation and Historical Research Associates—each generously provided professional support.

Paul Hirt more than any other person shaped the contours of this book, prompting many of the initial questions that framed my research agenda and helping to mold the chapters (sometimes many times over) as I completed them. I consider myself lucky to have such a generous mentor and friend. Stephen Pyne offered perceptive and useful comments throughout the writing process, redirecting me in matters of manuscript design and style. Thanks also go to Jessie Embry, Donald Fixico, Carla Homstad, Ed Iversen, Paul Nelson, and Neil Prendergast for reviewing chapters or providing research assistance.

Fred Swanson, a talented writer and editor with a deep knowledge of the redrock country, graciously read an early draft of the entire manuscript and offered perceptive and useful comments. The final product is better thanks to his kindness. Thanks, also, to E. Richard Hart and an anonymous reader for giving the manuscript a close reading and for offering insights that improved the final product.

In the world of western history publishing, John Alley has a lion's reputation, and I feel fortunate to have had him shepherd my manuscript through the publication process.

As cliché as it might be, despite all the help I have received, any errors are mine alone, and I own up to them all.

Notes

ABBREVIATIONS FOR MANUSCRIPT COLLECTIONS

GC-UT	Grand County Recorder's Office, Moab, Utah.
HC	James J. Hanks Collection, Cline Library Digital Archives, Northern Arizona University, Flagstaff.
KC-UT	Kane County Recorder's Office, Kanab, UT.
MFO-BLM	Moab Field Office, Bureau of Land Management, US Department of the Interior, Moab, UT.
MTFO-BLM	Monticello Field Office, Bureau of Land Management, US Department of the Interior, Monticello, UT.
PEA	Papers of Edward Abbey, MS 271, Special Collections, University of Arizona Library, Tucson.
PUCSC	Papers of the Utah Chapter of the Sierra Club, MSS 148, Special Collections and Archives, Merrill-Cazier Library, Utah State University, Logan.
UCTDO-UT	Uintah County Transportation District Office, Vernal, UT.
UC-UT	Uintah County Recorder's Office, Vernal, UT.
USAR.S.	Utah State Archives and Records Service, Salt Lake City.
USHS	Utah State Historical Society, Salt Lake City.
UWAC	Utah Wilderness Association Collection, MSS 200, Special Collections and Archives, Merrill-Cazier Library, Utah State University, Logan.
VFO-BLM	Vernal Field Office, Bureau of Land Management, US Department of the Interior, Vernal, UT.

WS-FCROR Wilderness Society Four Corners Regional Office Records, CONS227, Denver Public Library, Denver, CO.

WSR Wilderness Society Records, CONS130, Denver Public Library, Denver, CO.

PROLOGUE

1. I use *canyon country, plateau country, canyon lands,* and *redrock desert,* or some variation, interchangeably. Although the borders of this region are not entirely clear, they extend roughly from the Book Cliffs of the Tavaputs Plateau to the north-northeast, the mountains and high plateaus running to the west through central Utah and northern Arizona, and the Utah-Colorado border to the east. An east-west line through Lee's Ferry on the Colorado River could mark the canyon country's southern border, roughly demarcating the Glen Canyon and Grand Canyon stretches of the Colorado River. The Colorado Plateau—or Plateau Province, as John Wesley Powell called it—refers to the 140,000-square-mile region drained by the Colorado River encompassing a broad swath of land in Utah, Arizona, Colorado, and New Mexico.
2. John Wesley Powell, *Exploration of the Colorado River of the West and Its Tributaries: Explored in 1869, 1870, 1871, and 1872, under the Direction of the Secretary of the Smithsonian Institution,* 57–59, 69.
3. Edward Abbey, *Desert Solitaire: A Season in the Wilderness,* 127.
4. Charles Wilkinson, in *Fire on the Plateau: Conflict and Endurance in the American Southwest,* refers to the 1950s and 1960s on the Colorado Plateau as the Big Buildup, a period of intense and largely unrestrained development.
5. See, for example, Wallace Stegner, ed., *This Is Dinosaur: Echo Park and Its Magic Rivers;* Abbey, *Desert Solitaire;* T. H. Watkins, *Red Rock Chronicles: Saving Wild Utah;* and Terry Tempest Williams, *Red: Passion and Patience in the Desert.*
6. Mark W. T. Harvey, *A Symbol of Wilderness: Echo Park and the American Conservation Movement;* Jared Farmer, *Glen Canyon Dammed: Inventing Lake Powell and the Canyon Country;* James Lawrence Powell, *Dead Pool: Lake Powell, Global Warming, and the Future of Water in the West;* Byron E. Pearson, *Still the Wild River Runs: Congress, the Sierra Club, and the Fight to Save Grand Canyon.*
7. Section 8 of "An Act Granting the Right of Way to Ditch and Canal Owners over the Public Lands, and for Other Purposes," known as the Mining Act of 1866, 14 Stat. 251, 253.
8. Herbert E. Gregory and Raymond C. Moore, *The Kaiparowits Region: A Geographic and Geologic Reconnaissance of Parts of Utah and Arizona,* 4.
9. "R.S. 2477 Rights-of-Way Settlement Act of 1996," Statement of Senator Orrin G. Hatch before the Senate Energy and Natural Resources Committee, March 14, 1996.

CHAPTER 1. STORIES OF ORIGIN

1. This was the original directive of the San Juan Mission, or Hole-in-the-Rock expedition, as it was later called. See David E. Miller, *Hole-in-the-Rock: An Epic in the Colonization of the Great American West,* 14. I rely on Miller's account in my retelling of the Hole-in-the-Rock trek.
2. Donald Worster, *A River Running West: The Life of John Wesley Powell,* 128.
3. A number of books address the pre-nineteenth-century history of southeastern Utah. See in particular C. Gregory Crampton, *Standing Up Country: The Canyon Lands of Utah and Arizona;* Gary Topping, *Glen Canyon and the San Juan Country;* and Paul Thomas Nelson, "Utah's Canyon Country: Hope and Experience Approach an American Desert, 1500–1936."
4. William B. Smart, *Old Utah Trails,* 42–51.
5. D. Miller, *Hole-in-the-Rock,* 17–30.
6. Ibid., 34–42.
7. Wallace Stegner, *Beyond the Hundredth Meridian: John Wesley Powell and the Second Opening of the West,* 161.
8. Journal of Platte D. Lyman, November 4, 21, and 24, 1879, in *Hole-in-the-Rock,* by D. Miller, 160–61.
9. Ibid., 59.
10. Journal of Lyman, December 1, 1879, in ibid., 163.
11. Journal of Lyman, November 27, 1879, in ibid., 162.
12. Ibid., 63–66.
13. Journal of Lyman, December 17, 1879, in ibid., 164.
14. Ibid., 83–91.
15. Ibid., 96–97.
16. Ibid., 101–17.
17. L. Decker to Harrys Slideoff, February 22, 1880, in ibid., 197.
18. Journal of Lyman, February 9, 17, and 18, 1880, in ibid., 166–67.
19. Decker to Slideoff, February 22, 1880, in ibid., 197.
20. Ibid., 136–37.
21. Charles S. Peterson, *Look to the Mountains: Southeastern Utah and the La Sal National Forest,* 53.
22. "Second Annual Trip to Hole-in-the-Rock Written for the Record," *San Juan Record,* October 2, 1941.
23. Samuel Joseph Schmieding, "Visions of a Sculptured Paradise: The Colorado Plateau as American Sacred Space," 330.
24. Quoted in D. Miller, *Hole-in-the-Rock,* 140.
25. Ibid., 178.
26. Denver & Rio Grande report by B. D. Cutchlow, Preliminary survey—Farmington to Escalante, 1880–81, April 13, 1881, in Folder 11, Box 316, Geographical Section, Otis R. Marston Manuscript Collection, Huntington Library, San Marino, CA.
27. Quoted in Cornelia Perkins, Marian Nielson, and Lenora Jones, *Saga of the San Juan,* 78.

28. D. Miller, *Hole-in-the-Rock,* 138, 140.
29. Excerpts from the history of the life of James Davis, in ibid., 156.
30. Transcript of George W. Decker's speech at Hole-in-the-Rock, 1941, in ibid., 200–203.
31. I am indebted to Paul Thomas Nelson, author of "Utah's Canyon Country," for pointing out to me the possibility that Clyde Kluckhohn's travels represented an alternative to the Hole-in-the-Rock expedition. Kluckhohn first published *To the Foot of the Rainbow: A Tale of Twenty-Five Hundred Miles of Wandering on Horseback through the Southwest Enchanted Land.* His account of finally reaching the top of Wild Horse Mesa is found in *Beyond the Rainbow,* now out of print. For an overall view of Kluckhohn's work, see the posthumous volume *Culture and Behavior: The Collected Essays of Clyde Kluckhohn,* edited by his son, Richard Kluckhohn.
32. Quoted in Frederick H. Swanson, *Dave Rust: A Life in the Canyons,* 134.
33. C. Kluckhohn, *Beyond the Rainbow,* 13–14.
34. James Hanks to "Mother" [Mrs. Stanley Hanks], July 23, 1928, HC.
35. C. Kluckhohn, *Beyond the Rainbow,* 15–17.
36. Hanks to "Mother," June 22, 1928, HC.
37. C. Kluckhohn, *Beyond the Rainbow,* 14–15.
38. Aside from Clyde Kluckhohn's *Beyond the Rainbow,* information on the expedition comes from an excellent website maintained by Northern Arizona University, http://www6.nau.edu/library/sca/exhibits/hanks/index.cfm.
39. C. Kluckhohn, *Beyond the Rainbow,* 182–83.
40. Ibid., 125–32. That was the closest Kluckhohn had come to Wild Horse Mesa ("apparently so near, yet inaccessible"), boxed in by a swift river and impenetrable canyon walls. Hanks's attempt was made nearly equidistant from the Hole-in-the-Rock crossing upriver and the even earlier crossing of Francisco Atanasio Domínguez and Francisco Silvestre Veléz de Escalante at Crossing of the Fathers.
41. Hanks to "Mother," July 23, 1928, HC.
42. C. Kluckhohn, *Beyond the Rainbow,* 183–88.
43. Ibid., 188–91.
44. Ibid., 191–94.
45. John W. Van Cott, *Utah Place Names,* 211.
46. Gregory and Moore, *Kaiparowits Region,* 27, 35.
47. C. Kluckhohn, *Beyond the Rainbow,* 194–95.
48. Ibid., 204.
49. Swanson, *Dave Rust,* 171–72.
50. C. Kluckhohn, *Beyond the Rainbow,* 207–9.
51. Ibid., 268–71.
52. Ibid., 127, 270–71.
53. Quoted in Gary James Bergera, ed., *On Desert Trails with Everett Ruess,* 53. For more on Ruess's sojourns into the wild, see W. L. Rusho, *Everett Ruess: A Vagabond for Beauty.*

54. Quoted in Thomas J. Harvey, "The Storehouse of Unlived Years: Producing the Space of the Old West in Modern America," 257.
55. Ibid., 3.
56. Clyde Kluckhohn and Henry A. Murray, "The Determinants of Personality," in *Personality in Nature, Society, and Culture,* 45.

CHAPTER 2. ABBEY'S ROAD, BLACK'S HIGHWAY

1. Edward Abbey, "How It Was," in *Slickrock: Endangered Canyons of the Southwest,* photographs and commentary by Philip Hyde, 20 (emphasis added).
2. William Mulder, "The Mormons in American History," 26. Just prior to his death in June 1844, Joseph Smith had boldly articulated his religious *and* geopolitical aspirations: "I calculate to be one of the instruments of setting up the kingdom of Daniel by the word of the Lord, and I intend to lay a foundation that will revolutionize the whole world." Quoted in Joseph Smith Jr. et al., *History of the Church of Jesus Christ of Latter-day Saints: Period 1, History of Joseph Smith, the Prophet, by Himself,* 6:365.
3. Leonard Arrington, *Great Basin Kingdom: An Economic History of the Latter-day Saints,* 195–231.
4. See Peterson, *Look to the Mountains,* 92–100; Robert S. McPherson, "Monticello," in *Utah History Encyclopedia,* edited by Allan Kent Powell.
5. Schmieding, "Visions of a Sculptured Paradise," 317–18.
6. For a discussion of the agrarian myth, see Donald Worster, "The Kingdom, the Power, and the Water," in *The Wealth of Nations: Environmental History and the Ecological Imagination,* 117–22. See also Wallace Stegner, *Mormon Country,* 21–32; and Richard V. Francaviglia, *The Mormon Landscape.*
7. Peterson, *Look to the Mountains,* 47–49.
8. See ibid., 219.
9. Ibid., 46, 219–20.
10. Gary Topping, ed., "An Adventure for Adventure's Sake Recounted by Robert B. Aird," 288–89.
11. Quoted in Buckley Jensen, "Remarkable Life from Humble Start," *San Juan Record,* October 1, 2008.
12. Calvin Black, interview by Lynn Coppel, transcript; Black, interview by Milan Pavlovich and Jeffrey Jones, transcript.
13. Ted Capener, "Uranium in Them Hills!," in "The Life Story of Calvin 'F.' Black," compiled by Karl Lyman, 226; Black, interview by Pavlovich and Jones, 4, 8–10.
14. Lyman, "Life Story of Calvin 'F.' Black," 4; Black, interview by Pavlovich and Jones, 7–9.
15. See Gary Shumway, "A History of the Uranium Industry on the Colorado Plateau," 219–26; Christopher Smith, "Uranium Oxide: Yellowcake Not All It's Cooked Up to Be," *Salt Lake Tribune,* August 4, 2003; Allan Kent Powell, ed., *San*

Juan County, Utah: People, Resources, and History, 282–98; Michael Amundson, *Yellowcake Towns: Uranium Mining Communities in the American West.*

16. Black, interview by Pavlovich and Jones.
17. Capener, "Uranium in Them Hills!," in "Life Story of Calvin 'F.' Black," compiled by Lyman, 226.
18. Proceedings of dedication of Hite Road and Chaffin's Ferry at Chaffin's Ranch, Hite, UT, September 17, 1946 (hereafter cited as Hite booklet), 7, Folder 20, Box 311, Geographical Section, Otis R. Marston Manuscript Collection, Huntington Library, San Marino, CA. See also David H. Mann, "Missing (Road) Link Is Ready to Open," *Salt Lake Tribune,* September 1, 1946.
19. "Access Roads to Open Up Scenic Southeast Utah Wonderland," *San Juan Record,* May 17, 1951.
20. Utah State Road Commission, General Highway Map, San Juan County, UT, 1948, Folder 19, Box 390, Geographical Section, Marston Collection.
21. Hite booklet, 18.
22. Linda Lorraine Nash, "Transforming the Central Valley: Body, Identity, and Environment in California, 1850–1970," 192, 195.
23. See Abbey, "How It Was," in *Slickrock,* 18–31.
24. Hite booklet, 40–41.
25. James M. Cahalan, *Edward Abbey: A Life,* 24–25; Edward Abbey, *Desert Solitaire: A Season in the Wilderness,* 298; Abbey to Marian Skedgell, Managing Editor of E. P. Dutton & Co., March 10, 1970, Folder 6, Box 3, PEA.
26. Quoted in Cahalan, *Edward Abbey: A Life,* 28–29.
27. Abbey, "How It Was," in *Slickrock,* 18–31.
28. Thomas R. Dunlap, *Faith in Nature: Environmentalism as Religious Quest,* 19.
29. Virgil Hays to Abbey, November 8, 1970, Folder 6, Box 2, PEA. For more on Abbey's view of roads, see Winfred Blevins, "Mariah Interviews Edward Abbey, 'the Thoreau of the American Desert,'" 91; Abbey to Albright, March 13, 1970, Folder 6, Box 3, PEA.
30. "Access Roads to Open Up Scenic Southeast Utah Wonderland"; A. Powell, *San Juan County,* 234–35.
31. Julian D. Sears, *Geology of Comb Ridge and Vicinity North of San Juan River,* 176; A. Powell, *San Juan County,* 235–36.
32. Robert S. McPherson, *Comb Ridge and Its People: The Ethnohistory of a Rock,* 192.
33. Edward Abbey, *The Monkey Wrench Gang,* 120.
34. Dedication ceremony for the Colorado River Bridge, Dirty Devil River Bridge, White Canyon Bridge, June 3, 1966, Box 1, Series 9917, Road Commission, Department of Highways Dedication Program Booklets, USAR.S..
35. Statement of Harry Heland, from US Senate, Committee on Interior and Insular Affairs, Subcommittee on Parks and Recreation, *Canyonlands National Park and Glen Canyon National Recreational Area: Hearing, Ninety-First Congress, Second Session, on S. 26 and S. 27, May 5, 1970,* 85.
36. Frank G. Shields, BLM District Manager, Monticello, Notes, September 5, 1972; "Environmental Analysis, Bureau of Public Roads—U-6593, U-95 Atomic

Rock to White Canyon Segment," May 10, 1974; both documents on file in MTFO-BLM.

37. Sheridan Hansen, Area Manager, October 9, 1968; Thomas Moore, Chief Division Resource Management, to R/W U 6468 and U 6670, June 19, 1969, Folder "U-95, the Needle—U-261, UTU-6468"; "Comments on U-95 (White Canyon) Staff Report," June 28, 1973; "Environmental Analysis, Bureau of Public Roads—U-6593, U-95 Atomic Rock to White Canyon Segment," May 10, 1974; all documents on file in MTFO-BLM. See also Frank G. Shields, BLM District Manager, Monticello, to BLM State Director, November 3, 1972, Folder "U-95 U-6670 Federal H. A.," MTFO-BLM.
38. See "Negative Environmental Impact Declaration, U-95 White Canyon to Atomic Rock," [1973]; Frank G. Shields, BLM District Manager, Monticello, to BLM State Director, Utah, April 27, 1973, memorandum; "Analysis and Recommendations for Archeological Values—U-95," Staff Report written by Richard E. Fike, April 23, 1973, Folder "U-95 U-6670 Federal H. A."; all documents on file in MTFO-BLM. For the BLM's reaction to the damage, see Blaine J. Kay, Director, Utah State Department of Highways, to R. D. Nielson, BLM State Director, April 18, 1973; "Report of Meeting with Officials of Utah State Highway Department, University of Utah, and Bureau of Land Management in Reference to Highway U-95—May 30, 1973," written by R. D. Nielson, June 6, 1973, Folder "U-95 U-6670 Federal H. A."; both documents on file in MTFO-BLM.
39. Frank A. Ularich, Engineer, Utah State Department of Highways, Memorandum, August 14, 1973, MTFO-BLM.
40. Bob Brock, BLM, "U-95—Atomic Rock to White Canyon," Staff Report, June 27, 1973; Ularich, Memorandum, August 14, 1973; both documents on file in MTFO-BLM.
41. County Commission Minutes, November 18, 1974, Roll Accession 160296, Series 84229, San Juan County, UT, County Commission Minutes, USAR.S..
42. Abbey, *The Monkey Wrench Gang*, 77–78, 313.
43. Calvin Black, Commissioner, San Juan County Commission, to Henry C. Helland, Director, Utah State Department of Highways, [1972], MTFO-BLM. See also R. D. Nielson, State Director, BLM, to Helland, August 15, 1972, MTFO-BLM.
44. Black mentioned many of his business dealings in his journal. He bought stock and real estate in Carlsbad, New Mexico; considered buying land in California; and purchased property at Halls Crossing for a marina on the anticipated Lake Powell. He bought up additional mining claims or the interest of his partners, like Rust Black. In February 1965, he recorded "investigating the purchase of a sawmill" and a "Wax Museum." In 1966 he considered more land purchases, including land in Park City, Utah; ranches in Nevada and Loa, Utah; and a mine in Montezuma, Utah. And he discussed many other business deals. In March 1966 alone, he pondered purchasing a motel in Monticello, two motels in Blanding, and several other businesses and properties. He made an offer on a shopping center in Phoenix, leased an oil well in Tucson, and considered copper

leaching in Milford, Utah. His empire continued to grow. In 1968 he and a business partner bought Silver Saddle Café in Blanding, and he explored the possibility of a mortuary and a car dealership in Boise, Idaho. The next year he purchased the local radio station and another in Page, Arizona. To manage these holdings spread across the state, he kept a car in Salt Lake City, a truck in Kanab, a truck at Halls Crossing, and numerous vehicles and a small plane in Blanding. Excerpts from the Journals of Calvin Black, in "Life Story of Calvin 'F.' Black," compiled by Lyman, 113, 115, 116, 117, 120, 123.

45. Black to Helland, n.d., MTFO-BLM; "Life Story of Calvin 'F.' Black," compiled by Lyman, 7–8; Black, interview by Pavlovich and Jones, 57–58; Calvin Black, "History of the John Atlantic Burr."
46. Calvin Black, "Development of Halls Crossing," March 30, 1971, in "Life Story of Calvin 'F.' Black," compiled by Lyman, 97; Black, "History of the John Atlantic Burr"; "Narrative History of Halls Crossing," December 26, 1971, in "Life Story of Calvin 'F.' Black," compiled by Lyman, 105–7; Diary, in "Life Story of Calvin 'F.' Black," compiled by Lyman, 113, 115; "Interview with Son Alan Taylor (Buddy) Black," in "Life Story of Calvin 'F.' Black," compiled by Lyman, 51.
47. "Narrative History of Halls Crossing," December 26, 1971, in "Life Story of Calvin 'F.' Black," compiled by Lyman, 105–7; Black to Gerald Matthews, Utah Department of Highways, March 19, 1967, Folder 23, Box 1, Reel 1, Series 20902, Governor Rampton County Trip Records, USAR.S..
48. San Juan County to the Secretary of Commerce, n.d., Folder 3, Box 1, Reel 1, Governor Rampton County Trip Records, USAR.S.; Allan T. Howe to Black, May 24, 1971, in San Juan County Commission Minutes, June 7, 1971, San Juan County, UT, County Commission Minutes, USAR.S..
49. "Development of Halls Crossing," 98.
50. "Interview: Ken Sleight," in *Glen Canyon: A Dam, Water, and the West,* a production of KUED, http://www.kued.org/productions/glencanyon/interviews/sleight.html.
51. Cahalan, *Edward Abbey: A Life,* 108–9; Ken Sleight, interview by the author, April 20, 2009.
52. Edward Abbey, *Confessions of a Barbarian: Selections from the Journals of Edward Abbey, 1951–1989.*
53. Edward Abbey, "A Foreword to the New Ballantine Edition of *The Brave Cowboy,*" March 1970, Folder 6, Box 3, PEA.
54. Cahalan, *Edward Abbey: A Life,* 157–59.
55. Abbey, *The Monkey Wrench Gang,* 77–78.
56. Ibid., 241, 249, 250.
57. Interview with Abbey in Doug Biggers, "From Abbey's Tower," *Tucson's Mountain Newsreal,* September 1979, 6–7.
58. Abbey, *The Monkey Wrench Gang,* 225.
59. Ibid., 78–80.
60. Cahalan, *Edward Abbey: A Life,* 160–61; "U-95 Outlook Is Good," *San Juan Record,* January 29, 1976.

61. Sleight, interview by the author.
62. Carolyn Black, interview by the author, August 11, 2006.
63. Journal in "Life Story of Calvin 'F.' Black," compiled by Lyman, 119, 123.
64. See James Meadowcroft, "Green Political Perspectives at the Dawn of the Twenty-First Century," 176.
65. Ibid., 177.
66. For Joseph Smith's teachings on this subject, see *Teachings of the Prophet Joseph Smith,* 350–54.
67. On June 16, 1844, Joseph Smith declared that "every man who reigns in celestial glory is a God to his dominions. . . . They who obtain a glorious resurrection from the dead, are exalted far above principalities, powers, thrones, dominions and angels, and are expressly declared to be heirs of God and joint heirs with Jesus Christ, all having eternal power." Ibid., 374.
68. Lynn White Jr., "The Historical Roots of Our Ecological Crisis"; Roderick Nash, *Wilderness and the American Mind,* 13–20.
69. Quoted in Ken Sleight, "The Political Mark Maryboy," *Canyon Country Zephyr,* October–November 1998.
70. See Wendell Berry, *The Gift of Good Land: Further Essays Cultural and Agricultural;* Thomas G. Alexander, "Stewardship and Enterprises: The LDS Church and the Wasatch Oasis Environment, 1847–1930"; Hugh Nibley, "Brigham Young on the Environment."
71. Statement of Calvin Black, from US Senate, Committee on Interior and Insular Affairs, Subcommittee on Parks and Recreation, *Canyonlands National Park and Glen Canyon National Recreational Area,* 59, 62.
72. John Widtsoe, *Success on Irrigation Projects,* 138.
73. Stephen Trimble, *Bargaining for Eden: The Fight for the Last Open Spaces in America,* 41; see also 203–7.
74. Statement of Calvin Black, County Commissioner, San Juan County, UT, in US Senate, Committee on Interior and Insular Affairs, Subcommittee on Parks and Recreation, *Canyonlands National Park and Glen Canyon National Recreational Area,* 58.
75. Calvin Black, "San Juan County Roads and Resources," in *San Juan County,* edited by A. Powell, 244–45.
76. Christopher Smith, "Utahn's War: Let's Visit the Tomb of a Well-Known Sagebrush Soldier," *Salt Lake Tribune,* November 2, 1995.
77. Abbey, *Desert Solitaire,* 313–29.
78. Quoted in ibid., 293, 302, 334.
79. See Leo Marx, *The Machine in the Garden: Technology and the Pastoral Ideal in America.*
80. Abbey, "How It Was," in *Slickrock.*
81. John M. Morehead, National Park Service, to Rita Gordon, *American Heritage,* November 4, 1969; Abbey to Morehead, February 27, 1970; both documents in Folder 6, Box 3, PEA.
82. Quoted in Cahalan, *Edward Abbey: A Life,* 154. For a full discussion of the

contradictions and ironies in Abbey's life and work, see David Mark Pozza, "The Unity of Opposites in the Works of Edward Abbey."

83. Susan Zakin, *Coyotes and Town Dogs: Earth First! and the Environmental Movement,* 6–7.
84. Tom Austin to Edward Abbey, February 1986, Folder 4, Box 2, PEA.
85. Abbey, speech at the University of Utah, 1988, available on http://www.youtube.com; Abbey to Black, December 1, 1988, in "Life Story of Calvin 'F.' Black," compiled by Lyman.

CHAPTER 3. ROADLESS IN NEGRO BILL CANYON

1. John Riis, *Ranger Trails,* 83–84. John Riis, an employee of the US Forest Service in the early twentieth century, was son of the famous social reformer and journalist Jacob Riis.
2. Sterling C. Davis, Utah Department of Transportation, to Craig Rayle, Sierra Club, September 10, 1979, Folder 2, Box 8, UWAC; James Baker, "Winning (and Losing) the West."
3. Raymond Tibbetts, interview by the author, July 3, 2008.
4. R. Nash, *Wilderness and the American Mind,* 241–42; Wilderness Act of September 3, 1964 (PL 88-577, 78 Stat. 890).
5. In 1971 the Forest Service initiated a wilderness review of all its lands, known as the Roadless Area Review and Evaluation (RARE) study. After a court decision in the mid-1970s declared that RARE had major flaws, in 1977 the Forest Service began a second nationwide roadless review—dubbed RARE II—that recommended 15.6 million acres for wilderness, 10.6 million for further study, and release of the rest. See R. McGreggor Cawley, *Federal Land, Western Anger: The Sagebrush Rebellion and Environmental Politics,* 45; Doug Scott, *The Enduring Wilderness: Protecting Our Natural Heritage through the Wilderness Act,* 79–83.
6. The 1964 act established that existing mining claims would be recognized and that new mining claims could be filed until December 31, 1983; the president could authorize water development; and the secretary of agriculture could recognize existing grazing permits in wilderness areas. Some of the fiercest battles over wilderness designation have stemmed from these loopholes in the Wilderness Act. Among the more contentious debates were those centered around Bureau of Reclamation plans to build water developments in places like the Gila Wilderness in New Mexico, the Bob Marshall Wilderness in Montana, the Flat Top Wilderness in Colorado, and primitive areas in Idaho.
7. Quoted in Carol Edmonds, *Wayne Aspinall: Mr. Chairman,* 162.
8. James R. Skillen, *The Nation's Largest Landlord: The Bureau of Land Management in the American West;* Cawley, *Federal Land, Western Anger,* 35–36.
9. US Department of the Interior, Bureau of Land Management and Office of the Solicitor, *The Federal Land Policy and Management Act, as Amended,* 1–2.
10. US Department of the Interior, Bureau of Land Management, *Wilderness*

Inventory Handbook: Policy, Direction, Procedures, and Guidance for Conducting Wilderness Inventory of the Public Lands, 3–4. This handbook was updated in 2012 but with few changes. William Stevens, personal correspondence with the author, October 17, 2012.

11. US Department of the Interior, Bureau of Land Management, *Wilderness Inventory Handbook,* 13–14; Associate Director, BLM, to "All SD's," June 28, 1979, 6–7, Folder 5, Box 23, UWAC.
12. US Department of the Interior, Bureau of Land Management, *Wilderness Inventory Handbook,* 12–14, 27; Associate Director, BLM, to "All SD's," June 28, 1979, 4–6, 8, Folder 5, Box 23, UWAC.
13. Mark Harvey, *Wilderness Forever: Howard Zahnizer and the Path to the Wilderness Act,* 203.
14. Wilderness Act of September 3, 1964 (emphasis added).
15. Tibbetts interview.
16. See Kevin Marsh, *Drawing Lines in the Forest: Creating Wilderness Areas in the Pacific Northwest,* 71–76; John F. Tanner, Executive Director of Utah Association of Counties, to Scott M. Matheson, Governor of Utah, September 26, 1978, Folder 20, Box 4, Reel 4, Series 19269, Governor Matheson County Records, USAR.S..
17. Scott, *Enduring Wilderness,* 61.
18. House Report of the Endangered American Wilderness Bill (Report 95-540, July 27, 1977), quoted in Marsh, *Drawing Lines in the Forest,* 73, 125.
19. Wilderness Inventory, Situation Evaluation, Negro Bill Canyon, UT-060-138, MFO-BLM; Tibbetts interview.
20. Wilderness Inventory, Situation Evaluation, Negro Bill Canyon, UT-060-138B, MFO-BLM.
21. Amy Irvine, "Janet Ross: Claiming the Land on Her Own Terms," *Canyon Country Zephyr,* August–September 1999.
22. Moab District Staff Report, April 11–12, 1979, Reel 1, Series 19269, Governor Matheson County Records, USAR.S..
23. Ibid.
24. Mark Maryboy, "We Can't Drink Black Gold," speech to the Hinckley Institute of Politics, January 11, 1990, Folder 1, Box 1, Mss B 663, Mark Maryboy Papers, USHS.
25. Ed Scherick, Moab District Staff Report, May 24, 1979, Reel 1, Governor Matheson County Records, USAR.S..
26. Raymond Wheeler, "Boom! Boom! Boom! War on the Colorado Plateau," in *Reopening the Western Frontier,* edited by Ed Marston, 298. Black said something similar to Gunn McKay in Moab: "that residents are frustrated with federal agencies and are actually considering committing acts of vandalism on areas of land being considered for possible wilderness designation 'if they don't start paying attention to us.' 'People might get hurt. There's going to be a lot of vandalism.'" Letter to the editor, *San Juan Record,* April 26, 1979. In an undated

letter, Bill Haase wrote, "I was at the meeting [where Black threatened employees] so I know the threats by Black were *very* real, and not just what 'other' people were saying. Black got swept up in the emotionalism of his own rhetoric that evening. [Joseph] Bauman [of the *Deseret News*] concluded his article by saying that Black had better spread the gospel of non-violent dissent before someone gets hurt. Personally, I think Cal Black got burned over those statements. Rumor has it that Frank Gregg called some of the Utah congressional delegation and requested tham [*sic*] to put a lid on Black. This may be the case, as things have been relatively quiet down here." See Haase to Brian Beard, n.d., Folder 3, Box III.A: 12, PUCSC.

27. Dick Carter, letter to the editor, *Deseret News,* July 10, 1980; Haase to Beard, April 15, 1979, Folder 3, Box 12, Series III, PUCSC.
28. See Bernard DeVoto, "The West against Itself," 45–73, in *The Western Paradox: A Conservation Reader.*
29. Senator Orrin Hatch, *Congressional Record—Senate* (August 3, 1979): S. 11657.
30. "How about Cutting Back Utah's Biggest Landlord?," *Deseret News,* June 16, 1978.
31. Tibbetts interview.
32. D. H. Shields, letter to the editor, *Moab (UT) Times-Independent,* July 19, 1979; Margot Hornblower, "BLM Manager on Front Lines of Sagebrush Rebellion in Utah," *Los Angeles Times,* December 16, 1979.
33. Apparently, the dozer advanced up the road a mile and a half, the same distance Shumway had originally constructed it in 1978. US Department of the Interior, Interior Board of Land Appeal, "In Re: The Bureau of Land Management's Decision to Exclude Negro Bill Inventory Unit, UT-060-138 from Further Wilderness Review," IBLA 81-655, Sierra Club's Statement of Reasons, 4–5, Folder 3, Box 8, UWAC.
34. Tibbetts interview.
35. Hornblower, "BLM Manager on Front Lines of Sagebrush Rebellion in Utah"; Joseph Bauman, "BLM's Canyon Barricade Removed," *Deseret News,* August 7, 1979; Lee Holley, "U.S. Suing Grand County for Road," *Salt Lake Tribune,* August 16, 1979; "Vandalism Continues," *Moab (UT) Times-Independent,* August 30, 1979; "Pot Continues to Simmer over Disputed Road in Negro Bill Canyon," *Moab (UT) Times-Independent,* September 6, 1979; letter to Alfred Richins, Utah State Department of Transportation, September 2, 1979, Folder 2, Box 8, UWAC.
36. Helen Lacko, "The Good Ol' Boys vs. the BLM in Negro Bill Canyon," 12.
37. Beard to S. Gene Day, June 2, 1980; Rocco Dodson to Beard, June 5, 1980; both documents in Folder 3, Box 8, Series III, PUCSC.
38. "Initial Wilderness Inventory, Summary of Changes in the Situation Evaluation, Negro Bill Canyon, UT-060-138," unpublished report on file in MFO-BLM.
39. Grand County Commission Minutes, June 23, 1980, copies at GC-UT.
40. Tibbetts interview; Grand County Commission Minutes, July 1 and July 21, 1980, copies at GC-UT.

41. Joe Bauman, "250 Watch 'Rebellion' Dozer Cut BLM Land," *Deseret News*, July 5, 1980; Bill Davis, "County Action Aims to Challenge 'Organic Act,'" *Moab (UT) Times-Independent*, July 10, 1980.
42. Tibbetts interview; Jimmie Walker, interview by the author, July 2, 2008.
43. Rencher to Grand County Commissioners, July 22, 1980; Aldine J. Coffman Jr. to Rencher, July 30, 1980; both documents in Grand County Commission Minutes, August 4, 1980, copies at GC-UT.
44. Grand County Commission Minutes, August 4, 1980, copies at GC-UT.
45. Doug Goodman and Daniel McCool, eds., *Contested Landscape: The Politics of Wilderness in Utah and the West*, 44–45.
46. IBLA, Sierra Club, Statement of Reasons, 7, Folder 3, Box 8, UWAC; "BLM Settles Negro Bill Canyon Feud," *Cedar City Spectrum*, December 2, 1980; Memorandum of Understanding between Grand County and the BLM, November 24, 1980, Folder 4, Box 11, Series III, PUCSC.
47. Dave Foreman, *Confessions of an Eco-Warrior*, 16. For reference to the July 1980 Round River Rendezvous, see Cahalan, *Edward Abbey: A Life*, 192.
48. Dick Carter, "Defending the Desert," speech at the Utah Wilderness Association Annual Rendezvous, Salt Lake City, April 27, 1985, Folder 11, Box 7, UWAC.
49. IBLA, Sierra Club, Statement of Reasons, 8–9, Folder 3, Box 8, UWAC.
50. Supplemental Wilderness Inventory, UT-060-138, Negro Bill Canyon, May 4, 1982, MFO-BLM; "Final Wilderness Inventory Decision on Negro Bill Canyon," September 1, 1982, signed by state director Roland G. Robison, Series 8, Public Policy (Conservation) Department—Bureau of Land Management, WSR.
51. BLM District Manager to Katherine P. Kitchell, Slickrock Country Council, July 1982, Folder 21, Box 17, Series 8, WSR.
52. James Catlin, Conservation Chairman, Utah Chapter of the Sierra Club, to Roland Robison, Utah State Director, BLM, June 16, 1982, MFO-BLM.
53. Ibid.
54. Intervenor's Response, IBLA 83-99.
55. Quoted in "Negro Bill Battle Reheats," *Deseret News*, September 22, 1982.
56. Jim Woolf, "Negro Bill Canyon Battle Brewing Again," *Salt Lake Tribune*, June 7, 1982; Lynn Jackson, Memorandum, September 3, 1982, MFO-BLM.
57. "BLM Utah News Digest," November 5, 1982, MFO-BLM.
58. Ruling by the Interior Board of Land Appeals, IBLA 83-99, Answer of the Bureau of Land Management to Appellant's Statement of Reasons, February 10, 1983, Folder 21, Box 17, Series 8, WSR.
59. Scoping the Utah Statewide Wilderness EIS [Environmental Impact Statement]: Public Scoping Issues and Alternatives, [July 20, 1984], 27; Rock Pring to Utah BLM Wilderness Inventory Appellants, April 16, 1985, Folder 9, Box 2, UWAC.
60. Utah State Wilderness Study Report (1991), http://www.blm.gov/ut/st/en/prog/blm_special_areas/wilderness_study_areas/ut_wilderness_study.html. The present size of the Negro Bill Canyon WSA is 7,560 acres.
61. Skillen, *Nation's Largest Landlord*, 109–11.

62. Goodman and McCool, *Contested Landscape,* 41.
63. US Department of the Interior, Office of Hearings and Appeals, Interior Board of Land Appeals, "In Re: BLM Decision to Identify 7,620 Acres as a WSA in Unit UT-060-138," Statement of Reasons, IBLA 83-99, filed by Red Rock 4-Wheelers, written January 4, 1983, Folder 21, Box 17, Series 8, WSR.
64. R. Nash, *Wilderness and the American Mind,* 264.
65. George Wuerthner, "Wagon Wilderness," *Earth First!,* March 20, 1986, 21.
66. Abbey, *Desert Solitaire,* 45.
67. Wallace Stegner, "The Marks of Human Passage," in *This Is Dinosaur.*
68. Wallace Stegner's "Wilderness Letter," written to the Outdoor Recreation Resources Review Commission, December 3, 1960, http://wilderness.org/content/wilderness-letter.
69. Wallace Stegner, "The Geography of Hope."

CHAPTER 4. POSTURING ON THE BURR TRAIL

1. Kenneth Reich, "Utah Parks Expansion Infuriates Small Town," *Los Angeles Times,* November 23, 1969, copy in Folder 8, Box 316, Geographical Section, Otis R. Marston Manuscript Collection, Huntington Library, San Marino, CA.
2. Quoted in Swanson, *Dave Rust,* 167.
3. Linda King Newell and Vivian Linford Talbot, *A History of Garfield County,* 183.
4. "Current Research," *American Antiquity* 56, no. 4 (1991): 729.
5. Jack Hillers diary, June 11–18, 1872, in *"Photographed All the Best Scenery": Jack Hillers's Diary of the Powell Expeditions, 1871–1875,* 119–23. For Frederick S. Dellenbaugh's account, see his book *The Romance of the Colorado River,* 310–14.
6. John Wesley Powell, *Report on the Lands of the Arid Regions of the United States,* 6–7. See chapters by Powell, "The Lands of Utah," 93–112; Clarence Dutton, "Irrigable Lands of the Valley of the Sevier River," 128–49; and A. H. Thompson, "Irrigable Lands of That Portion of Utah Drained by the Colorado River and Its Tributaries," 150–64.
7. Hillers diary, June 9, 1872, in *"Photographed All the Best Scenery,"* 118.
8. See Newell and Talbot, *A History of Garfield County,* 181–91, 302–3.
9. Grant Johnson, personal communication to the author, July 24, 2012.
10. Lincoln Lyman, quote printed on a sign at the border of the Grand Staircase–Escalante National Monument on the Burr Trail.
11. Kenneth Creer to Scott Matheson, February 14, 1979; Garfield County Commission to Governor Matheson, March 5, 1979; both on Reel 1, Series 19269, Governor Matheson County Records, USAR.S..
12. See Utah State Department of Highways, "Access Roads for the Golden Circle: America's Newest Playground," n.d. [circa 1965], Series 21104, State Department of Highways, Tourist Access Roads Publication, USARS; Utah State Department of Highways, "Scenic Roads for the Golden Circle," Folder 17, Box 32, MSS 132, Gary Smith Papers, Special Collections and Archives, Merrill-Cazier Library, Utah State University, Logan.

13. Paul Nelson, "Not Getting Along: A Brief History of Conflict in Utah's Canyon Country."
14. See Jake Garn to Howard M. Metzenbaum, July 31, 1986, Folder 2, Box 5, Series VIII, PUCSC.
15. Iver Peterson, "Blacktop for a Desert Trail Spurs Southwest Tourism Debate," *Special to the New York Times,* n.d., Folder 13, Box 15, Series 8, Public Policy (Conservation) Department—Bureau of Land Management, WSR; "At Four Corners, 2 Views on Trail," *Milwaukee Journal,* October 21, 1983, 17.
16. See draft letter to editor, June 4, 1984, Folder 13, Box 3, Reel 6, Matheson Natural Resources Files, USAR.S.. For Matheson's aide's proposed changes to the language in the letter, see Jim Butler to Matheson, June 4, 1984, Folder 13, Box 3, Reel 6, Matheson Natural Resources Files, USAR.S..
17. In 1965 Ken Sleight, as president of the Escalante Chamber of Commerce, had endorsed a proposal for a road "across the Circle Cliffs and the Burr Trail area" as an alternative to the Trans-Escalante Highway. See Sleight to Utah governor Calvin L. Rampton, October 28, 1965; and Minutes of the Five County Organization, October 1, 1965; both in Folder 10, Box 27, Series III, PUCSC.
18. Ruth A. Frear, Chair of the Burr Trail Committee, to Senator Jake Garn, June 16, 1984, Folder 20, Box 15, Series 8, WSR.
19. Form letter to newspaper editor signed by Governor Matheson, Senator Orrin Hatch, Senator Jake Garn, Congressman James Hansen, Congressman Howard Nielson, and Congressman Dan Marriott, June 11, 1984, Folder 20, Box 15, Series 8, WSR.
20. Jim Catlin, "Paving the Burr Trail, Motives and Reasons," *Utah Sierran,* n.d., copy in Folder 9, Box 6, Series VIII, PUCSC.
21. Clive Kincaid, "My View: Preserve the Unique Character of Picturesque Burr Trail," *Deseret News,* February 14, 1986.
22. Ruth A. Frear, "The Burr Trail?," Folder 10, Box 6, Series VIII, PUCSC.
23. US Department of the Interior, Bureau of Land Management and National Park Service, *Draft Environmental Assessment on Paving Boulder-to-Bullfrog Road, Garfield County, Utah,* 13–18.
24. Burr Trail Update, Folder 13, Box 15, Series 8, WSR.
25. See Clive Kincaid to Mr. Sigma, September 16, 1985, Folder 20, Box 15, Series 8; Terry [Sopher] to Chuck [Clusen], Memorandum, November 13, 1985, Folder 13, Box 15, Series 8; both in WSR.
26. "Paving to Begin in Spring on 27 Miles of Burr Trail," *Deseret News,* January 24, 1987, B2; Katie Thomas, "Official Defends Plan to Pave Burr Trail," *Salt Lake Tribune,* January 29, 1987, A12; Wayne Petty and Lori Potter to Roland Robison, February 9, 1987, Folder 2, Box 16, Series 8, WSR.
27. *Sierra Club, National Parks and Conservation Association, Southern Utah Wilderness Alliance, Wilderness Society, Plaintiffs v. Donald P. Hodel, U.S. Department of the Interior, Bureau of Land Management, Garfield County, Harper Excavating, Inc., Defendants,* Complaint, Folder 5, Box VIII.A: 5: Burr Trail, PUCSC; Darrell Knuffke to George Frampton, Peter Coppelman, Chuck Clusen, John McComb,

and Terry Sopher, February 9, 1987, Folder 2, Box 16, WSR; Plaintiffs' Brief in Support of Their Motion for Preliminary Injunction or Temporary Restraining Order, Folder 2, Box 16, Series 8, WSR; Joseph Bauman, "Groups Sue to Block Burr Trail Road Work," *Deseret News,* February 18–19, 1987, B9.

28. William J. Lockhart, Attorney for SUWA, to Robison, April 14, 1984; Robison to Lockhart, May 16, 1984, both in Folder 2, Box 5, Series VIII, PUCSC; Petty to Harper Excavating, February 12, 1987; Plaintiffs' Brief in Support of Their Motion for Preliminary Injunction or Temporary Restraining Order, Folder 2, Box 16, Series 8, WSR; Roland G. Robison to Wayne G. Petty, February 13, 1987, Folder 5, Box VIII.A: 5: Burr Trail, PUCSC.
29. Margie Spence, Statement under Oath in Re: Boulder-Bullfrog Road, Reported by Paul G. McMullin of St. George, February 21, 1987, 1, 4–5, 10–11; Thomas Hatch, Statement under Oath in Re: Boulder-Bullfrog Road, February 21, 1987, 13, both in Special Collections, J. Willard Marriott Library, University of Utah, Salt Lake City; Joseph Bauman, "Teacher Testifies about Terrors of Commuting on the Burr Trail," *Deseret News,* February 26–27, 1987, 6B. Spence probably exaggerated her experience on the Burr Trail. Grant Johnson, who has lived on that road since 1975, claims she actually traveled through Wayne County. Johnson, personal communication to the author, July 20, 2012.
30. John Williams, Statement under Oath in Re: Boulder-Bullfrog Road, February 21, 1987, Special Collections, J. Willard Marriott Library, University of Utah, Salt Lake City.
31. Rodd G. Wagner, "Judge Delays Burr Trail, Calls for Further Study," *Salt Lake Tribune,* March 11, 1987, B1; "'Pave Burr Trail,' 7 of 8 Speakers Say," *Deseret News,* January 5, 1988.
32. Rodd G. Wagner, "Judge Gives Go-Ahead to Burr Trail Improvements," *Salt Lake Tribune,* December 1, 1987; Joseph Bauman, "Burr Trail Suspect Vows to Fight," *Deseret News,* December 19, 1987.
33. *SUWA Bulletin,* no. 3 (December 22, 1987), Folder 6, Box 5, Series VIII, PUCSC; Bauman, "Burr Trail Suspect Vows to Fight."
34. Joseph Bauman, "Naturalists Deny Responsibility for Cartoon," *Deseret News,* February 27, 1987; Patrick B. Nolan to Petty, February 17, 1987, Folder 2, Box 16, Series 8, WSR; Petty to Nolan, February 26, 1987, Folder 2, Box 16, Series 8, WSR.
35. Biographical information on Johnson comes from Iver Peterson, "Blacktop for a Desert Trail Spurs Southwest Tourism Debate," *Special to the New York Times,* n.d., in Folder 13, Box 15, Series 8, WSR; and Grant Johnson, interview by the author, April 22, 2009.
36. Bauman, "Burr Trail Suspect Vows to Fight"; Johnson interview. For the resolution of the case, see Katie Thomas, "Suspect in Burr Trail Vandalism Admits to Two Drug Charges," *Salt Lake Tribune,* October 18, 1990.
37. Johnson, personal communication to the author, July 24, 2012.
38. Bauman, "Burr Trail Suspect Vows to Fight"; Johnson interview; Larry Davis, conversation with the author, Boulder, UT, October 26, 2008.

39. Johnson interview; "Charges Dismissed in Burr Vandalism," *Deseret News,* December 22, 1988; Knuffke to George Frampton, Syd Butler, and Ron Tipton, September 29, 1988, Folder 34, Box 11, Series 10, WSR; *SUWA Bulletin,* no. 3 December 22, 1987, Folder 6, Box 5, Series VIII, PUCSC.
40. Edward Abbey, speech at the University of Utah, 1988, available on http://www.youtube.com
41. See Doug Scott, Conservation Leader of the Sierra Club, to Chuck Clusen, John McComb, Terry Sopher, Debbie Sease, Darrell Knuffke, and Maggie Fox, February 12, 1986, Folder 3, Box 17, Series 8, WSR.
42. Terry to Chuck [Clusen], November 13, 1985, Memorandum, Folder 13, Box 15, Series 8, WSR; Terri Martin to Maggie Fox, Darrell Knuffke, Clive Kincaid, Bill Lienisch, and Fred Swanson, January 21, 1986, Folder 2, Box 5, Series VIII, PUCSC.
43. Edward Abbey, "Statement for Glen Canyon National Recreation Area Hearing, Kanab, Utah, May 15, 1975," Folder 6, Box 7, PEA.
44. For a discussion of Earth First! monkey-wrenching activities, see Zakin, *Coyotes and Town Dogs;* and Derek Wall, *Earth First! and the Anti-roads Movement: Radical Environmentalism and Comparative Social Movements.* In Utah incidences of sabotage reportedly spiked; Sheriff Rigby Wright of San Juan County investigated fifty-plus cases of sabotage to machinery in five years, although few of these cases could be solved. Law enforcement and authorities sometimes kept instances of sabotage quiet to avoid inspiring more attacks. See "Lobbying Forsaken for 'Ecotage,'" *Rocky Mountain News,* October 17, 1982, 14.
45. George Wuerthner, "Wilderness: A Bioregional Approach," *Earth First!,* December 21, 1985, 23; "Earth First! Proposes 16 Million Acres of Wilderness for Utah BLM," *Earth First!,* May 1, 1986, 1.
46. Head of Joaquin, "Sleaze from the Slickrock," *Earth First!,* December 21, 1985, 26. See also Leslie Lyon, "Lessons from the Utah Wilderness Battle," *Earth First!,* May 1, 1991, 14.
47. Grant Johnson, "A Personal Early SUWA History," http://www.canyoncountryzephyr.com/oldzephyr/aug-sept2005/feedback.html. Although critical of the Forest Service wilderness bill of 1984, Johnson gives Carter a lot of credit for the conservation works he has done in Utah. "Dick Carter was among the most important early wilderness advocates because he spent a lot of time educating the public and softening up Utahns to the issue of wilderness and he should go down in history as such. I hold him in high regards for that." Johnson, personal communication to the author, July 24, 2012.
48. "Garn Assails Wild Proposal," *Deseret News,* October 14, 1988. For Earth First!'s wilderness proposal, see "Earth First! Proposes 16 Million Acres of Wilderness for Utah BLM," 1, 4. The Utah Chapter of the Sierra Club and the Wilderness Society were the other coordinators of the Utah Wilderness Coalition.
49. "The Burr Trail," January 10, 1985, Folder 10, Box 6, Series VIII, PUCSC.
50. Dick Carter to Terri Martin, May 29, 1985, Folder 8, Box 1, UWAC.

51. Doug Scott to Chuck Clusen, John McComb, Terry Sopher, Debbie Sease, Darrell Knuffke, and Maggie Fox, February 12, 1986, Folder 3, Box 17, Series 8, WSR.
52. Lawson LeGate to Dick Carter, [1988]; handwritten notes, n.d. (circa October–November 1988); both in Folder 20, Box 15, Series 8, WSR.
53. Handwritten notes, n.d. (circa October–November 1988); Confidential Internal Memo: Burr Trail Opening Positions, October 30, 1988; both in Folder 20, Box 15, Series 8, WSR. See also Mike Medberry to Peter Coppelman, Syd Butler, and Ron Tipton, June 8, 1988, Folder 20, Box 15, Series 8, WSR.
54. Handwritten notes, n.d. (circa October–November 1988); Confidential Internal Memo: Burr Trail Opening Positions, October 30, 1988, Folder 20, Box 15, Series 8, WSR.
55. Brant [Calkin] to Lawson, Terry, Mike, Darrell, Wayne, SUWA Board, and others, December 14, 1988, Folder 20, Box 15, Series 8, WSR. For information on Calkin's background, see Scott Groene, "Brant Calkin," *Canyon Country Zephyr,* August–September 1999, 16.
56. Brant to Lawson, et al., December 14, 1988, Folder 20, Box 15, Series 8, WSR.
57. "Unnecessary Legislative Haste on Latest Burr Trail Paving," *Salt Lake Tribune,* October 8, 1988, A10; Wayne Petty to Ronald Thompson, November 18, 1988, Folder 20, Box 15, Series 8, WSR; Mike Medberry to George Frampton et al., December 4, 1988, Folder 20, Box 15, Series 8, WSR.
58. Wayne Petty to Ronald Thompson, November 30, 1988; Aldon J. Anderson (judge), December 2, 1988, Order Partially Dissolving Injunction, Civil No. 87C-0120A, in the US Court for the District of Utah, Central Division, *Sierra Club et al. v. Donald P. Hodel et al.;* Petty to S[ierra] C[lub], N[ational] P[arks] C[onservation] A[ssociation], SUWA, W[ilderness] S[ociety], December 5, 1988; all in Folder 20, Box 15, Series 8, WSR. See also Rodd G. Wagner, "Judge Scolds County for Rushing Burr Trail Work," *Salt Lake Tribune,* December 12, 1987.
59. "Garfield Gets OK to Use Nearby Gravel on Burr Trail," *Salt Lake Tribune,* August 12, 1989.
60. Wayne Petty to Sierra Club et al., March 27, 1989, Folder 20, Box 15, Series 8, WSR; Louise Liston, Garfield County Commissioner, to Paul Young, March 25, 1991, Folder 5, Box 6, Series VIII, PUCSC.
61. Louise Liston to Paul Young, March 25, 1991, Folder 5, Box 6, Series VIII, PUCSC. See also "Notes on a KUED Live Production in Escalante," March 1, 1988, Folder 13, Box 1, UWAC.
62. Memorandum from Secretary of the Interior Donald Hodel to Assistant Secretaries, Subject: Departmental Policy on Section 8 of the Act of July 26, 1866, Revised Statute 2477 (Repealed), Grant of Right-of-Way for Public Highways (R.S.-2477).
63. Wendell Chappell, Wayne County Roads Commission, to Kay Erickson, BLM, August 26, 1991; Brian Bremner to Kay Erickson, September 26, 1991; Bill Lockhart to Stan Sloss, October 29, 1991; all in Folder 10, Box 30, Series III, PUCSC.
64. See Ronald W. Thompson, Attorney for Thompson, Hughes & Reber, to

Wayne G. Petty, Attorney for Moyle & Draper, January 7, 1991, Folder 9, Box 6, Series VIII, PUCSC; letter to Charles Lundy, January 28, 1991, Folder 7, Box 5, Series VIII, PUCSC.

65. Hillary M. Hoffmann, "Signs, Signs, Everywhere Signs: *The Wilderness Society v. Kane County* Leaves Everyone Confused about Navigating a Right-of-Way Claim under Revised Statute 2477," 12.
66. Quoted in Elizabeth Manning, "Utah's Burr Trail Still Leads to Court," *High Country News,* 1994. See also Joe Costanzo, "Federal Judge Rejects Burr Trail Right of Way," *Deseret News,* April 30, 1998, B2; Elizabeth G. Daerr, "Court Rules for NPS at Burr Trail," *NPCA Park News* (January–February 2001): 19–20.
67. Quoted in Reich, "Utah Parks Expansion Infuriates Small Town."
68. See handwritten notes "Trials of the Burr Trail," n.d., Folder 9, Box 1, UWAC.
69. Ibid.
70. Elaine Roundy, conversation with the author, October 27, 2008.
71. Davis conversation; LeFevre quote in Matthew Brown, "A Town in Turmoil," *Salt Lake Tribune,* September 3, 1996.
72. Russ Henrie, letter to the editor, "Forget Paving," *Garfield County News* (Panguitch, Utah), June 28, 1984.
73. Johnson, personal communication to the author, July 20, 2012. On how westerners have grappled with the issue of boosterism and tourism, see Hal K. Rothman, *Devil's Bargains: Tourism in the Twentieth-Century American West.*

CHAPTER 5. ABUNDANCE AND SCARCITY IN THE BOOK CLIFFS

1. *Deseret News,* September 25 and 28, 1861, quoted in Jedediah S. Rogers, "One Vast 'Contiguity of Waste': Documents from an Early Attempt to Expand the Mormon Kingdom into the Uinta Basin, 1861," 250.
2. Quoted in Smart, *Old Utah Trails,* 54.
3. Mike Milligan, *Westwater Lost and Found,* 17–19. Milligan evaluates Marston's claim on 19–22.
4. "Road Creates Misconceptions," *Vernal Express,* November 20, 1991.
5. US Department of the Interior, Bureau of Land Management, *Utah: Westwater,* BLM Edition, Surface Management Status, 1993; US Department of the Interior, Bureau of Land Management, *Utah: Seep Ridge,* BLM Edition, Surface Management Status, 1999.
6. See "Green River Basin Oil Shale Formation—Oil Field," http://oilshalegas.com/greenriveroilshale.html.
7. Howard G. Wilshire, Jane E. Nielson, and Richard W. Hazlett, *The American West at Risk: Science, Myth, and Politics of Land Abuse and Recovery,* 317–18.
8. Appendix B: Tar Sands Development Background and Technology Overview, B-16, http://ostseis.anl.gov/documents/fpeis/vol3/OSTS_FPEIS_vol3_App_B.pdf.
9. See US Department of the Interior, Bureau of Land Management, Moab and Vernal Districts, Utah, *Draft EIS Ouray to Interstate 70 Highway,* 3-39–3-45,

MFO-BLM; "Highway Funding Possible with Mineral Development," *Vernal Express,* November 20, 1991. For statistics on global oil and natural gas reserves, see "World Proved Reserves of Oil and Natural Gas, Most Recent Estimates," http://www.eia.doe.gov/international/reserves.html.

10. Uintah County Commission Minutes, June 17, 1985, UC-UT. See also John Maynard, "Counties Working Together on Road over the Book Cliffs," *Moab (UT) Times-Independent,* February 23, 1989.
11. Raymond Tibbetts, interview by the author, July 3, 2008.
12. Jim Stiles, "The Book Cliffs Highway: Half a Million Dollars and Still Flushing," *Catalyst* (November 1992): 10–11.
13. Jimmie Walker, interview by the author, July 2, 2008.
14. Uintah Special Service District, news release, August 14, 1989, UCTDO-UT.
15. Jim Stiles, "Twenty Years of the Zephyr," *Canyon Country Zephyr,* February–March 2009; "A Candid Conversation with Commissioner David Knutson," *Canyon Country Zephyr,* September 1989, 6.
16. See Stiles, "Book Cliffs Highway," 12.
17. Quoted in Steve Howe, "Big Times for the Book Cliffs," *Sports Guide* (October 1992): 26, Folder 9, Box 4, PUCSC; Janet Lunt, "BLM Waiting for EIS on Ouray to Cisco Highway," *Uintah Basin Standard,* February 5, 1992. See also Uintah Special Service District, Minutes, December 19, 1989, UCTDO-UT; Minutes of the Regular Public Meeting of the Uintah County Commission, February 21, 1989, UC-UT.
18. Uintah Special Service District, Public Meeting, May 17, 31, and September 26, 1989, UCTDO-UT.
19. Uintah Special Service District, Minutes, April 10, 1989; Uintah Special Service District, Joint Meeting, Minutes, April 12, 1989; Uintah Special Service District, Minutes, May 17, 1989; Uintah Special Service District, Minutes, September 21, 1989; all on file in UCTDO-UT.
20. Vicki J. Barker, "In-Depth EIS Recommended on Book Cliffs Proposal," *Deseret News,* July 29, 1989; Uintah Special Service District, Minutes, December 11, 1989; Uintah Special Service District, news release, December 19, 1989; both on file in UCTDO-UT. Concerned that a less comprehensive environmental assessment would not stand up in court considering the extraordinary level of environmental impacts, county officials worked out an agreement with BLM manager Gene Nodine for the preparation of an EIS before construction contracts would be awarded. The BLM and county road districts signed a memorandum of understanding (MOU) outlining the BLM's responsibility for the EIS and the districts' responsibility to fund it.
21. US Department of the Interior, Bureau of Land Management, *Wilderness Inventory, State of Utah,* April 1979; US Department of the Interior, Bureau of Land Management, *Utah BLM Intensive Wilderness Inventory, Wilderness Study Areas,* November 1980, MFO-BLM.
22. For a map of the BLM wilderness proposal, see http://www.suwa.org/site/PageServer?pagename=ARRWAclickablemap.
23. Utah Wilderness Association, "Utah Wilderness Association Files Suit against

BLM for Road Building in Book Cliffs Wilderness Inventory Units," Folder 9, Box 2, UWAC.

24. US Department of the Interior, Bureau of Land Management, *Management Situation Analysis for the Grand Resource Area Resource Management Plan/Environmental Impact Statement, Moab District, Utah, Grand Resource Area,* 4-9, 4-10, Box III.A: 2, PUCSC. The RMP acknowledged the threat of motorized use and energy development: "Changes in the nature and extent of vehicle use in the Book Cliffs could result in serious damage to the fragile watershed, wildlife and wilderness values. It is possible that recreational vehicle use will increase over the next several years as oil and gas exploration activity introduces more people to the area and results in the building of new roads. Hence, it is important that the BLM monitor the Book Cliffs area."
25. Statement of Debbie Sease, Washington Representative for the Sierra Club, Regarding the Reauthorization of the BLM before the House Interior Subcommittee on National Parks and Public Lands, Honorable Bruce Vento, Chairman, April 11, 1989, Folder 12, Box III.A:5, PUCSC.
26. US Department of the Interior, Bureau of Land Management, Moab and Vernal Districts, Utah, *Draft EIS Ouray to Interstate 70 Highway,* 3–19, MFO-BLM; Bison Herd Unit Management Plan, Book Cliffs, Bitter Creek and Little Creek, Herd Unit #10A and #10C, Wildlife Board Approval, November 29, 2007, http://wildlife.utah.gov/hunting/biggame/pdf/bison_10.pdf.
27. Minutes of the Regular Public Meeting of the Uintah County Commission, September 8, 1987, UC-UT.
28. Uintah Special Service District, Minutes, December 19, 1989, UCTDO-UT.
29. Grand County Roads Special Service District No. 1, Minutes, July 18, 1992, GC-UT. See also "Michelle Nijhuis, "Oil Clashes with Elk in the Book Cliffs," *High Country News,* April 13, 1998.
30. S.B. 114, *An Act Relating to the Division of Wildlife Resources; Providing for a $2,000,000 Appropriation to the Division of Wildlife Resources to Purchase the S & H Book Cliffs Ranch for the Book Cliffs Conservation Initiative; Providing for Administration of the Land; and Providing an Effective Date,* February 13, 1992, Folder 6, Box 2, UWAC.
31. See "BLM Approves Road Survey in Wilderness Study Area," *Vernal Express,* October 2, 1991; Paul M. Andrews, Area Manager, BLM, to Tom Wardell, Uintah Service Special District, October 29, 1991, Folder 6, Box 4, PUCSC; "Wilderness Groups Protest Seep Ridge Road," *Vernal Express,* November 6, 1991; "Seep Ridge Road Project Creates Concerns for Environmental Special-Interest Groups," *Uintah Basin Standard* (Roosevelt, UT), November 27, 1991; Utah Chapter Sierra Club and Utah Wildlife Leadership Coalition, IBLA 92-77, Utah EA-1991-19, Proposed Ouray to Cisco Highway, Order, January 7, 1992, Folder 9, Box 4, PUCSC; Sierra Club Utah Chapter Issue Alert, Book Cliffs Highway Hearings Upcoming in Salt Lake, Vernal, and Moab, n.d., Folder 6, Box 4, PUCSC.
32. Mark MacAllister, "Orton Paves the Way for Book Cliffs Highway," *Utah Sierran* 24, no. 12 (1991): 1–2.

33. See pamphlet in Folder 1, Box 12, UWAC.
34. Glenn Anderson, letter to the editor, *Vernal Express,* December 11, 1991.
35. Gary Martin, letter to the editor, *Vernal Express,* December 11, 1991.
36. Will Durrant, letter to the editor, *Vernal Express,* November 27, 1991.
37. Proposed Ouray to Cisco Highway, Scoping for Draft Environmental Impact Statement (DEIS), Public Comment Analysis, n.d., Folder 1, Box 27, Series III, PUCSC.
38. Grand County Roads Special Service District No. 1, Minutes, May 16, 1992, GC-UT.
39. Grand County Roads Special Service District No. 1, Minutes, August 15, 1992, GC-UT.
40. See "Chamber Backs Highway through Book Cliffs Area," *Vernal Express,* June 3, 1992; Aldon Rachele, "Roosevelt, Vernal Mayors Give Pros and Cons to Road," *Basin Life,* November 17, 1992; Stiles, "Book Cliffs Highway," 12.
41. *Draft EIS Ouray to Interstate 70 Highway,* 2–4, MFO-BLM.
42. Assistant Field Supervisor, US Fish and Wildlife Service, to Moab District Manager, BLM, January 9, 1992, in *Draft EIS Ouray to Interstate 70 Highway,* C-6, MFO-BLM; Grand County Roads Special Service District No. 1, Minutes, July 18, 1992, GC-UT; Jerry McNeil, interview by the author, October 28, 2008.
43. Mark MacAllister, "Book Cliff's Update," *Utah Sierran,* December 1992–January 1993; Public Hearing on Book Cliffs Highway DEIS, Salt Lake City, November 4, 1992, Folder 1, Box 12, UWAC. See also Grand County Roads Special Service District No. 1, Minutes, September 19 and November 21, 1992, GC-UT.
44. William R. Russell to Daryl Trotter, BLM, November 18, 1992, Folder 1, Box 12, UWAC.
45. George Nickas, Assistant Coordinator, UWA, to Daryl Trotter, BLM, December 8, 1992, Folder 1, Box 12, UWAC. For even stronger language, see the draft letter in Folder 1, Box 12, UWAC.
46. Jim Stiles dedicated a full issue of the October 1992 *Canyon Country Zephyr* to the issue, which reflected the concerns of many locals.
47. William Riebsame, ed., *Atlas of the New West: Portrait of a Changing Region,* 55.
48. Charles Wilkinson, "Paradise Revised," in ibid., 17–18, 22. See also William R. Travis, *New Geographies of the American West: Land Use and the Changing Patterns of Place.*
49. Charlie Peterson, Chairman of the Grand County Council, to Roger Zortman, BLM Moab District Manager, May 14, 1993, VFO-BLM.
50. See Zortman to Wardell, May 20, 1993, VFO-BLM.
51. Layne Miller, "Residents Debate Merits of Book Cliffs Road," *Sun Advocate,* December 17, 1992, in Folder 1, Box 12, UWAC; Walker interview.
52. Tibbetts interview.
53. John F. Wilson to Daryl Trotter, November 28, 1992, Folder 1, Box 12, UWAC.
54. Letter from Stephen Lewis, November 4, 1992, Folder 1, Box 12, UWAC.

55. William B. Smart, *Mormonism's Last Colonizer: The Life and Times of William H. Smart*, 303–4.
56. Utah Governor's Office, *The Structure and Economic Impact of Utah's Oil and Gas Exploration and Production Industry, Phase I—the Uinta Basin*, Prepared by Bureau of Economic and Business Research, October 2007, 1–3.

CHAPTER 6. HERITAGE ON THE GRAND STAIRCASE-ESCALANTE

1. Pahreah is one of several abandoned pioneer-era sites in what is now the Grand Staircase–Escalante National Monument. Another is Adairville, situated downstream on the Paria River in the Rimrocks area. The newly restored Watson cabin in Hackberry Canyon, a tributary of Cottonwood Wash, was home to a man from Wisconsin who tried unsuccessfully to wash gold dust out of the Chinle Shale Formation. See "Watson Cabin . . . Preserving the Past," *Grand Staircase–Escalante Partners News* (Summer–Fall 2012): 1–2.
2. The controversies surrounding the monument's creation and management have been well covered in newspaper articles, magazines, journals, and books. For book-length treatments, see Robert B. Keiter, Sarah B. George, and Joro Walker, eds., *Visions of the Grand Staircase–Escalante: Examining Utah's Newest National Monument;* Paul Larmer, ed., *Give and Take: How the Clinton Administration's Public Lands Offensive Transformed the American West;* and Sarah Fleisher Trainor, "Conflicting Values, Contested Terrain: Mormon, Paiute, and Wilderness Advocate Values of the Grand Staircase–Escalante National Monument (Utah)."
3. Steven H. Heath, "A Historical Sketch of the Scientific Exploration of the Region Containing the GSENM," in *Learning from the Land: GSENM Science Symposium Proceedings*, 439–41, 444.
4. Wilkinson, *Fire on the Plateau*, 232–33; "Coal Mining vs. Wilderness on the Kaiparowits Plateau," in *Canyons, Cultures, and Environmental Change: An Introduction to the Land-Use History of the Colorado Plateau*, edited by John D. Grahame and Thomas D. Sisk.
5. William Least Heat-Moon, *Blue Highways: A Journey into America*, 178.
6. Office of Energy and Resource Planning, "Summary of the Coal Resources of Kaiparowits Plateau and Its Value," October 9, 1996, http://geology.utah.gov/online/c/c-93/gsekcoal.htm. The World Energy Council estimates that some 850 billion tons of recoverable coal are available worldwide. See "Survey of Energy Resources 2007," http://www.worldenergy.org/publications/survey_of_energy_resources_2007/coal/627.asp.
7. See Kane County response to environmental assessment of the Gulf Mineral Resource Company's Proposed Uranium Drilling Project, October 19, 1981, Folder 24, Box 6, Reel 13, Series 19161, Governor Matheson Natural Resources Working Files, USAR.S..
8. Dixie Brunner, "Kane County—a National Monument?," *Southern Utah News*,

September 11, 1996; Western States Coalition, "Federal Government Land-Grab: First Utah, Then ?????," n.d., File UT: Andalex Mine, Box 26, WS-FCROR.

9. Dixie Brunner, "SUWA Objects to Andalex Mine Permit Application," *Southern Utah News,* October 5, 1994; SUWA, "Smoky Hollow Mine Proposal," n.d., File UT:BLM:GSENM:TWS Proposal, Box 26, WS-FCROR.
10. Brunner, "SUWA Objects to Andalex Mine Permit Application." For more on the proposed Andalex mine, see Marta Murvosh, "Funding Sought to Plan Southern Corridor," *Spectrum,* November 14, 1995; Phillip Bimstein to Bill Clinton, September 16, 1996, File UT: Andalex Mine, Box 26, WS-FCROR; Wilkinson, *Fire on the Plateau,* 326–27.
11. Kane County Commission to Mike Noel, BLM, January 22, 1996, File UT: Andalex Mine, Box 26, WS-FCROR.
12. See Elmo R. Richardson, "Federal Park Policy in Utah: The Escalante National Monument Controversy of 1935–1940." For the Freeman quote, see Swanson, *Dave Rust,* 260.
13. See documents in Box 7, Series: Cedar City District, RG: BLM, MSS 200, UWAC.
14. "Canyons of the Escalante, a National Ecoregion," Staff Conceptual Paper for Discussion Only, July 22, 1994, Folder 2, Box 5, Series 25985, USAR.S..
15. Brad T. Barber to Citizens Interested in Canyons of the Escalante, November 9, 1994; Escalante Community Workshop Comments, Boulder, UT, September 20, 1994; Dick Carter to Brad Barber, September 5, 1994; Thomas C. Jensen to Michael O. Leavitt, Governor of Utah, October 21, 1994; Terri Martin to Leavitt, October 18, 1994; all in Folder 2, Box 7, UWAC.
16. See hand- and typewritten notes, January 22, 1996, File UT: Andalex Mine, Box 26, WS-FCROR.
17. William B. Smart, "Stewardship of the Earth."
18. Bill Clinton, *My Life,* 727–28.
19. Quoted in Skillen, *Nation's Largest Landlord,* 152. See Proclamation No. 6920, 3 C.F.R § 64 (2008).
20. Dixie Brunner, "President Inks National Monument," *Southern Utah News,* September 25, 1996; Carol Sullivan, "Former Commissioner Esplin Thinks Rait Is in the SUWA," *Southern Utah News,* September 25, 1996; Gerald Berry, "Letter to Pres. Clinton," *Southern Utah News,* September 25, 1996.
21. "Dixie Speaks," editorial, *Southern Utah News,* September 11, 1996.
22. Kane County Commission Minutes, April 23, 1996, originals on file in KC-UT.
23. Carol Sullivan, "Local Reps Arrive from Washington, DC, in Time for Press Conference," *Southern Utah News,* September 25, 1996. See also Dixie Brunner and Carol Sullivan, "Commission Gets Public Reaction to National Monument Designation," *Southern Utah News,* September 18, 1996; and Kane County Commission Minutes, October 11, 1996, originals on file in KC-UT.
24. Larry Warren, "UT Counties Bulldoze the BLM, Park Service," *High Country News,* October 28, 1996.
25. See Alex Levinson and Jessica Woodhouse to Phil Berry et al., October 25, 1996, Folder 7, Box 4, PUCSC.

26. Susan Sweigert, "Garfield County's Revenge," *Catalyst,* December 1996, n.p.; Levinson and Woodhouse to Berry et al., October 25, 1996; both documents in Folder 7, Box 4, PUCSC. See also Susan Sweigert, "On the 'Road' in Southern Utah," *Catalyst,* April 1997, 16–17; Cheryl Fox, "'Road Warriors' Spread Out over Utah," *High Country News,* August 4, 1997.
27. US Government Accountability Office, "Recognition of R.S. 2477 Rights-of-Way under the Department of the Interior's FLPMA Disclaimer Rules and Its Memorandum of Understanding with the State of Utah"; "Background on R.S. 2477," Folder 7, Box 4, PUCSC. See US Department of the Interior, *Report to Congress on R.S. 2477: The History and Management of R.S. 2477 Right-of-Way Claims on Federal and Other Lands,* 25–26; "Revised Statute 2477 Rights-of-Way," 59 Fed. Reg. (August 1, 1994) 39216.
28. Letter to the editor, *Southern Utah News,* September 18, 1996. For SUWA's reaction to an NPS-managed monument, see SUWA Staff to SUWA Members, n.d., File UT: BLM/wilderness/GSENM?clips, Box 26, WS-FCROR.
29. Clinton went on to establish fourteen other monuments in seven western states to be managed by the BLM, touching off a new era in federal land management. See Mark Squillace, "The Antiquities Act and the Exercise of Presidential Power: The Clinton Years," in *The Antiquities Act: A Century of American Archaeology, Historic Preservation, and Nature Conservation,* edited by David Harmon, Francis P. McManamon, and Dwight T. Pitcaithley; Skillen, *Nation's Largest Landlord,* 211.
30. Valerie P. Cohen to Bruce Babbitt, November 17, 1997; Ted Zukoski to Pam Eaton and Suzanne Jones of the Wilderness Society and Valerie Cohen of the Taxpayers for Safe Utah Road, November 18, 1996; both documents in File UT: Andalex Mine, Box 26, WS-FCROR.
31. Eaton to Fran Hunt and Ken Rait, August 16, 1996; Zukoski to Eaton, Hunt, and Rait, August 16, 1996; Zukoski to Eaton and Jones of the Wilderness Society and Cohen of the Taxpayers for Safe Utah Road, November 18, 1996; all documents in File UT: Andalex Mine, Box 26, WS-FCROR.
32. Wilkinson, *Fire on the Plateau,* 330–31.
33. Roger Holland, editorial, *Southern Utah News,* October 9, 1996.
34. Press briefing by Babbitt, Mike McCurry, and Joe Lockhart, Grand Canyon National Park, September 18, 1996, File UT:BLM:GSENM:TWS Proposal, Box 26, WS-FCROR.
35. "Andalex Yanks Request to Mine at Kaiparowits," *Deseret News,* January 25, 1997.
36. Porter Arbogast, "Strength Comes from Diversity," *Southern Utah News,* October 2, 1996. See also Rinda Alldredge, "'Black Wednesday,'" *Southern Utah News,* October 9, 1996; Carol Sullivan, "New Monument Continues to Consume Commissioners," *Southern Utah News,* October 30, 1996; "Dixie Speaks," *Southern Utah News,* June 11, 1997.
37. Kane County Commission Minutes, April 2, 1997, Reel 7, Series 83799, Kane County (UT), County Commission Minutes, USARS.
38. Melvin K. Dalton, "Letter to Gov. Leavitt," *Southern Utah News,* October 2, 1996.

39. Kane County Commission Minutes, October 3, 1996, Reel 6, Kane County (UT), County Commission Minutes, USAR.S..
40. Carol Sullivan, "Public Hearing on Monument Brings Some Answers, More Questions," *Southern Utah News,* February 5, 1997.
41. Kane County Commission Minutes, January 14, 1997, Reel 7, Kane County (UT), County Commission Minutes, USAR.S..
42. Dixie Brunner, "Monument Director Meets with Community Members," *Southern Utah News,* December 18, 1996. See also Sullivan, "Public Hearing on Monument," 14.
43. Kane County Commission Minutes, June 12, 1997, Reel 7, Kane County (UT), County Commission Minutes, USAR.S..
44. Ibid., January 11 and February 22, 1999.
45. Ibid., February 22, 1999; Carol Sullivan, "Tempers Flare over Roads in the Monument," *Southern Utah News,* March 3, 1999.
46. Ibid.; Sullivan, "Cattleman Worried about Changes Taking Place in the Monument," *Southern Utah News,* March 31, 1999; Kane County Commission Minutes, May 24, 1999, Reel 7, Kane County (UT), County Commission Minutes, USAR.S..
47. Kane County Commission Minutes, June 14, 1999, Reel 7, Kane County (UT), County Commission Minutes, USAR.S..
48. Kane County Commission Minutes, June 28, 1999, KC-UT.
49. Ibid., July 12, 1999.
50. Ibid., July 26, 1999.
51. Ibid., August 23, 1999.
52. US Government Accountability Office, "Recognition of R.S. 2477 Rights-of-Way"; Michael Leavitt, "Governor Suggests 'Common Ground' Solution," *Salt Lake Tribune,* April 20, 2003, AA4.
53. Heidi McIntosh, "Activist Says Governor's Process Is Flawed, Unfair," *Salt Lake Tribune,* April 20, 2003, AA4.
54. Mark Udall, House of Representatives, to Gale Norton, Secretary of the Interior, April 16, 2003, http://www.suwa.org. See also US Government Accountability Office, "Recognition of R.S. 2477 Rights-of-Way."
55. Earthjustice, "Kane County Signage & R.S. 2477," http://www.earthjustice.org/our_work/cases/2005/kane-county-signage-rs-2477; Joshua Zaffos, "Serendipity in the Desert," *High Country News,* January 24, 2011, 18. For a legal perspective on the road-closure controversy and the ensuing lawsuit, see Hoffmann, "Signs, Signs, Everywhere Signs," 3–35.
56. Mark Habbeshaw to the People of Kane County, May 3, 2009, http://kane.utah.gov/att/38/store/u34_Kane-County-Commission-Letter-to-the-People-of-Kane-County-re-the-closure-of-the-Paria-Canyon-Road.pdf.
57. See Laurel Hagen, "Report from the Paria River," Wildlands CPR, http://www.wildlandscpr.org/blog/report-paria-river-protests; Mark Havnes, "Protesters Roar through Fed Lands," *Salt Lake Tribune,* May 10, 2009; Zaffos, "Serendipity in the Desert," 17.

58. At the turn of the twenty-first century, official road claims in Utah numbered more than five thousand. See Christa Powell and Buck Swaney, "Divided Highway: The Politics of the Roadless Debate," in *Contested Landscape,* edited by Goodman and McCool, 180. Udall to Norton, April 16, 2003, noted that Utah claimed fifteen thousand R.S. 2477 routes on public lands.
59. Zaffos, "Serendipity in the Desert," 14, 16.
60. Quoted in ibid., 19.
61. Brent Israelsen, "Staircase Still Strikes Sparks among Utahns," *Salt Lake Tribune,* September 16, 2000.
62. Gregory Aplet and Pamela Pride Eaton to A. J. Meredith, October 29, 1997, File UT:BLM:GSENM:TWS Management Plan Project, Box 26, WS-FCROR. See also Internal Discussion Draft, "Shaping the Future of the Grand Staircase–Escalante National Monument, Utah: A Project of the Wilderness Society," File UT:BLM:GSENM:TWS Management Plan Project, Box 26, WS-FCROR.
63. Bruce Bolander, "Keep All of Our Trails Open," *Southern Utah News,* January 2, 2008.
64. Thomas V. Hatch, Utah Representative, and D. Maloy Dodds, Garfield County Commissioner, "What Has Happened in America," *Southern Utah News,* September 25, 1996.

CHAPTER 7. OFF-ROADING IN ARCH CANYON

1. Scott Groene, Attorney, SUWA, to James Parker, State Director, BLM, November 3, 1989, in MTFO-BLM.
2. Affidavit of William Browning in Opposition to San Juan County, n.d. (circa 1990), in MTFO-BLM.
3. Fred Blackburn, BLM, Staff Report, June 11, 1978, Folder 3, Box 8, Series III, PUCSC.
4. US Department of the Interior, BLM, Moab District Office, San Juan Resource Area, Kane Gulch Ranger Station, Incident Report, Incident No. GG-79-45, Cedar Mesa, August 12, 1979, Folder 3, Box 8, Series III, PUCSC. See also Jerry W. Ballard, Outdoor Recreation Planner, BLM, Staff Report, May 19, 1980, Folder 3, Box 8, Series III, PUCSC.
5. William R. Haase, Public Comment Sheet, Unit No. UT-060-205, Mule and Arch Canyons, n.d., Folder 3, Box 8, Series III, PUCSC.
6. See US Department of the Interior, BLM, Moab District Office, San Juan Resource Area, Kane Gulch Ranger Station, Incident Reports, 1979–1980, Folder 3, Box 8, Series III, PUCSC.
7. Utah Wilderness Coalition, *Wilderness at the Edge: A Citizen Proposal to Protect Utah's Canyons and Deserts,* 19–21.
8. Abbey to editors, *Esquire,* September 11, 1976, Folder 10, Box 3, PEA.
9. Jerry W. Ballard, Outdoor Recreation Planner, BLM, Staff Report, May 19, 1980, Folder 3, Box 8, Series III, PUCSC.

10. Brian Beard, President, Utah Chapter of the Sierra Club, to Gene Day, District Manager, BLM, May 17, 1979; "Destruction of Arch Canyon," Utah Chapter Sierra Club Newsletter, n.d.; both in Folder 3, Box 8, Series III, PUCSC.
11. Letter to Rocco Dodson, Sierra Club Legal Defense Fund, September 6, 1980, Folder 3, Box 8, Series III, PUCSC.
12. Groene to Parker, November 3, 1989; untitled document, February 23, 1990, MTFO-BLM.
13. Groene to Parker, November 3, 1989; Michael F. Heyrend, Staff Council, SUWA, Jane Leeson, Utah Representative, Wilderness Society, and Rudy Lukez, Conservation Chair, Utah Chapter of the Sierra Club, to Gene Nodine, District Manager, BLM, February 23, 1990, MTFO-BLM.
14. Ibid.
15. Kenneth Rhea, District Manager, BLM, to Michael Heyrend, SUWA, March 9, 1990, MTFO-BLM.
16. Calvin Black to Ed Scherick, BLM, January 25, 1990, MTFO-BLM. See also Cleal Bradford, Executive Director, White Mesa Ute Council, to Dan J. Gliniecki, Manager, Chrysler Motors Corporation, March 23, 1990; statement by Lynn F. Lyman of Blanding, Utah, November 28, 1989, MTFO-BLM.
17. "Four-Wheel Drives Overrun Arch Canyon," *SUWA Newsletter* 7, no. 1 (1990): 1, 3–5; Joseph Bauman, "Who Is Forcing Wilderness Issue?," *Deseret News,* April 13, 1990, A7.
18. Joseph Bauman, "Environmentalists Angry at Renegade 4-Wheelers Driving Up Arch Canyon," *Deseret News,* April 11–12, 1990.
19. Joseph Bauman, "Charges Are Possible against 4-Wheel-Drive Group, BLM Chief Says," *Deseret News,* April 12–13, 1990.
20. BLM, Administrative Decision, April 30, 1990, MTFO-BLM; "BLM Rules Arch Canyon Road Remains Open, Despite Protest," *Moab (UT) Times-Independent,* May 3, 1990; Lawson LeGate, "'Public Road' Is a Jeep Trail," *Deseret News,* June 19, 1990.
21. Reply, San Juan County, April 20, 2004, MTFO-BLM.
22. Quoted in Lisa J. Church, "BLM Renews Red-Rock 4-Wheelers' Jeep Safari Permits," *Moab (UT) Times-Independent,* n.d., http://www.moabtimes.com/view/full_story/66793/article-BLM-renews-Red-Rock-4-Wheelers--Jeep-Safari-permits.
23. Liz Thomas, SUWA, to Sandy Meyers, Manager, BLM Monticello Field Office, October 13, 2006, MTFO-BLM.
24. Sandra Meyers, telephone conversation with Liz Thomas, October 19, 2006; Sandra Meyers to Liz Thomas, December 19, 2006, MTFO-BLM; "S.P.E.A.R. Sponsors Road Repair Efforts in Beautiful Arch Canyon," *San Juan Record,* November 29, 2006, 2.
25. SUWA, "SUWA: BLM Ignores Request to Protect Arch Canyon," *San Juan Record,* March 21, 2007; "Petition to Preserve Arch Canyon's Natural and Cultural Heritage," December 2006, iii–iv, http://www.suwa.org/site/DocServer/Arch_Petition_final_reduced.pdf?docID=861; John Hollenhorst, "Petition

Filed to Ban Vehicles in Arch Canyon, Near Blanding," December 26, 2006, MTFO-BLM.

26. "SUWA: BLM Ignores Request to Protect Arch Canyon," *San Juan Record,* March 21, 2007.
27. Decision Record on Southern Utah Wilderness Alliance "Petition to Preserve Arch Canyon's Natural and Cultural Heritage," October 13, 2010, http://www.suwa.org/site/DocServer/archCanyon_BLMDecision.pdf.
28. Abbey to editors, *Esquire,* September 11, 1976, Folder 10, Box 3, PEA.
29. Ken Davey, "Jeepers v Environmentalists," *Canyon Country Zephyr,* March 1991, 22.
30. Edward Abbey and Renee Abbey to Hearing Officer, c/o Superintendent, Canyonlands National Park, September 9, 1974, Folder 8, Box 3, PEA.
31. Veronica Egan to Sandra Meyers, November 21, 2006, in MTFO-BLM.
32. Quoted in Carol Poster, "Arch Canyon Road: To Be or Not to Be," 46.

CHAPTER 8. MAKING A DESERT LANDSCAPE

1. Quoted in Michael Williams, "Historical Geography and the Concept of Landscape," 95.
2. Craig Childs, *The Secret Knowledge of Water: Discovering the Essence of the American Desert,* xii–xiii.
3. John Seelye, *Beautiful Machine,* 8–9.
4. John R. Stilgoe, *Common Landscape of America, 1580 to 1845,* 21–23.
5. Quoted in Nathan Miller, *The Enterprise of a Free People: Aspects of Economic Development in New York State during the Canal Period, 1792–1838,* 30.
6. Quoted in Stilgoe, *Common Landscape of America,* 132.
7. Originally published in Walt Whitman, *Leaves of Grass,* 120–29.
8. Wilshire, Nielson, and Hazlett, *American West at Risk,* 138–40. See also *Killing Roads: A Citizens' Primer on the Effects & Removal of Roads,* produced by Earth First!, May 1, 1990, Folder 7, Box 4, PUCSC; R. T. T. Forman and L. E. Alexander, "Roads and Their Major Ecological Effects."
9. See Paul Sutter, *Driven Wild: How the Fight against Automobiles Launched the Modern Wilderness Movement.*
10. Marx, *Machine in the Garden.*
11. Quoted in Thomas E. Rinaldi and Robert J. Yasinsac, *Hudson Valley Ruins: Forgotten Landmarks of an American Landscape,* 69–70.
12. Timothy Davis, "The Rise and Decline of the American Parkway," in *The World beyond the Windshield: Roads and Landscapes in the United States and Europe,* edited by Christof Mauch and Thomas Zeller, 36.
13. Heat-Moon, *Blue Highways.*
14. This is an argument advanced by Sutter in *Driven Wild* and by Thomas R. Vale in *The American Wilderness: Reflections on Nature Protection in the United States,* 134–35.

15. Quoted in Wallace Stegner, *Where the Bluebird Sings to the Lemonade Springs: Living and Writing in the West,* 131.
16. Thomas G. Alexander, *Utah: The Right Place,* 424.
17. Michael Frome, *Battle for the Wilderness,* 260; US Department of the Interior, Bureau of Land Management, "Wilderness Areas," http://www.blm.gov/ut/st/en/prog/blm_special_areas/utah_wilderness.html.
18. Dick Carter, "Defending the Desert," speech at the Utah Wilderness Association Annual Rendezvous, Salt Lake City, April 27, 1985, Folder 11, Box 7, UWAC.
19. Andrew Fitzgerald and Deborah Schwabach, "Drawing Lines in the Desert Sand: The Politics of Public-Interest Groups," in *Contested Landscape,* edited by Goodman and McCool, 74–75; Brent Israelsen, "Battle Likely over Utah Wilderness," *High Country News,* June 26, 1995; "Utah Wilderness Bills," http://www.utahwildernessatlas.net/documents/bills/index.htm.
20. Fitzgerald and Schwabach, "Drawing Lines in the Desert Sand," 78–79.
21. "Statement of Hon. James V. Hansen, a U.S. Representative from Utah and Chairman, Subcommittee on National Parks, Forests and Lands," 1, in *Rights-of-Way: Hearing before the Subcommittee on National Parks, Forests, and Lands of the Committee on Resources, House of Representatives, One Hundred Fourth Congress, First Session, on H.R. 2081,* July 27, 1995. By 1996 about five thousand claims had been made in Utah; the number has since increased to as many as twenty thousand by some counts.
22. Thomas Reed Petersen, ed., *A Road Runs Through It: Reviving Wild Places,* 2.
23. Quoted in Fitzgerald and Schwabach, "Drawing Lines in the Desert Sand," 78–79.
24. William Cronon, "The Trouble with Wilderness; or, Getting Back to the Wrong Nature."
25. Scott, *Enduring Wilderness,* 15.
26. See J. R. McNeill, "Observations on the Nature and Culture of Environmental History," 34.
27. Statement of Louise Liston, Garfield County Commissioner, 19, in *Rights-of-Way,* July 27, 1995.
28. Joseph Smith, "Manuscript History of the Church," compiled from 1838 to 1856, Vol. A-1, 127, josephsmithpapers.org/paperSummary/history-1838-1856-volume-a-1.
29. Klaus J. Hansen, *Mormonism and the American Experience,* 69–70.
30. For an excellent discussion of how early Mormons and other premodern groups confronted the region, see Paul Thomas Nelson, "Utah's Canyon Country: Hope and Experience Approach an American Desert, 1500–1936."
31. Frederick Jackson Turner, "The Significance of the Frontier in American History," paper presented at the American Historical Association conference, Chicago, July 12, 1893, http://nationalhumanitiescenter.org/pds/gilded/empire/text1/turner.pdf.
32. Donald H. Dyal, "Mormon Pursuit of the Agrarian Ideal."
33. "Religion, Progress, and Privileges of the Saints, &c.," 83.

34. Robert Redd, Oral History, interviewed by Jessie Embry, February 8, 2011, Provo, UT, San Juan County Public Lands Oral History Project, Charles Redd Center for Western Studies, L. Tom Perry Special Collections, Harold B. Lee Library, Brigham Young University, Provo, UT (hereafter San Juan County Public Lands).
35. Charlotte Palfreyman Smith, ed., *Stories Told: Life on the Public Lands in San Juan County,* 14–15.
36. Andrew Gulliford, Oral History, phone interview by Jessie Embry, March 8, 2011, San Juan County Public Lands.
37. Oliver Harris, Oral History, interviewed by Jessie Embry, March 22, 2011, Blanding, UT, San Juan County Public Lands.
38. Harris interview.
39. Gary Shumway, Oral History, interviewed by Carly Smith, February 19, 2011, Blanding, UT, San Juan County Public Lands.
40. Phyllis Rose, "Pioneers on a Mission: American Popular Culture Glorifies Cowboys and Other Heroes of Frontier Individualism. But the West's Most Successful Settlers—the Mormons—Followed Orders, Worked in Groups, and Rejected the American Dream," 59.
41. See Stephen C. Sturgeon, "The Disappearance of Everett Ruess and the Discovery of Utah's Red Rock Country," 30–31.
42. Ward J. Roylance, *The Enchanted Wilderness: A Red Rock Odyssey,* 94 (emphasis in the original).
43. See Sherry L. Smith, ed., *The Future of the Southern Plains,* 226; Marsha Weisiger, *Dreaming of Sheep in Navajo Country.*
44. Gulliford interview.
45. Stegner, *Mormon Country,* 62.
46. Terry Tempest Williams, William B. Smart, and Gibbs M. Smith, eds., *New Genesis: A Mormon Reader on Land and Community,* is an attempt by members of the LDS faith "to begin the storytelling of sustainability with our own spiritual tradition" (ix).
47. Leonard J. Arrington, *Utah's Audacious Stockman: Charlie Redd,* 243–46.
48. Gulliford interview.
49. Loch Wade, "The Stagnation of the Environmental Movement," *Canyon Country Zephyr,* April–May 2006, 4.
50. See Jim Stiles, "Take It or Leave It . . . ," *Canyon Country Zephyr,* April–May 2006, 2–3; Robert Redford, "Utah Approves a Mine Next to Bryce Canyon for Coal America Doesn't Need," *Huffington Post,* December 14, 2010, http://www.huffingtonpost.com/robert-redford/utah-approves-a-mine-next_b_795955.html.
51. Michael P. Conzen, ed., *The Making of the American Landscape,* xv.
52. Grant Johnson, "A Personal Early SUWA History," http://www.canyoncountryzephyr.com/oldzephyr/aug-sept2005/feedback.html.
53. Quoted in Lisa J. Church, "BLM Renews Red-Rock 4-Wheelers' Jeep Safari Permits," *Moab (UT) Times-Independent,* n.d., http://www.moabtimes.com/view/full_story/66793/article-BLM-renews-Red-Rock-4-Wheelers--Jeep-Safari-permits.

EPILOGUE

1. The best source of the trail is still LeRoy R. Hafen and Ann W. Hafen, *Old Spanish Trail: Santa Fe to Los Angeles, with Extracts from Contemporary Records and Including Diaries of Antonio Armijo and Orville Pratt.* See also C. Gregory Crampton, "Utah's Spanish Trail"; Smart, *Old Utah Trails;* and C. Gregory Crampton and Steven K. Madsen, *In Search of the Spanish Trail: Santa Fe to Los Angeles, 1829–1848.*
2. Jeremy Miller, "Map Quest," *High Country News,* March 19, 2012, 10, 24.
3. Stephen H. Lekson, *The Chaco Meridian: Centers of Political Power in the Ancient Southwest,* 114–17.
4. Quoted in ibid., 117, 118, 126, 129–30.
5. George Washington Martin, *How the Oregon Trail Became a Road* (Salt Lake City: Deseret News, 1906), 52, Folder 63, Box 13, MS 120, Howard R. Driggs Collection, Special Collections and Archives, Gerald R. Sherratt Library, Southern Utah University, Cedar City.

Bibliography

Abbey, Edward. *Confessions of a Barbarian: Selections from the Journals of Edward Abbey, 1951–1989.* Boston: Little, Brown, 1994.

———. *Desert Solitaire: A Season in the Wilderness.* 1968. Reprint, New York: Ballantine Books, 1971.

———. *Hayduke Lives!* Boston: Little, Brown, 1990.

———. *The Monkey Wrench Gang.* 1975. Reprint, New York: HarperCollins, 2000.

Abbey, Edward, and Philip Hyde. *Slickrock: Endangered Canyons of the Southwest.* New York: Sierra Club Books/Charles Scribner and Sons, 1971.

Alexander, Thomas G. "Stewardship and Enterprises: The LDS Church and the Wasatch Oasis Environment, 1847–1930." *Western Historical Quarterly* 25 (Autumn 1994): 341–66.

———. *Utah: The Right Place.* Rev. ed. Salt Lake City: Gibbs Smith, 2003.

Amundson, Michael. *Yellowcake Towns: Uranium Mining Communities in the American West.* Boulder: University Press of Colorado, 2002.

Arrington, Leonard. *Great Basin Kingdom: An Economic History of the Latter-day Saints.* Cambridge, MA: Harvard University Press, 1958.

———. *Utah's Audacious Stockman: Charlie Redd.* Logan: Utah State University Press, 1995.

Athearn, Robert. *The Mythic West in Twentieth-Century America.* Lawrence: University Press of Kansas, 1980.

Aton, James M., and Robert S. McPherson. *River Flowing from the Sunrise: An Environmental History of the Lower San Juan.* Logan: Utah State University Press, 2000.

Babbitt, Bruce. *Cities in the Wilderness: A New Vision of Land Use in America.* Washington, DC: Island Press, 2005.

Baden, John A., and Donald Snow, eds. *The Next West: Public Lands, Community, and Economy in the American West.* Washington, DC: Island Press, 1997.

Baker, James. "Winning (and Losing) the West." *Sierra,* May–June 1985.

Behan, Richard. *Plundered Promise: Capitalism, Politics, and the Fate of the Public Lands.* Washington, DC: Island Press, 2001.

Benson, Jackson J. *Wallace Stegner: His Life and Work.* New York: Penguin Books, 1996.

Bergera, Gary James, ed. *On Desert Trails with Everett Ruess.* Commemorative ed. Salt Lake City: Gibbs Smith, 2000.

Berry, Wendell. *The Gift of Good Land: Further Essays Cultural and Agricultural.* San Francisco: North Point, 1981.

Bishop, James, Jr. *Epitaph for a Desert Anarchist: The Life and Legacy of Edward Abbey.* New York: Atheneum, 1994.

Black, Calvin. "History of the John Atlantic Burr." May 4, 1985. In possession of Blue Mountain Shadows, Blanding, UT.

———. Interview by Lynn Coppel. May 29, 1978. Southeastern Utah Project, Utah State Historical Society and California State University, Fullerton, Oral History Program.

———. Interview by Milan Pavlovich and Jeffrey Jones. July 24, 1970. Southeastern Utah Project, Utah State Historical Society and California State University, Fullerton, Oral History Program.

Blevins, Winfred. "Mariah Interviews Edward Abbey, 'the Thoreau of the American Desert.'" *Mariah: The Complete Outdoor Magazine* (October–November 1978).

Brennan, Amy E. "Grassroots in the Desert: An Analysis of the Roles of the Utah Wilderness Association and the Southern Utah Wilderness Alliance in the Debate over Wilderness Designation of Bureau of Land Management Lands in Southern Utah." Master's thesis, Utah State University, 1998.

Brick, Philip D, and R. McGreggor Cawley. *A Wolf in the Garden: The Land Rights Movement and the New Environmental Debate.* Lanham, MD: Rowman and Littlefield, 1996.

Brooks, Joanna. "'Genealogy Is in Our Blood': Terry Tempest Williams and the Redemption of 'Native' Mormonism." In *True West: Authenticity and the American West,* edited by William R. Handley and Nathaniel Lewis. Lincoln: University of Nebraska Press, 2004.

Brower, David, ed. *The Place No One Knew.* San Francisco: Sierra Club, 1963.

Brown, Kenneth. *Four Corners: History, Land, and People of the Desert Southwest.* New York: HarperCollins, 1995.

Cahalan, James M. *Edward Abbey: A Life.* Tucson: University of Arizona Press, 2001.

Cawley, R. McGreggor. *Federal Land, Western Anger: The Sagebrush Rebellion and Environmental Politics.* Lawrence: University Press of Kansas, 1993.

Child, Craig. *The Secret Knowledge of Water: Discovering the Essence of the American Desert.* Seattle: Sasquatch Books, 2001.

Clawson, Marion. *The Bureau of Land Management.* New York: Praeger, 1971.

———. *The Federal Lands since 1956: Recent Trends in Use and Management.* Washington, DC: Resources for the Future, distributed by Johns Hopkins University Press, [1967].

Clinton, Bill. *My Life.* New York: Alfred A. Knopf, 2004.

Conzen, Michael P., ed. *The Making of the American Landscape.* New York: Routledge, 1994.

Crampton, C. Gregory. *Standing Up Country: The Canyon Lands of Utah and Arizona.* New York: Alfred A. Knopf, 1964.

———. "Utah's Spanish Trail." *Utah Historical Quarterly* 47 (Fall 1979): 361–83.

Crampton, C. Gregory, and Steven K. Madsen. *In Search of the Spanish Trail: Santa Fe to Los Angeles, 1829–1848.* Layton, UT: Gibbs Smith, 1994.

Cronon, William. "Modes of Prophecy and Production: Placing Nature in History." *Journal of American History* 76 (March 1990): 1122–31.

———. "The Trouble with Wilderness; or, Getting Back to the Wrong Nature." In *Uncommon Ground: Rethinking the Human Place in Nature,* edited by William Cronon, 69–90. New York: W. W. Norton, 1995.

Davis, Charles, ed. *Western Public Lands and Environmental Politics.* Boulder, CO: Westview Press, 1997.

Decker, Peter R. *Old Fences, New Neighbors.* Tucson: University of Arizona Press, 1998.

Dellenbaugh, Frederick S. *The Romance of the Colorado River.* 1902. Reprint, New York: Knickerbocker Press, 1982.

DeVoto, Bernard. "The West Against Itself." In *The Western Paradox: A Conservation Reader,* edited by Douglas Brinkley and Patricia Nelson Limerick. New Haven, CT: Yale University Press, 2001.

Dunlap, Thomas R. *Faith in Nature: Environmentalism as Religious Quest.* Seattle: University of Washington Press, 2001.

Durning, Alan Thein. *This Place on Earth: Home and the Practice of Permanence.* Seattle: Sasquatch Books, 1996.

Dyal, Donald H. "Mormon Pursuit of the Agrarian Ideal." *Agricultural History* 63, no. 4 (1989): 19–35.

Edmonds, Carol. *Wayne Aspinall: Mr. Chairman.* Lakewood, CO: Great America Printing, 1980.

Ellis, Jeffrey C. "On the Search for a Root Cause: Essentialist Tendencies in Environmental Discourse." In *Uncommon Ground: Rethinking the Human Place in Nature,* edited by William Cronon. New York: W. W. Norton, 1995.

Farmer, Jared. *Glen Canyon Dammed: Inventing Lake Powell and the Canyon Country.* Tucson: University of Arizona Press, 1999.

———. *On Zion's Mount: Mormons, Indians, and the American Landscape.* Cambridge, MA: Harvard University Press, 2008.

Firmage, Richard A. *A History of Grand County.* Salt Lake City: Utah State Historical Society and Grand County Commission, 1996.

Fleck, Richard F., ed. *A Colorado River Reader.* Salt Lake City: University of Utah Press, 2000.

Flores, Dan. *The Natural West: Environmental History in the Great Plains and Rocky Mountains.* Norman: University of Oklahoma Press, 2001.

Foreman, Dave. *Confessions of an Eco-Warrior.* New York: Harmony Books, 1991.

Forman, R. T. T., and L. E. Alexander. "Roads and Their Major Ecological Effects." *Annual Review of Ecology and Systematics* 29 (1998): 207–31.

Foss, Phillip O., ed. *Politics and Ecology.* Belmont, CA: Duxbury Press, 1972.

———. *Politics and Grass: The Administration of Grazing on the Public Domain.* Seattle: University of Washington Press, 1960.

Fradkin, Philip L. *A River No More: The Colorado River and the West.* Tucson: University of Arizona Press, 1981.

Francaviglia, Richard V. *Believing in Place: A Spiritual Geography of the Great Basin.* Reno: University of Nevada Press, 2003.

———. *The Mormon Landscape.* New York: AMS Press, 1978.

Frome, Michael. *Battle for the Wilderness.* Rev. ed. Salt Lake City: University of Utah Press, 1997.

Geary, Edward A. *A History of Emery County.* Salt Lake City: Utah State Historical Society and Emery County Commission, 1996.

———. *The Proper Edge of the Sky: The High Plateau Country of Utah.* Salt Lake City: University of Utah Press, 1992.

Gomez, Arthur R. *Quest for the Golden Circle: The Four Corners and the Metropolitan West, 1945–1970.* Albuquerque: University of New Mexico Press, 1994.

Goodman, Doug, and Daniel McCool, eds. *Contested Landscape: The Politics of Wilderness in Utah and the West.* Salt Lake City: University of Utah Press, 1999.

Grahame, John D., and Thomas D. Sisk, eds. *Canyons, Cultures, and Environmental Change: An Introduction to the Land-Use History of the Colorado Plateau.* http://cpluhna.nau.edu/Places/gsenm3.htm.

Gregory, Herbert E., and Raymond C. Moore. *The Kaiparowits Region: A Geographic and Geologic Reconnaissance of Parts of Utah and Arizona.* Geological Survey Professional Paper 164. Washington, DC: Government Printing Office, 1931.

Gressley, Gene M., ed. *Old West/New West: Quo Vadis?* Worland, WY: High Plains, 1994.

Grey, Zane. *Riders of the Purple Sage.* 1912. Reprint, New York: Random House, 2007.

Hafen, LeRoy R., and Ann W. Hafen. *Old Spanish Trail: Santa Fe to Los Angeles, with Extracts from Contemporary Records and Including Diaries of Antonio Armijo and Orville Pratt.* Glendale, CA: Arthur H. Clark, 1954.

Hansen, Klaus J. *Mormonism and the American Experience.* Chicago: University of Chicago Press, 1981.

Harmon, David, Francis P. McManamon, and Dwight T. Pitcaithley, eds. *The Antiquities Act: A Century of American Archaeology, Historic Preservation, and Nature Conservation.* Tucson: University of Arizona Press, 2006.

Harper, Kimball, Jr., ed. *Natural History of the Colorado Plateau and Great Basin.* Niwot: University Press of Colorado, 1994.

Harvey, Mark W. T. *A Symbol of Wilderness: Echo Park and the American Conservation Movement.* 1994. Reprint, Seattle: University of Washington Press, 2000.

———. *Wilderness Forever: Howard Zahnizer and the Path to the Wilderness Act.* Seattle: University of Washington Press, 2005.

Harvey, Thomas J. *Rainbow Bridge to Monument Valley: Making the Modern Old West.* Norman: University of Oklahoma Press, 2011.

———. "The Storehouse of Unlived Years: Producing the Space of the Old West in Modern America." PhD diss., University of Utah, 2004.

Havlick, David G. *No Place Distant: Roads and Motorized Recreation on America's Public Lands.* Washington, DC: Island Press, 2002.

Hays, Samuel P. *Beauty, Health, and Permanence: Environmental Politics in the United States, 1955–1985.* Cambridge: Cambridge University Press, 1987.

Heat-Moon, William Least. *Blue Highways: A Journey into America.* 2nd ed. Boston: Houghton Mifflin, 1991.

Hess, Karl, and John A. Baden, eds. *Writers on the Range.* Niwot: University Press of Colorado, 1998.

Hillers, Jack. *"Photographed All the Best Scenery": Jack Hillers's Diary of the Powell Expeditions, 1871–1875.* Edited by Don D. Fowler. Salt Lake City: University of Utah Press, 1972.

Hirt, Paul. *Conspiracy of Optimism: Management of the National Forests since World War Two.* Lincoln: University of Nebraska Press, 1994.

Hoffmann, Hillary M. "Signs, Signs, Everywhere Signs: *The Wilderness Society v. Kane County* Leaves Everyone Confused about Navigating a Right-of-Way Claim under Revised Statute 2477." *Hastings West-Northwest Journal of Environmental Law & Policy* 18, no. 1 (2012).

Huggard, Christopher J., and Arthur R. Gomez, eds. *Forests under Fire: A Century of Ecosystem Management in the Southwest.* Tucson: University of Arizona Press, 2001.

Jackson, Richard. "Righteousness and Environmental Change: The Mormons and the Environment." In *Charles Redd Monographs in Western History,* edited by Thomas G. Alexander, 21–43. No. 5. Provo, UT: Brigham Young University Press, 1975.

Johnson, Barbara H., ed. *Forging a West That Works: An Invitation to the Radical Center; Essays on Ranching, Conservation, and Science.* Santa Fe, NM: Quivira Coalition, 2003.

Keiter, Robert B., Sarah B. George, and Joro Walker, eds. *Visions of the Grand Staircase–Escalante: Examining Utah's Newest National Monument.* Salt Lake City: Utah Museum of Natural History and Wallace Stegner Center, 1998.

Kemmis, Daniel. *This Sovereign Land: A New Vision for Governing the West.* Washington, DC: Island Press, 2001.

Ketcham, Christopher. "Off-Road Rules: Timber, Mining, and Off-Road-Vehicle Lobbyists Advocate Staking Road Claims All over the West." *Mother Jones,* July 2007.

Kluckhohn, Clyde. *Beyond the Rainbow.* Boston: Christopher, 1933.

———. *To the Foot of the Rainbow: A Tale of Twenty-Five Hundred Miles of Wandering on Horseback through the Southwest Enchanted Land.* 1927. Reprint, Albuquerque: University of New Mexico Press, 1992.

Kluckhohn, Clyde, and Henry A. Murray, eds. *Personality in Nature, Society, and Culture.* New York: Alfred A. Knopf, 1948.

Kluckhohn, Richard, ed. *Culture and Behavior: The Collected Essays of Clyde Kluckhohn.* New York: Free Press, 1962.

Kneese, Allen V., and F. Lee Brown. *The Southwest under Stress: National Resource Development Issues in a Regional Setting.* Baltimore: Johns Hopkins University Press, 1981.

Knowlton, Ezra C. *History of Highway Development in Utah.* Salt Lake City: Utah Department of Transportation, 1967.

Lacko, Helen. "The Good Ol' Boys vs. the BLM in Negro Bill Canyon." *Utah Holiday* (August 1979).

Lamm, Richard D., and Michael McCarthy. *The Angry West: A Vulnerable Land and Its Future.* Boston: Houghton Mifflin, 1982.

Lang, William L. "From Where We Are Standing: The Sense of Place and Environmental History." In *Northwest Lands, Northwest Peoples: Readings in Environmental History,* edited by Dale D. Goble and Paul W. Hirt. Seattle: University of Washington Press, 1999.

———. "Using and Abusing Abundance: The Western Resource Economy and the Environment." In *Historians and the American West,* edited by Michael P. Malone. Lincoln: University of Nebraska Press, 1983.

Larmer, Paul, ed. *Give and Take: How the Clinton Administration's Public Lands Offensive Transformed the American West.* Paonia, CO: High Country News Books, 2004.

Learning from the Land: GSENM Science Symposium Proceedings. Southern Utah University Hunter Conference Center, Cedar City, UT, November 4–5, 1997. Salt Lake City: Bureau of Land Management, Utah State Office, n.d.

Lekson, Stephen H. *The Chaco Meridian: Centers of Political Power in the Ancient Southwest.* Walnut Creek, CA: AltaMira Press, 1999.

Levine, Andrew. *The American Ideology: A Critique.* New York: Routledge, 2004.

Limerick, Patricia Nelson, Clyde A. Milner, II, and Charles E. Rankin, eds. *Trails: Toward a New Western History.* Lawrence: University Press of Kansas, 1991.

Limerick, Patricia Nelson. *Desert Passages: Encounters with the American Desert.* Albuquerque: University of New Mexico Press, 1985.

———. *The Legacy of Conquest: The Unbroken Past of the American West.* New York: W. W. Norton, 1987.

Louter, David. *Windshield Wilderness: Cars, Roads, and Nature in Washington's National Parks.* Seattle: University of Washington Press, 2006.

Luke, Adam M. "Manufacturing the Wilderness: The Role of Local Communities, Activists, and Industry in Creating Wilderness and Public Land Policy." Master's thesis, Utah State University, 2007.

Lyman, Karl. "The Life Story of Calvin 'F.' Black." In possession of Blue Mountain Shadows, Blanding, UT.

MacDonald, Bonney. "Authoring an Authentic Place: Environmental and Literary

Stewardship in Stegner and Kittredge." In *True West: Authenticity and the American West,* edited by William R. Handley and Nathaniel Lewis. Lincoln: University of Nebraska Press, 2004.

Marsh, Kevin. *Drawing Lines in the Forest: Creating Wilderness Areas in the Pacific Northwest.* Seattle: University of Washington Press, 2007.

Marston, Ed, ed. *Reopening the Western Frontier.* Washington, DC: Island Press, 1989.

Martin, George Washington. *How the Oregon Trail Became a Road.* Salt Lake City: Deseret News, 1906.

Martin, Russell. *A Story That Stands Like a Dam: Glen Canyon and the Struggle for the Soul of the West.* New York: Henry Holt, 1989.

Marx, Leo. *The Machine in the Garden: Technology and the Pastoral Ideal in America.* New York: Oxford University Press, 1964.

Matheson, Scott M., and James M. Kee. *Out of Balance.* Salt Lake City: Peregrine Smith, 1986.

Mauch, Christof, and Thomas Zeller, eds. *The World beyond the Windshield: Roads and Landscapes in the United States and Europe.* Athens: Ohio University Press, 2008.

Mayer, Carl, and George Riley. *Public Domain, Private Dominion.* San Francisco: Sierra Club Books, 1985.

McKinney, Matthew, and William Harmon. *The Western Confluence: A Guide to Governing Natural Resources.* Washington, DC: Island Press, 2004.

McNeill, J. R. "Observations on the Nature and Culture of Environmental History." Special issue, "Environment and History." *Theory and History* 42, no. 4 (2003): 5–43.

McPhee, John. *Basin and Range.* New York: Farrar, Straus, and Giroux, 1980.

———. *The Control of Nature.* New York: Farrar, Straus, and Giroux, 1989.

———. *Encounters with the Archdruid.* New York: Farrar, Straus, and Giroux, 1971.

McPherson, Robert S. *Comb Ridge and Its People: The Ethnohistory of a Rock.* Logan: Utah State University Press, 2009.

———. *A History of San Juan County: In the Palm of Time.* Salt Lake City: Utah State Historical Society and San Juan County Commission, 1995.

Meadowcroft, James. "Green Political Perspectives at the Dawn of the Twenty-First Century." In *Reassessing Political Ideologies: The Durability of Dissent,* edited by Michael Freeden, 175–92. New York: Routledge: 2001.

Meinig, Donald. "The Mormon Culture Region." In *Cultural Geography: Selected Reading.* New York: Thomas Crowell, 1967.

Merrill, Karen R. *Public Lands and Political Meaning: Ranchers, the Government, and the Property between Them.* Berkeley: University of California Press, 2002.

Miller, David E. *Hole-in-the-Rock: An Epic in the Colonization of the Great American West.* Salt Lake City: University of Utah Press, 1959.

Miller, Nathan. *The Enterprise of a Free People: Aspects of Economic Development in New York State during the Canal Period, 1792–1838.* Ithaca, NY: Cornell University Press, 1962.

Milligan, Mike. *Westwater Lost and Found.* Logan: Utah State University Press, 2004.

Milner, Clyde A., II, Carol A. O'Connor, and Martha A. Sandweiss, eds. *The Oxford History of the American West.* New York: Oxford University Press, 1994.

Muhn, James, and Hanson R. Stuart. *Opportunity and Challenge: The Story of BLM.* Washington, DC: US Department of the Interior, 1988.

Mulder, William. "The Mormons in American History." *University of Utah Bulletin* 48, no. 11 (1957).

Mumford, Lewis. *The Highway and the City.* New York: Harcourt, Brace, and World, 1963.

Nash, Gerald D. *The Federal Landscape: An Economic History of the Twentieth Century West.* Tucson: University of Arizona Press, 1999.

Nash, Linda. *Inescapable Ecologies: A History of Environment, Disease, and Knowledge.* Berkeley: University of California Press, 2006.

———. "Transforming the Central Valley: Body, Identity, and Environment in California, 1850–1970." PhD diss., University of Washington, 2000.

Nash, Roderick. *The Rights of Nature: A History of Environmental Ethics.* Madison: University of Wisconsin Press, 1989.

———. *Wilderness and the American Mind.* 3rd ed. New Haven, CT: Yale University Press, 1982.

Nelson, Lowry. *The Mormon Village: A Pattern and Technique of Land Settlement.* Salt Lake City: University of Utah Press, 1952.

Nelson, Paul Thomas. "Not Getting Along: A Brief History of Conflict in Utah's Canyon Country." Unpublished article in the author's possession.

———. "Utah's Canyon Country: Hope and Experience Approach an American Desert, 1500–1936." PhD diss., Southern Methodist University, 2009.

Nelson, Robert H. *Public Lands and Private Rights: The Failure of Scientific Management.* Lanham, MD: Rowman and Littlefield, 1995.

Newell, Linda King, and Vivian Linford Talbot. *A History of Garfield County.* Utah Centennial County History Series. Utah State Historical Society and Garfield County Commission, 1998.

Nibley, Hugh. "Brigham Young on the Environment." In *To the Glory of God: Mormon Essays on Great Issues—the Environment, Commitment, Love, Peace, Youth, Man,* edited by Truman Madsen and Charles D. Tate, 3–29. Salt Lake City: Deseret Book, 1972.

Nicholas, Liza, Elaine M. Bapis, and Thomas J. Harvey, eds. *Imagining the Big Open: Nature, Identity, and Play in the New West.* Salt Lake City: University of Utah Press, 2003.

Nie, Martin A. "In Wilderness Is Dissension: The Contentious Battle over Utah's Wilderness Is Marked by a Cultural Clash." *Forum for Applied Research and Public Policy* 14 (1999).

Oelschlaeger, Max. *The Idea of Wilderness: From Prehistory to the Age of Ecology.* New Haven, CT: Yale University Press, 1991.

———, ed. *The Wilderness Condition: Essays on Environment and Civilization.* San Francisco: Sierra Club Books, 1992.

Pearson, Byron E. *Still the Wild River Runs: Congress, the Sierra Club, and the Fight to Save Grand Canyon.* Tucson: University of Arizona Press, 2002.

Perkins, Cornelia, Marian Nielson, and Lenora Jones. *Saga of the San Juan.* N.p.: San Juan County Daughters of Utah Pioneers, 1957.

Petersen, Thomas Reed, ed. *A Road Runs Through It: Reviving Wild Places.* Boulder, CO: Johnson Books, 2006.

Peterson, Charles S. *Look to the Mountains: Southeastern Utah and the La Sal National Forest.* Provo, UT: Brigham Young University Press, 1975.

Poster, Carol. "Arch Canyon Road: To Be or Not to Be." *Utah Holiday* (July 1990).

Powell, Allan Kent, ed. *San Juan County, Utah: People, Resources, and History.* Salt Lake City: Utah Historical Society, 1983.

———, ed. *Utah History Encyclopedia.* Salt Lake City: University of Utah Press, 1994.

Powell, James Lawrence. *Dead Pool: Lake Powell, Global Warming, and the Future of Water in the West.* Berkeley: University of California Press, 2008.

Powell, John Wesley. *Exploration of the Colorado River of the West and Its Tributaries: Explored in 1869, 1870, 1871, and 1872, under the Direction of the Secretary of the Smithsonian Institution.* Washington, DC: Government Printing Office, 1875.

———. *Report on the Lands of the Arid Regions of the United States.* 2nd ed. Washington, DC: Government Printing Office, 1879.

Pozza, David Mark. "The Unity of Opposites in the Works of Edward Abbey." PhD diss., Indiana University of Pennsylvania, 2001.

Rasband, James R. "Questioning the Rule of Capture Metaphor for Nineteenth Century Public Land Law: A Look at R.S. 2477." *Environmental Law* 35 (Fall 2005): 1005–48.

———. "Utah's Grand Staircase: The Right Path to Wilderness Preservation?" *University of Colorado Law Review* (Spring 1999): 483–562.

Reisner, Marc. *Cadillac Desert: The American West and Its Disappearing Water.* New York: Viking, 1986.

"Religion, Progress, and Privileges of the Saints, &c." Remarks by President Brigham Young, June 12, 1860. In vol. 8 of *Journal of Discourses.* Liverpool: George Q. Cannon, 1861.

Relph, E. *Place and Placelessness.* London: Pion, 1976.

Revised Statute 2477 Rights-of-Way." 59 Federal Register (August 1, 1994), 39216.

Richardson, Elmo R. "Federal Park Policy in Utah: The Escalante National Monument Controversy of 1935–1940." *Utah Historical Quarterly* 33 (Spring 1965): 109–33.

Riebsame, William, ed. *Atlas of the New West: Portrait of a Changing Region.* New York: W. W. Norton, 1997.

Riis, John. *Ranger Trails.* Richmond, VA: Dietz Press, 1937.

Rinaldi, Thomas E., and Robert J. Yasinsac. *Hudson Valley Ruins: Forgotten Landmarks of an American Landscape.* Hanover, NH: University Press of New England, 2006.

Ringholz, Raye G. *Uranium Frenzy: Boom and Bust on the Colorado Plateau.* Albuquerque: University of New Mexico Press, 1989.

Roche, Vaughn. "'Seldom Seen Smith' Mourns a Lost Canyon and Dead Foes." *High Country News* (Paonia, CO), October 18, 1993.
Rogers, Jedediah S. "One Vast 'Contiguity of Waste': Documents from an Early Attempt to Expand the Mormon Kingdom into the Uinta Basin, 1861." *Utah Historical Quarterly* 73, no. 3 (2005): 249–64.
Rose, Phyllis. "Pioneers on a Mission: American Popular Culture Glorifies Cowboys and Other Heroes of Frontier Individualism. But the West's Most Successful Settlers—the Mormons—Followed Orders, Worked in Groups, and Rejected the American Dream." *Civilization,* February—March 1997.
Roth, Dennis. *The Wilderness Movement and the National Forests: 1964–1980.* Washington, DC: US Department of Agriculture, Forest Service, 1984.
Rothman, Hal K. *America's National Monuments: The Politics of Preservation.* Lawrence: University Press of Kansas, 1989.
———. *Devil's Bargains: Tourism in the Twentieth-Century American West.* Lawrence: University Press of Kansas, 1998.
———. *Preserving Different Pasts: The American National Monuments.* Urbana: University of Illinois Press, 1989.
———, ed. *Reopening the American West.* Tucson: University of Arizona Press, 1998.
Rowley, William D. *U.S. Forest Service Grazing and Rangelands: A History.* College Station: Texas A&M University Press, 1985.
Roylance, Ward J. *The Enchanted Wilderness: A Redrock Odyssey.* Torrey, UT: Four Corners West, 1986.
Rusho, W. L. *Everett Ruess: A Vagabond for Beauty.* Salt Lake City: Gibbs Smith, 1983.
Sawyer, Timothy Leighton. "Writing the American Desert: Abbey, Austin, Stegner, and Williams and the Preservation of the Arid West." PhD diss., University of New Mexico, 2001.
Sayre, Nathan. *Working Wilderness: The Malpai Borderlands Group Story and the Future of the Western Range.* Tucson, AZ: Rio Nuevo, 2006.
Schmieding, Samuel Joseph. "Visions of a Sculptured Paradise: The Colorado Plateau as American Sacred Space." PhD diss., Arizona State University, 2002.
Scott, Doug. *The Enduring Wilderness: Protecting Our Natural Heritage through the Wilderness Act.* Golden, CO: Fulcrum, 2004.
Sears, Julian D. *Geology of Comb Ridge and Vicinity North of San Juan River.* US Geological Survey Bulletin 1021-E. San Juan County, UT: US Geological Survey, 1956.
Seelye, John. *Beautiful Machine.* New York: Oxford University Press, 1991.
Shanks, Bernard. *This Land Is Your Land: The Struggle to Save America's Public Land.* San Francisco: Sierra Club Books, 1984.
Shepard, Paul. *Man in the Landscape: A Historical View of the Esthetics of Nature.* New York: Alfred A. Knopf, 1966.
Shumway, Gary. "A History of the Uranium Industry on the Colorado Plateau." PhD diss., University of Southern California, 1970.
Skillen, James R. *The Nation's Largest Landlord: The Bureau of Land Management in the American West.* Lawrence: University Press of Kansas, 2009.

Smart, William B. *Mormonism's Last Colonizer: The Life and Times of William H. Smart.* Logan: Utah State University Press, 2008.

———. *Old Utah Trails.* Salt Lake City: Utah Geographic Series, 1988.

———. "Stewardship of the Earth." Unpublished manuscript in the author's possession.

Smith, Charlotte Palfreyman, ed. *Stories Told: Life on the Public Lands in San Juan County.* Provo, UT: Charles Redd Center for Western Studies, 2012.

Smith, Henry Nash. *Virgin Land: The American West as Symbol and Myth.* Cambridge, MA: Harvard University Press, 1950.

Smith, Joseph. *Teachings of the Prophet Joseph Smith.* Compiled by Joseph Fielding Smith. Salt Lake City: Deseret Book, 1977.

Smith, Joseph, Jr., et al. *History of the Church of Jesus Christ of Latter-day Saints: Period 1, History of Joseph Smith, the Prophet, by Himself.* Edited by B. H. Roberts. 6 vols. Salt Lake City: Published by the Church and Deseret Book, 1902–12.

Smith, Sherry L., ed. *The Future of the Southern Plains.* Norman: University of Oklahoma Press, 2003.

Starrs, Paul F. *Let the Cowboy Ride: Cattle Ranching in the American West.* Baltimore: Johns Hopkins University Press, 1998.

Stegner, Wallace. *Beyond the Hundredth Meridian: John Wesley Powell and the Second Opening of the West.* Boston: Houghton Mifflin, 1954.

———. "The Geography of Hope." *Living Wilderness* 44 (December 1980): 12–17.

———. *Mormon Country.* Lincoln: University of Nebraska Press, 1942.

———, ed. *This Is Dinosaur: Echo Park and Its Magic Rivers.* 1955. Reprint, Boulder, CO: Roberts Rinehart, 1985.

———. *Where the Bluebird Sings to the Lemonade Springs: Living and Writing in the West.* 1992. Reprint, New York: Wings Books, 1995.

———. "Wilderness Letter." Written to the Outdoor Recreation Resources Review Commission, December 3, 1960. http://wilderness.org/content/wilderness-letter.

Stilgoe, John R. *Common Landscape of America, 1580 to 1845.* New Haven, CT: Yale University Press, 1982.

Sturgeon, Stephen C. "The Disappearance of Everett Ruess and the Discovery of Utah's Red Rock Country." In *Utah in the Twentieth Century,* edited by Brian Q. Cannon and Jessie L. Embry. Logan: Utah State University Press, 2009.

Sutter, Paul. *Driven Wild: How the Fight against Automobiles Launched the Modern Wilderness Movement.* Seattle: University of Washington Press, 2004.

Swanson, Frederick H. *Dave Rust: A Life in the Canyons.* Salt Lake City: University of Utah Press, 2007.

Switzer, Jacqueline Vaughn. *Green Backlash: The History and Politics of the Environmental Opposition in the U.S.* Boulder, CO: Lynne Rienner, 1997.

Thybony, Scott. *Canyon Country Parklands: Treasures of the Great Plateau.* Washington, DC: National Geographic Society, 1993.

Topping, Gary, ed. "An Adventure for Adventure's Sake Recounted by Robert B. Aird." *Utah Historical Quarterly* 62, no. 3 (1994): 275–88.

———. *Glen Canyon and the San Juan Country.* Moscow: University of Idaho Press, 1997.

Trainor, Sarah Fleisher. "Conflicting Values, Contested Terrain: Mormon, Paiute, and Wilderness Advocate Values of the Grand Staircase–Escalante National Monument (Utah)." PhD diss., University of California, Berkeley, 2002.

Travis, William R. *New Geographies of the American West: Land Use and the Changing Patterns of Place.* Washington, DC: Island Press, 2007.

Trimble, Stephen. *Bargaining for Eden: The Fight for the Last Open Spaces in America.* Berkeley: University of California Press, 2008.

———. *Blessed by Light: Visions of the Colorado Plateau.* Layton, UT: Peregrine Smith Books, 1986.

Tuan, Yi-Fu. *Passing Strange and Wonderful: Aesthetics, Nature, and Culture.* Washington, DC: Island Press, 1993.

Turner, Frederick. *Beyond Geography: The Western Spirit against the Wilderness.* New Brunswick, NJ: Rutgers University Press, 1983.

Udall, Stewart, Patricia Nelson Limerick, Charles F. Wilkinson, John M. Volkman, and William Kittridge. *Beyond the Mythic West.* Salt Lake City: Peregrine Smith, 1990.

US Department of the Interior. *Report to Congress on R.S. 2477: The History and Management of R.S. 2477 Right-of-Way Claims on Federal and Other Lands.* Washington, DC: Government Printing Office, June 1993.

US Department of the Interior, Bureau of Land Management. *Management Situation Analysis for the Grand Resource Area Resource Management Plan/Environmental Impact Statement, Moab District, Utah, Grand Resource Area.* Washington, DC: Government Printing Office, 1982.

———. *Wilderness Inventory Handbook: Policy, Direction, Procedures, and Guidance for Conducting Wilderness Inventory of the Public Lands.* Washington, DC: Government Printing Office, September 27, 1978.

US Department of the Interior, Bureau of Land Management, Moab and Vernal Districts, Utah. *Draft EIS Ouray to Interstate 70 Highway.* Prepared for Uintah and Grand Counties, Utah. Washington, DC: Government Printing Office, September 1992.

US Department of the Interior, Bureau of Land Management, Utah State Office. *Utah BLM Statewide Wilderness Environmental Impact Statement: Final.* Washington, DC: Government Printing Office, 1990.

US Department of the Interior, Bureau of Land Management and National Park Service. *Draft Environmental Assessment on Paving Boulder-to-Bullfrog Road, Garfield County, Utah.* Washington, DC: Government Printing Office, May 1985.

US Department of the Interior, Bureau of Land Management and Office of the Solicitor. *The Federal Land Policy and Management Act, as Amended.* Washington, DC: Government Printing Office, 2001.

US Government Accountability Office. "Recognition of R.S. 2477 Rights-of-Way under the Department of the Interior's FLPMA Disclaimer Rules and Its

Memorandum of Understanding with the State of Utah." February 6, 2004. http://www.gao.gov/decisions/other/300912.htm.

US Senate, Committee on Interior and Insular Affairs, Subcommittee on Parks and Recreation. *Canyonlands National Park and Glen Canyon National Recreational Area: Hearing, Ninety-First Congress, Second Session, on S. 26 and S. 27, May 5, 1970.* Washington: Government Printing Office, 1970.

Utah Wilderness Coalition. *Wilderness at the Edge: A Citizen Proposal to Protect Utah's Canyons and Deserts.* Salt Lake City: Utah Wilderness Coalition, 1990.

Vale, Thomas R. *The American Wilderness: Reflections on Nature Protection in the United States.* Charlottesville: University of Virginia Press, 2005.

Van Cott, John W. *Utah Place Names.* Salt Lake City: University of Utah Press, 1990.

Wall, Derek. *Earth First! and the Anti-roads Movement: Radical Environmentalism and Comparative Social Movements.* New York: Routledge, 1999.

Watkins, T. H. *Red Rock Chronicles: Saving Wild Utah.* Baltimore: Johns Hopkins University Press, 2000.

Webb, Robert H., Jayne Belnap, and John S. Weisheit. *Cataract Canyon: A Human and Environmental History of the Rivers in Canyonlands.* Salt Lake City: University of Utah Press, 2004.

Weisiger, Marsha. *Dreaming of Sheep in Navajo Country.* Seattle: University of Washington Press, 2009.

Wells, Christopher W. *Car Country: An Environmental History.* Seattle: University of Washington Press, 2012.

White, Lynn, Jr. "The Historical Roots of Our Ecological Crisis." *Science,* n.s., 155, no. 3767 (1967): 1203–7.

White, Richard. "Are You an Environmentalist or Do You Work for a Living? Work and Nature." In *Uncommon Ground: Rethinking the Human Place in Nature* edited by William Cronon. New York: W. W. Norton, 1996.

White, Richard, and John Findlay, eds. *Power and Place in the North American West.* Seattle: University of Washington Press, 1999.

Whitman, Walt. *Leaves of Grass.* Philadelphia: David McKay, 1891–92.

Widtsoe, John. *Success on Irrigation Projects.* New York: John Wiley and Sons, 1928.

Wiley, Peter, and Robert Gottlieb. *Empires in the Sun: The Rise of the New American West.* New York: Putnam, 1982.

Wilkinson, Charles. *Crossing the Next Meridian: Land, Water, and the Future of the West.* Washington, DC: Island Press, 1992.

———. *Fire on the Plateau: Conflict and Endurance in the American Southwest.* Washington, DC: Island Press, 1999.

Williams, Michael. "Historical Geography and the Concept of Landscape." *Journal of Historical Geography* 5, no. 1 (1989): 92–104.

Williams, Terry Tempest. *Red: Passion and Patience in the Desert.* New York: Pantheon Books, 2001.

Williams, Terry Tempest, William B. Smart, Gibbs M. Smith, eds. *New Genesis: A Mormon Reader on Land and Community.* Salt Lake City: Gibbs Smith, 1998.

Wilshire, Howard G., Jane E. Nielson, and Richard W. Hazlett. *The American West at Risk: Science, Myth, and Politics of Land Abuse and Recovery.* New York: Oxford University Press, 2008.

Worster, Donald. *Nature's Economy: A History of Ecological Ideas.* 2nd ed. New York: Cambridge University Press, 1994.

———. *A River Running West: The Life of John Wesley Powell.* New York: Oxford University Press, 2001.

———. *Rivers of Empire: Water, Aridity, and the Growth of the American West.* New York: Pantheon Books, 1985.

———. *Under Western Skies: Nature and History in the American West.* New York: Oxford University Press, 1992.

———. *The Wealth of Nations: Environmental History and the Ecological Imagination.* New York: Oxford University Press, 1993.

Wuerthner, George. "Wagon Wilderness." *Earth First!*, March 20, 1986.

———. "Wilderness: A Bioregional Approach." *Earth First!*, December 21, 1985.

Zakin, Susan. *Coyotes and Town Dogs: Earth First! and the Environmental Movement.* New York: Viking, 1993.

Zaslowsky, Dyan. *These American Lands: Parks, Wilderness, and the Public Lands.* New York: Henry Holt, 1984.

Index